International Screen Industries

Series Editors:
Michael Curtin, University of California, Santa Barbara, USA
and Paul McDonald, King's College London, UK.

The International Screen Industries series offers original and probing analysis of media industries around the world, examining their working practices and the social contexts in which they operate. Each volume provides a concise guide to the key players and trends that are shaping today's film, television and digital media.

Published titles:
The American Comic Book Industry and Hollywood *Alisa Perren and Gregory Steirer*
The American Television Industry *Michael Curtin and Jane Shattuc*
Arab Television Industries *Marwan M. Kraidy and Joe F. Khalil*
The Chinese Television Industry *Michael Keane*
East Asian Screen Industries *Darrell Davis and Emilie Yueh-yu Yeh*
European Film Industries *Anne Jäckel*
European Television Industries *Petros Iosifidis, Jeanette Steemers and Mark Wheeler*
Global Television Marketplace *Timothy Havens*
Hollywood in the New Millennium *Tino Balio*
Latin American Film Industries *Tamara L. Falicov*
Latin American Television Industries *John Sinclair and Joseph D. Straubhaar*
Localising Hollywood *Courtney Brannon Donoghue*
The New Screen Ecology in India *Smith Mehta*
Nollywood Central *Jade L. Miller*
Screen Industries in East-Central Europe *Petr Szczepanik*
Video and DVD Industries *Paul McDonald*
The Video Game Business *Randy Nichols*

Supply Chain Cinema:
Producing Global Film Workers

Kay Dickinson

THE BRITISH FILM INSTITUTE
Bloomsbury Publishing Plc, 50 Bedford Square, London, WC1B 3DP, UK
Bloomsbury Publishing Inc, 1359 Broadway, New York, NY 10018, USA
Bloomsbury Publishing Ireland, 29 Earlsfort Terrace, Dublin 2, D02 AY28, Ireland

BLOOMSBURY is a trademark of Bloomsbury Publishing Plc

First published in Great Britain by Bloomsbury in 2023
Paperback edition published 2025
on behalf of the
British Film Institute
21 Stephen Street, London W1T 1LN
www.bfi.org.uk

The BFI is the lead organization for film in the UK and the distributor of Lottery funds for film. Our mission is to ensure that film is central to our cultural life, in particular by supporting and nurturing the next generation of filmmakers and audiences. We serve a public role which covers the cultural, creative and economic aspects of film in the UK.

Copyright © Kay Dickinson, 2024

Kay Dickinson has asserted her right under the Copyright, Designs and Patents Act, 1988, to be identified as author of this work. For legal purposes the Acknowledgements on p. viii constitute an extension of this copyright page.

Cover design: Louise Dugdale
Cover image: Harry Potter Studio Tour London, model of Hogwarts School/Hemis/Alamy Stock Photo

All rights reserved. No part of this publication may be: i) reproduced or transmitted in any form, electronic or mechanical, including photocopying, recording or by means of any information storage or retrieval system without prior permission in writing from the publishers; or ii) used or reproduced in any way for the training, development or operation of artificial intelligence (AI) technologies, including generative AI technologies. The rights holders expressly reserve this publication from the text and data mining exception as per Article 4(3) of the Digital Single Market Directive (EU) 2019/790.

Bloomsbury Publishing Plc does not have any control over, or responsibility for, any third-party websites referred to or in this book. All internet addresses given in this book were correct at the time of going to press. The author and publisher regret any inconvenience caused if addresses have changed or sites have ceased to exist, but can accept no responsibility for any such changes.

A catalogue record for this book is available from the British Library.

A catalog record for this book is available from the Library of Congress.

ISBN: HB: 978-1-8390-2462-7
       PB: 978-1-8390-2466-5
       ePDF: 978-1-8390-2464-1
       eBook: 978-1-8390-2463-4

Series: International Screen Industries

Typeset by RefineCatch Limited, Bungay, Suffolk

For product safety related questions contact productsafety@bloomsbury.com.

To find out more about our authors and books visit www.bloomsbury.com and sign up for our newsletters.

For, about and impossible without: Adam

Contents

Acknowledgements	viii
1 'How Incredible is That?': The Extent of the Supply Chain	1
2 Hollywood Offshores to British Shores: Riding the Rise of the Creative Economy	35
3 Training Creative Wizardry: UK Supply Chain Filmmaking Education	63
4 Greasing the Wheels of Transnational Film Production: The United Arab Emirates' Post-Oil Vision for Education	87
5 Production Migrates to the Migrants: Logistics, Service and Precarity in the UAE's Creative Economy Free Zones	113
Conclusion	135
Notes	141
Bibliography	143
Index	167

Acknowledgements

In the Warner Bros. Studio Tour – the Making of Harry Potter (which this book visits presently), there lies a room containing over four thousand 'wand boxes', each honouring in full name someone who worked on the franchise. As my investigations uncover, many more participated who have not been recognized and, likewise, this will sadly also prove true of these acknowledgments.

Notwithstanding, from the very outset, I wish to express my sincere appreciation to the film professionals and aspirants who managed to find rare moments amidst unremitting and punishing schedules to talk to me about these very same conditions. Counter to the 'wand box' ideal, the majority elected to remain uncredited by their real names so they could speak freely from within a climate of job insecurity that the coming pages mean to expose. I am immeasurably indebted to those choosing to be called Ben, Emilia, Jessica, Muhammad, Pamela, Rami, Ruaa, Serena, Shaima and Tom, and the others simply labelled 'friends', who preferred our relationship, rather than a pseudonym, to stand for them. Everyone I interviewed volunteered unremunerated time that, in this format, now siphons some form of capital to the corporate university: both outcomes which this book means to roundly critique. All I can hope is that I have contributed a little something to the struggles we share over and above any of the ways in which I might have profited personally.

Similarly, a number of academic friends spared not insignificant hours under comparatively pressurized circumstances to read this entire manuscript before it was submitted to the press. Masha Salazkina, I thank for her intellect, rigour and reliability, for embodying everything I could wish for in a comrade, as well as a reader. It is rare to find the comprehensively combatable research interests and principles I share with Charles Acland, whose expertise, enthusiasm and perspicacity never fail to sharpen my thinking. Nikolaus Perneczky brought his singular combination of political conviction and precision to this manuscript with a generosity he displays in so many other circumstances. Shane Boyle, my stalwart travelling companion amidst scholarship on logistics, has consistently helped me hone how we investigate its influence over culture. And Patrick Brodie's kindred approaches to the Irish context have greatly inspired, as well as surpassed, my own inquiries in their ambition and imaginativeness. BFI Publishing took on two (now not so) anonymous reviewers, Bridget Conor and Kevin Sanson, to evaluate this project; their enduring support and judicious suggestions have animated welcome improvements. Amy Holdsworth and Inge Sørensen made astute observations about the UK-focused chapters at a moment when, as a new returnee to the country, I felt a little rusty. Along with the other Glasgow colleagues in our current research group – Mhairi Brennan, Abigail Jenkins and Lisa Kelly – they foster thoughtful and exciting opportunities to bring some of the urgent concerns explored in this book into the classroom. Alia Yunis, who experiences what I write about much more comprehensively than I, graciously encouraged my research in the United Arab Emirates. Like Alia, Dale Hudson kindly proffered insightful feedback on two of my chapters that engage with people and situations to which they often both introduced me. Viviane Saglier and Stefan Tarnowski, to my mind, two of the most inventive and activist thinkers of SWANA region media culture, served as fantastic interlocutors about these portions too. I have had the pleasure of co-writing, from slightly different angles, with Priya Jaikumar and Pooja Thomas on matters that this monograph addresses and I thank them both for deepening and extending how I approach these issues.

This book's subject, the supply chain, holds together a disparate production process over considerable geographical distance. In smaller part, the same remains true of this study, although the links in its own chain have been forged from a more collective spirit. My friendships with Glyn Davis, Helen De Witt, Seb Franklin, Lee Grieveson, Michael Lawrence, Jo Littler, Arshad Makhdum, John David Rhodes, Arabella Stanger and all of the Precarious Workers Brigade inspired this project in subtle and meaningful ways. I have had the good fortune to share drafts in various settings, including at the Universities of Anger, Cambridge, Carleton, Concordia, George Washington, Glasgow, MICA, NYU, NYU Abu Dhabi, Pennsylvania, Sheffield, SOAS, Sussex, Toronto, UC Santa Barbara and at numerous conferences, as well as through conversations that have led to earlier publications. Along these ways, the following people (and more whom I will have neglected to name) ventured stimulating questions, enriching discussions and pointers towards new ideas and people: Montiana Ashour, Farah Atoui, Jasper Bernes, Patricia Caillé, Michelle Cho, Deborah Cowen, Michael Curtin, Donatella Della Ratta, Lindiwe Dovey, Hatim El-Hibri, Yuriko Furahata, Toral Gajarawala, Bishnupriya Ghosh, David Hesmondhalgh, Matthew Hockenberry, Brian Jacobson, Alisa Lebow, Peter Limbrick, Masha Kirasirova, Sheetal Majithia, Anna McCarthy, Bindu Menon, Rahul Mukherjee, Jules O'Dwyer, Lisa Parks, Xin Peng, Damien Pollard, Karen Redrobe, Bhaskar Sarkar, Robert Stam, Nicole Starosielski, Samhita Sunya, Kate Taylor-Jones and Susan Zieger. Much of this book was conceived at Concordia University where it benefitted from conversations with fantastic colleagues (particularly Luca Caminati, Marc Steinberg, Ishita Tiwary and Haidee Wasson) and students (most foundationally, the Labour of Media (Studies) collective, all three of the 'Academic Labour' classes and the attention of Céline Nassar, who helped format its bibliography).

Michael Curtin and Paul McDonald's series International Screen Industries was my only choice as a home for this monograph. I am grateful to them both, along with Rebecca Barden and Veidehi Hans at British Film Institute/Bloomsbury, for their welcome and their guidance, along with Sarah Cook, who copy-edited it and Merv Honeywood who project managed its journey to press. Thanks to all the other workers, activists, educators and thinkers who have shaped this book and to whom I have failed to attribute 'wand boxes' here, but who weave their magic nonetheless.

Elements of Chapters 2 and 3 were first developed in the following essay: 'Supply Chain Cinema, Supply Chain Education: Training Creative Wizardry for Offshored Exploitation', in Matthew Hockenberry et al. (eds), *Assembly Codes: The Logistics of Media* (Durham NC: Duke University Press, 2021), pp. 171–187.

1

'How Incredible is That?': The Extent of the Supply Chain

We open with a pan across a pristine desertscape. The next brief shot reveals an exhausted and sweaty Finn (played by John Boyega) trailing his presumed-dead companion Poe's jacket across the sand. A voice announces, 'We are here on day one of *Star Wars Episode 7.*' The image catches up to reveal director J.J. Abrams addressing an assembly of crew members. 'How incredible is that?'

Across its three-minute duration, this YouTube video, *Exclusive Behind the Abu Dhabi Scenes of Star Wars: The Force Awakens*, respects the conventions of the making-of documentary (2454abudhabi 2015). It both demystifies and spectacularizes Abrams' 'how incredible is that?' by detailing ways in which an ambitious production like this actually comes together. Along the way, it purposefully advertises the capacities of the United Arab Emirates, the subject of this book's fourth and fifth chapters, as a consummate provider of services for anything a visiting blockbuster project could need. This comes as no surprise, given that the video's publisher is twofour54, the emirate of Abu Dhabi's economic free zone dedicated to media production. Tommy Gormley, the first assistant director, lists how 'We're building a big set there, we have many extras and aliens and people to accommodate. It's a huge operation.' The video parades spacecraft being detonated on delicate ecosystems and it makes sure to mention the logistical assistance provided by the UAE's military, Civil Defence and Ministry of the Interior. Tommy Harper, an executive producer, adds, 'The ability to get it all on camera at the time it needs to happen is something that is extremely difficult to pull off... We had a fantastic team in Abu Dhabi... and we all grabbed arms and did it together.' Off camera, this will have also involved everything from transporting and accommodating cast, crew, props and costumes to hiring locally based workers to build sets, cater, and serve as background artists or unpaid interns. The *Star Wars* juggernaut has rolled into the UAE not just because of its photogenic desert, but on account of all these provisions. Like almost all big-budget films, it will press onwards across an array of similarly obliging sites during its passage to completion.

My core proposition in this book is that journeys like these exemplify the principles of a supply chain, a mode of manufacturing that exerts control over so many other sectors globally. Supply chains do not simply bring commodities to consumers. They nimbly and opportunistically route *manufacturing* through wherever is most amenable and efficient. They subcontract, outsource and offshore, assembling and transfiguring ever-modulating workforces tasked with inputting portions into their wares, smoothly harmonizing these globally scattered stages into an integrated whole. As this chapter will illuminate, supply chains take advantage of, even bully into existence, facilities, infrastructures, logistical support, creative expertise and specially created tax loopholes.

Sites like the UAE now aggressively compete to attract incoming film business. These desert scenes could have been shot in Jordan, Morocco or Tunisia, as was the case for the first film in the franchise. In the intervening three decades, regions have advanced from reactively or haphazardly welcoming the odd movie production into their suitably eye-catching location to vociferously touting for film business by anticipating the supply chain's needs, of which the making-of video stands as one small example. Remaining viable amidst an ever-mounting number of rivals entails offering more for less, the upshots ricocheting across a landscape encompassing everything from national policy to individual employees. This chapter gives a taster of what these are for the UAE, with the final two more fully plumbing these depths. Wherever the supply chain chooses to go (usually multiple, otherwise disconnected sites), its coordinated operational strategies increasingly determine the ways in which movies come into being, the sheer scale of these interventions proving difficult to grasp. *Supply Chain Cinema* devotes itself to this endeavour, its highest priority the assessment of how these manoeuvres impact communities on the ground in lasting, material ways.

First, to apprehend the supply chain's extent and influence. Any ten-minute-plus final credit sequence from a blockbuster movie will give an inkling of its wide conscription of supporting agents: specialized equipment rental houses, airlines, shipping groups, local authorities, energy companies, the army. In pursuit of profitably lean and just-in-time production processes, the supply chain engulfs many sectors, some fairly unexpected for the average film fan, often because they remain unacknowledged in the film's closing moments. University-based film-making education, this book contends, increasingly administers to supply chain cinema's demands. Robustly supported by national governments, film production curricula accustom learners to not only supply chain-amenable technological standards, but also its globalized work cultures, socialities, and languages. Furthermore, such schooling helps frame this career path as (excitingly) unpredictable, competitive and precarious, denuded of welfare or corporate safety nets, a valorization of self-sufficiency that does much to shave costs.

These training and principal photography stages of supply chain cinema comprise the subject of this book. The current chapter elucidates the spatial, temporal and economic characteristics of supply chain cinema, its impact on host states, workers and their education. Chapter 2 zeros in on why Hollywood giants elect to make more of their films in Britain than in the USA, precisely because the country is so supply chain cinema-amenable. Chapter 3 then explores how this industry, in concert with the UK government, has massaged filmmaking education to fit its needs. Following on, Chapter 4 examines how the UAE has geared up its creative economy policy and education systems, largely through English-medium foreign franchise universities, to train a supply chain-ready workforce. Lastly, Chapter 5 asks: what does the UAE furnish to the now-hundreds of incoming (often big-budget) projects like *Star Wars* and at what cost to a precarious and largely migrant workforce?

HOW AND WHERE THE SUPPLY CHAIN FUNCTIONS

As consumers, we tend to construe supply chains as product delivery systems. An accurate definition to be sure, but it falls prey to how restricted our interpretation of 'delivery' can be. Supply chains are not simply commodity distribution circuits. Rather, they take charge of distributing the entire conception-to-purchase process to wherever and however they can maximize profit. A concrete example might help strike the difference here. A streaming platform's superlative means of providing us with, say, a film-on-demand within a matter of seconds would epitomize the former understanding of a supply chain. By contrast, the latter animates us to delve into how platforms like Netflix and Amazon use viewer data (far more sophisticated and closely guarded than traditional box office figures) to establish a responsive content production line that reacts quickly enough to meet (often fleeting) consumer desire and cheaply enough to reap the highest rewards. This book deliberately forfeits the elucidating endeavour of following given products along an entire supply chain so as to instead unfurl how deeply these techniques will penetrate even just two phases carried out in two countries.

Throughout this book, I consider the supply chain more a character (an antagonist, the villain much of the time) than a leading actor. When I invoke 'the supply chain', I mean it as a bundle of unremitting principles and intentions that motivate performance, rather than something that holds a steady and singular appearance. No less vivid for this, the supply chain in fact takes form as a shape shifter, brought to life in multiple ways simultaneously, through improvisation, and rarely answerable to a unique or identifiable director. As Miriam Posner, one of its theorists, explains:

> these supply pathways are never static... large companies' supply chains can change on a dime, triggered by global economic conditions or events on the ground. It is

hard to take a snapshot of a supply chain because it moves too fast... Like most consumers, corporations themselves are often at least partly in the dark. (Posner 2021: n.p.)

In the chapters that follow, I probe specific iterations, but more so to tease out the supply chain's operational predilections than to declare my case studies to be hard, fast and enduring embodiments of its links. 'What does it look like?' is best replaced by 'how does it behave?'

To stress the magnitude of what the supply chain orchestrates, my study elects to focus beyond distribution in the straightforward sense in order to expand our awareness of it to encompass film education and production. Crucially, these stages premise the supply chain's dependence on specific spaces: the film studio, the university and, for *Star Wars*, the desert. Somewhat interchangeable, yet ultimately indispensable, these places give generously to the supply chain and could do more to keep it in check. They draw workers from near and far, present and future, and this monograph's central concern is how the supply chain manipulates the contours and features of these groupings.

To conduct these analyses, I derive significant inspiration from anthropologist Anna Tsing's essay, 'Supply Chains and the Human Condition'. Tsing's scholarship attends to neither the film industry nor education; it is the pervasive globality of the system she describes that renders it pertinent to this book's objects of study. Tsing defines supply chain capitalism, from which I extrapolate supply chain cinema, as a web of specifically and differentially disciplined contributors, embroiled in commodity production and distribution. She opens us up to how:

> Supply chains offer a model for thinking simultaneously about global integration, on the one hand, and the formation of diverse niches, on the other. Supply chains stimulate both global standardization and growing gaps between rich and poor, across lines of color and culture, and between North and South. Supply chains refocus critical analysis of diversity in relation to local and global capitalist developments. (Tsing 2009: 150)

Let us pause for a minute to dwell on a few of these characteristics: global integration, standardization and then – in seeming, but distinctly opportunistic tension – the exploitation of diversity.

Global integration presumes a geography of production that is no longer centralized, as it was under the more in-house, Fordist regimes of the Hollywood studio system. Rather, in the words of containerization researcher Alexander Klose, the world itself has been converted into 'a gigantic assembly line' (Klose 2015: 21). One of supply chain management's primary techniques is to optimize savings on labour and resources by deftly assessing where to locate its various acts of creation. Or, to pick up on how logistics scholars Jorge Budrovich Sáez and Hernán Cuevas Valenzuela describe it, it is an approach that 'allows economic activities to be fragmented, externalized, and scheduled in a deterritorialized manner according to the competitive advantages of each economy so that the parts and/or processes can then be articulated for the benefit of capital' (Budrovich Sáez and Cuevas Valenzuela 2018: 164). While certain sectors prove awkward to snap into this schema, cinema has been testing these waters for quite some time now. In its larger-budget formats, film has long been transnationally produced (not to mention financed and distributed), offshored, reliant on sectional, fragmented and project-by-project reconfigurations of precarious labour.

Where the supply chain exceeds serving as a synonym for transnational or globalized production is in how it draws its strength from its attention to linkage, the integration as well as the standardization to which Tsing alerts us. Upon its post-Second World War overseas ventures, Hollywood quickly recognized that local contributors would need to be familiar with the dominant industry's work methods (Steinhart 2019: 113), which is one of the many ways in which education will play a role. As Ramyar D. Rossoukh and Steven C. Caton's anthology *Anthropology, Film Industries, Modularity* plots out, everything from strict job definitions to a largely unwavering sequence of production consolidates an ease of interaction through conformity (Rossoukh and Caton 2021: 19 & 22). Processes of standardization (to do with equipment, protocol and so forth) reduce friction on movement and likewise relieve Hollywood of an exclusive grasp on expertise and facilities. A globalized Hollywood can avail itself of competitive transportation, digital networks, globalized financial systems and fiscal incentives from host locales to make blockbusters elsewhere (Cucco 2015: 80).

Interoperability thus becomes paramount, but Tsing underscores that this is no mere act of homogenization. As she convincingly continues, when supply chains 'link up dissimilar firms... diversity forms a part of the *structure* of capitalism rather than an inessential appendage' (Tsing 2009: 150). Ultimately, the supply chain secures its routes around the globe in order to feed on economic and legislative *differences*. Film production history overflows with examples of this (as charted in, for example, Gasher 2002; Elmer and Gasher 2005; Tinic 2005; Goldsmith et al. 2010; Champion 2016; Szczepanik 2016; Kokas 2017; Mayer 2017; Acland 2018). Upon the collapse of Eastern European communism, Hollywood flocked towards the sturdy, previously nationalized film production infrastructures of cities like Prague with their attractively cheap studios, skilled technicians and handsome locations, now disabused of state subsidy and keen to remain buoyant in a capitalist economy. At the beginning of the millennium, costs for filming in Canada sat around 25 per cent cheaper than in Hollywood, all within easy geographical reach of and, in cities like Vancouver, within the same time zone as California (Scott and Pope 2007: 1371; see Tinic 2005: 29–38 & 51–57 for a fuller picture).

The supply chain hungrily sniffs out racialized divisions of labour too and purposefully takes advantage of naturalized diminishments of rights and recompense. The liberal-humanist outlook predominating in the industry would suppose otherwise and, as Miriam Posner asserts, the convoluted compartmentalized structure of the supply chain makes these moves less evident to all involved, 'but', she continues, 'in truth, of course, they depend intimately on the kind of logic that categorizes and assigns lower value to the labor of people in the global South; otherwise, we wouldn't have global supply chains, at least not to any great extent' (Posner 2021: n.p.). The *Star Wars* making-of video reveals how supply chain cinema ratifies one such technical class composition. We hear the creative visions of the directors, producers and designers who are white and speak in American or British accents. Yet we see, too, numerous support and 'below-the-line' personnel at their disposal (and easy disposability), who are racialized workers, providing a few weeks of temporary service. Their wages will be lower not only than those of the creative cadre, but also their counterparts in the USA or UK, and the same goes for their suppressed worker and (non-)citizen rights. The host state is far from oblivious to these inequalities; to the contrary, it purposefully confects these injustices as a fundamental element of its competitive advantage. The UAE's populous low-waged migrant construction sector (predominantly from other Asian countries) brings to screen for *Star Wars* the fictional marketplace of Jakku and a dilapidated spacecraft at drastically lowered costs, abetted by government-run twofour54 and the Abu Dhabi Film Commission, who will have helped arrange these contracts.

Such actions substantiate political theorists Sandro Mezzadra and Brett Neilson's assertion that, 'Gaps, discrepancies, conflicts, and encounters as well as borders are understood not as obstacles but as parameters from which efficiencies can be produced' (Mezzadra and Neilson 2013a: 206). Their scholarship adds depth to such analyses through how it acknowledges the global alignments of labour, capitalism and migration in ways atypical to the usual study of cinema. Productions like *Star Wars: The Force Awakens* are waived across the UAE border as it simultaneously calibrates an intricate and ever-shifting migrant workforce of millions and thus a globalized class system, a sub-section of which gives birth to an 'international division of creative labour', as Toby Miller, Nitin Govil, John McMurria, Richard Maxwell and Ting Wang dub it (Miller et al. 2005: 111–172).

With such iniquities in how big-budget filmmaking is engineered in the foreground, established definitions like 'split location production' (Goldsmith et al.

2010: 87) seem not quite to do justice to what is actually going on. In comparison, supply chain cinema bestows more of the resonance of how capital homes in on optimal production conditions, seamlessly marshalled into a more embracing and regulated sequence, aided by an ever-developing array of logistical mechanisms for coordinating labour and the mobility of capital across international borders.

Compositionally, this stations crews at strategic distances from each other. Even though they are ostensibly co-workers, many will never meet, as they might have more readily done in the days of more centralized studio production. The geographical span of supply chain cinema and the roles borders play to constrain certain workers decreases this likelihood, but so too does another fundamental characteristic of supply chain manufacturing: the outsourcing and subcontracting of work, parcelled out far and wide. The result is not simply a globalized assembly line, but, as I go on to argue, a highly limber and dynamic one that reorients the course of the chain whenever it sees more profitable opportunities.

Paul Hayes, the construction manager for *Star Wars* alludes to this practice in the promotional video when he mentions, 'We decided that we were going to make most of the set there. We contacted people over there and managed to find a crew.' As noted, the brutality of borders allows only certain privileged film workers like Hayes to move with the production when it travels the supply chain and to retain top-end Global Northern salaries in so doing. However, his comment also alludes to the short-term contracting of workers so typical of the industry and, most likely, how Hayes earns his living as well. Supply chain cinema constitutes its crews as separately hired units or individuals (and this goes for most of the arriving workers too) for only as long as it feels it can get away with. Such subcontracting shrugs off the costs of legal, financial, disciplinary and welfare responsibility in manifold ways whose outcomes will recur as a major theme within this book. Governments will be quick to celebrate the (largely temporary) jobs that supply chain cinema begets, but at what other costs? When an industry casualizes its employees in this way, they become highly dependent on stringing together a portfolio of contracts in order to make a living. In this scenario, they will push to their limits to advertise themselves as worthy of future work. Their understandable efforts both contribute at reduced cost to the overall profits of the film enterprise and normalize competitive, piecemeal employment. Charles Acland oxymoronically names this 'sustainable precarity... a calculated feature of this corner of the cultural industries', making clear the deliberate intent behind these practices (Acland 2018: 151).

As Andrew Ross argues of subcontracting's close relative, outsourcing:

> it is not in the actual tally of jobs or dollars lost, but rather in downward wage pressure, and the establishment of a permanent climate of job insecurity, that we are

likely to see the most sustained impact... It is fast becoming a way of life, regarded more and more as a social as well as an economic norm, and inevitably it is altering our perception of what a job entails. (Ross 2006: 20)

Terminologically, outsourcing also usefully spotlights the geographical dimensions in play. Anthropologist Kimberly Chong provides concrete examples from her in-depth study of American companies' outsourcing operations to China. Their encroachment into (largely cheaper) labour pools is not the simple substitution of one job for another for lower pay. The competition and threat of replacement engendered across the globalized job market disciplines all workers and advances hiring practices stripped to a bare minimum (Chong 2018: 99). Collective politics and rights bargaining prove harder to initiate amidst such deliberate distancing, both geographical and social. The suppleness of the supply chain means it can reconfigure or re-route around organized remonstrance.

Given these qualities, which unfold in a purposefully cunning transnational manner, I would like to consider what is happening here a form of *offshoring*. Situating such practices as a variant of offshoring trains the gaze on who the ultimate beneficiaries might be, framing supply chain cinema's ways and means more squarely as mechanisms to reduce costs, even avoid taxation, through judicious selections of the sites in which to manufacture. Outsourcing, as mentioned, shirks any number of responsibilities to workers and is, indeed, common practice in the industry. Offshoring sees this in league with averred avoidance of certain territorially determined legislative and financial responsibilities. While scholars like Andrew Ross have helpfully extended the rubrics of offshoring analysis to skilled, creative work (for instance, in the high-tech sector) (Ross 2006) and certain film researchers aim to expose the motivations of big-budget cinema as detrimental to its hosts (Goldsmith et al. 2010: 27; Curtin 2016: 677–678), few connect the dots to a wider practice of offshoring.

What's in a name? As Hollywood began to shoot elsewhere with increasing frequency in the years following the Second World War, US labour groups (and, since then, many scholars) have popularized another term for this process: 'runaway production' (Scott and Pope 2007: 1365; Cucco 2015; Steinhart 2019; Sayfo 2020). However, 'runaway' as a descriptor comes loaded with the harm such mobility exacts upon a 'home' workforce, cutting jobs for those presumed to 'own' them (Gasher 2002: 5 & 42–51; Goldsmith and O'Regan 2003: 9; McNutt 2015: 61). Without diminishing these hardships and insecurities, the lens provided by critiques of offshoring will also acknowledge the rights of non-Hollywood workers. The consequent restructuring towards the supply chain cinema model that attracted international features to the Czech Republic, for instance, brought about 1,700 redundancies in the country's Barrandov Studios

(Goldsmith and O'Regan 2003: 47). Faced with these devastating losses, reading supply chain cinema's techniques of offshoring as 'runaway' encourages workers to pit themselves against each other, rather than understand the situation as a 'race to the bottom' (see Sanson 2018: 361). This framework denudes us concomitantly of the scope to conceive of how similar insecurities might bring about transnational unity or allow us to organize against the exigencies of the supply chain above and beyond the divisions it deliberately strikes.

Ben Goldsmith, Susan Ward and Tom O'Regan's moniker 'Hollywood satellites' thankfully smacks of none of these same presumptions about who should be employed while still emphasizing an imbalance of power that is spatialized (Goldsmith et al. 2010: 87). John Urry's book *Offshoring* lends further nuance to this arrangement by stressing how digital flows of finance, trade and intellectual property work to significantly 'delocalize' space (Urry 2014: 9). This delocalization cuts in multiple directions. A dispersed internationalization of investment and production certainly complicates any geographically grounded understanding of 'Hollywood', which, in turn, picks away at the logic of the 'runaway' (Acland 2020: 69). Media multinationals delocalize in a totally different fashion when they strategically offshore via in-place subsidiaries who can take advantage of affordances designed for resident investors.

Such capitalistic unscrupulousness prompts another fundamental reason for my preference for classifying these supply chain cinema tactics as offshoring. John Urry argues how 'Offshoring provides a different theory of the workings of the contemporary world to that of "globalisation". It is an account that emphasizes avoidance, rule-breaking, irresponsibility, and secrets as the "rich class" remade the world in its interests' (Urry 2014: 14). The book you are reading, unlike others, does not stop short at paying due respect to the central undertakings of non-Hollywood workers in bringing such features onto our screens (see, for example, Goldsmith et al. 2010: 263). Rather, it aims to expose how the elite interests of supply chain cinema, in hunting down lower labour costs, infringed worker rights, favourable exchange rates and tax credits, take part in a systemic remodelling of economies hellbent on diminishing union power and social securities, from pensions and paid holidays to the welfare state more generally. In order to begin to understand how this happens, it proves necessary to appraise the onshoring role national governments play within this simultaneously transnational process.

THE STATE, THE SUPPLY CHAIN AND THEIR WORKERS

The supply chain specifically targets willing partner countries on the journeys it wends. The particular coordinates that have attracted it to the UK, for instance, comprise that country's decades of policies dedicated to deregulation, including in the entertainment sectors, and its concerted effort to lessen the power of organized labour. In the UAE, the majority of workers are migrant, thus in a particular state of job-needy suspension, subject to differential pay scales and weakened labour rights, which Chapters 4 and 5 will more fulsomely describe.

Yet the supply chain does more than work with what is already in place. Alexander Klose acknowledges a distinct agency on its part to initiate, 'administrative, legal, and conceptual reorganization' in its interests (Klose 2015: 176) and Chapter 3's investigation of industry influence over British film education will prove a case in point. Whatever lobbying and other such negotiations take place behind closed doors, the end result is often a country or region that is falling over itself to welcome supply chain cinema, 'often wrangling', as Kevin Sanson points out, 'with the most effective policies to ensure a location's sustainability as a global destination' (Sanson 2018: 365). Ben Goldsmith, Susan Ward and Tom O'Regan put forward the term 'film friendliness' to capture the lengths to which a site will go to attract productions, from the fiscal and infrastructural to service and training considerations (Goldsmith et al. 2010: 23). Film and other media scholars Susan Christopherson, Serra Tinic, Ben Goldsmith, Tom O'Regan, Michael Curtin, Kevin Sanson and Vicki Mayer variously chart how governments have sculpted trade agreements, dissolved elements of sovereignty, pared down workers' bargaining rights, built supply chain standard infrastructure, offered incentives and subsidies, and provided guiding intermediary services such as film commissions – all in the name of luring big-budget productions (Christopherson 2005; Tinic 2005; Goldsmith and O'Regan 2005b; Christopherson 2008: 164–165; Goldsmith et al. 2010; Curtin and Sanson 2016a; Mayer 2017). From Hungary to South Africa to Australia to Canada, upsurges in competing film friendliness bestow supply chain cinema with the upper bargaining hand. What offerings does it prize most?

Most would assume that supply chain cinema's primary reason for charting a course through any given country would be the visual attributes of a location: *Star Wars*' need for Abu Dhabi's pristine sand dunes, for instance. These matter, unquestionably, but our planet abounds with deserts beyond this one. All told, various financial measures that governments put in place to attract film business more squarely motivate big-budget productions. Supply chain cinema navigates through a constantly shifting global landscape of incentives and tax breaks, which, at the time of the *Star Wars* shoot in Abu Dhabi, amounted to a 30 per cent rebate on eligible production spend. Such enticements come in the guise of wage credits for hiring local crew, sales tax rebates, reductions or waivers on capital tax. Historically, governmental support for film had set its sights on bolstering a national industry, perhaps even to allay Hollywood's domination of local markets. Contemporary policy trends in many countries now reverse this principle by instead directing funds towards coaxing in such projects. Producers and investors collect substantial interest- and risk-free 'soft money', provided courtesy of local taxpayers, to float their endeavours. They understandably deem this preferable to borrowing upfront sums from a bank that will seek to profit from a loan (Cohen 2017: 140). Tax expert Joseph N. Cohen explains how, 'The studios were spoiled by these tax shelters, which often represented a negative cost of capital... a net benefit that effectively reduced their cost of production' (Cohen 2017: 132). In return, the country sees a rise in (predominantly temporary) employment, spending, prestige, on-screen location branding and even intensified tourism. Studio executives, though, largely determine the rules of this game, insisting on incentives as a prerequisite, pressuring governments to retain them or to outbid other hubs (Morawetz et al. 2007: 430 & 433).

To repeat, I categorize such manipulations as offshoring, a term that solidly implies tax evasion. Tax lawyer Schuyler M. Moore validates this assessment and Joseph N. Cohen expounds how governmental subsidies, 'typically represent "freebies" – that is, they are outright cash rebates or they can be monetized by selling the tax credits to tax-paying entities in the jurisdiction – and don't have to be repaid nor do they participate in the film's profits' (Cohen 2017: 81. See also Moore 2016: 116). The guaranteed security of this state-sponsored financing has drawn to the industry larger than ever numbers of risk-averse investors or those canny enough to work out how to finagle their tax bill through investing in cinema. While this remains a secretive, shadowy world through which it is hard to follow the money, Vicki Mayer's inventive Prologue to *Almost Hollywood, Nearly New Orleans* plots out such circumventions from the perspective of a film tax credit whose imagined voice narrates those pages (Mayer 2017: ix–xi). Brokers bundle these government-endowed sums, amalgamating them into the portfolios of hedge and private equity funds, which, in turn, offset the taxes of buyers in sectors like oil and gas. They are then traded as mercurially as other financial assets, bought and sold for short-term advantage, in the end advantaging these agents arguably more than the local film industry. The next section of this chapter will pick up on how the supply chain's imperative towards speed invigorates a context that is fecund for this sort of trading, but considerably less tolerable for film workers. As Charles Acland observes, while jobs are created in the immediate, and at a cost (in large part to the everyday citizen taxpayer), bankruptcies and redundancies result when incentives change or dissolve, or a more attractive opportunity arises in another country (Acland 2018: 148–149). In short, public funds, at the very least, float increased financialization of the sector and the country at large.

Where else is public money pumped? Specialized facilities, whose upkeep and updating to the supply chain's high spec standardizations devolves variously to state or private enterprise, often to individual contractors, but, noticeably, less and less to those plotting the course of the supply chain. In the UAE, the emirates' governments have built studios and other permanent physical amenities for media production from scratch and specifically in free zones with the hope of bringing offshored productions to those areas. Broader infrastructural capacity and compatibility fall too on the shoulders of the state: superlative digital and transport networks, reliable power, political and economic stability. Ned Rossiter's conceptualization of 'the logistical city' comprehensively classifies the favoured terrain as:

> elastic; its borders are flexible and determined by the ever-changing coordinates of supply chain capitalism... [manifesting] juridical power in the form of labor laws or extra-state forms of governance such as manufacturing and industrial design standards, communication protocols, and the politics of affect as it modulates the diagram or relations special to subjectivity. (Rossiter 2016: xiii & 65).

Such reach: from policy to individual comportment, with its workers, as will soon be signalled, mediating tirelessly between these registers. Also focusing on the built environment, Michael Curtin converges on the 'media capital', less a space of production for national needs and tastes than a service hub for multinationals, 'a nexus or switching point, rather than a container' (Curtin 2003: 204). Free zones – which is where transnational media production and private universities sit within the UAE – incarnate these qualities of the logistical city and the media capital. Government-designed to accommodate and speed through flighty foreign investment and workers, they have been meticulously engineered to extract capital with the least trace or liability. In effect, as Chapters 4 and 5 will lay out, the free zone nourishes offshoring gains with state oversight and subsidy.

These architectures are customized to transnational disaggregation and apportionment. Ben Goldsmith and Tom O'Regan call attention to how 'The contemporary production logic is a logic of parts and therefore a logic of clustered parts. Studio complexes are, in this sense, modelled as vehicles for organising a range of "plug-in" services' (Goldsmith and O'Regan 2003: 67). Tellingly, Dubai's media production quarters sit cheek by jowl with various universities, themselves both attractors of globalized revenues and means of converting education itself into a 'plug-in'. Various film commissions also dwell within the free zones and roundly exemplify the plug-in ethos with a film friendly face. Film commissions, at local or national level, pitch any number of can-do capacities, including securing shooting and work permits, suggesting locations and hiring on-the-ground crew. They also run training initiatives of various orders. Although public concerns, Ben Goldsmith, Susan Ward and Tom O'Regan observe that their mission has been diverted from an orientation 'towards nurturing aspiring local filmmakers and developing films and programs... to attracting production from beyond the city, state or region' (Goldsmith et al. 2010: 181). In this respect, film commissions and smaller scale, private-sector production services agencies, typically in conversation with the major producers and their satellite offices, do much to synchronize the passage of the supply chain.

Given all these outgoings, what are the perceived advantages of greenlighting supply chain cinema? With film commissions traditionally close allies of the tourism sector, there will be economic feed-through from what appears on screen: stunning views attracting the casual viewer and the die-hard franchise fan who checks off film locations alike (see Jaikumar 2019: 235–258 for a superlative class analysis of how location managers and other service personnel intersect with tourism promotion). High in the edit of the state-produced *Star Wars* making-of video sit comments like production designer Rick Carter's 'we're going to a real desert. It's a beautiful desert' and Tommy Gormley's 'the sand dunes in Abu Dhabi are actually unbeatable. They're the most amazing ones I've ever seen in my life.' A desert to visit on holiday, perhaps?

More quantifiably and immediately, its champions proclaim that supply chain cinema lifts the economy, although Phil Ramsey, Stephen Baker and Robert Porter's itemized investigations of government versus production spending on *Game of Thrones* in Ireland concludes sceptically on the overall benefits (Ramsey et al. 2019). The supply chain unequivocally provides jobs, around 928 full-time temporary ones, according to Marco Cucco's calculations for a high-budget vehicle (Cucco 2015: 81). These are specific in nature and this book places their composition centre stage. In its earlier days of moving production beyond its Californian base, Hollywood established a pattern that remains pretty much intact to this day: department heads were transported along with the project, but other jobs designated less creative control were filled locally (Steinhart 2019: 102–103). As I have already argued, the territorialized and racialized tenor of this division rings out even from a promotional YouTube video. A lot of these local jobs fall under the category of *production services*, which Ben Goldsmith and Tom O'Regan note as having mushroomed of late, thanks, often, to policy and film commission schemes (Goldsmith and O'Regan 2005b: 60). Production services concentrate on the mechanics of 'making it happen', as showcased in the making-of short. In Abu Dhabi, these contracts bundle almost entirely around interceding, coordinating, hiring, building, driving, and booking travel and hospitality (for a fuller description of the role that film services provide, see: Curtin and Sanson 2017: 137 and Sanson 2018: 362). Employees must be one step ahead, manage expectations, pick up the slack and take the blame. Deft and largely unnoticed. As a constellation of public and private providers, they, in the words of Michael Curtin and Kevin Sanson, negotiate 'a tangled mess of creative demands, local bureaucracies, thorny finances, and cultural differences, a complicated riddle that globe-trotting producers demand their local counterparts solve on their behalf' (Curtin and Sanson 2017: 136). 'Service' thus classifies a type of labour (noticeably distanced from creative input) as well as a social relation.

It is outsourced work, frequently subsidized by taxpayers, but also small-scale-entrepreneurial in disposition, temporary, precarious, non-unionized (exclusively so in the UAE, where free zones legally outlaw organized labour) and set at a remove from employer accountability and substantial creative agency alike. The modular and opportunistic structure of the supply chain offers no loyalty. In fact, from his research into how Canadian companies have regularly been driven into bankruptcy after Hollywood contracts dry up, Charles Acland concludes this to be '"fickleness" by design' (Acland 2018: 152). State expenditure thus services a deliberately inconstant industry where all local infrastructural and human capital investments remain a gamble.

Large productions typically hop from country to country in order to patchwork together a portfolio of all these aforementioned enticements. In each place, the projects hire a near-exact equivalent team of supply chain-ready workers, whose short-term tenancy casts them at a remove from the ongoing creative process (Morawetz et al. 2007: 434). As an assembly of independent firms or even one-person operations, they sustain the tension between difference and standardization that Tsing identifies as so beloved of the supply chain. Difference through the unlikelihood that the employees Hayes has hired enjoy anything like an equivalent status and may not even meet him. Yet still standardized. In order for these autonomous units to worker together efficiently, they must be deeply committed to teamwork and ready to slot into pre-conceived protocols, including those to do with crew hierarchy and sociality, knowing full well their replaceability in this schematization of flexible hiring. Ben Goldsmith, Susan Ward and Tom O'Regan observe the heavy emphasis within productions like these on 'project thinking', the exacting coordination of diverse contributors with an insistence on each's pliability for the greater good of the end result (Goldsmith et al. 2010: 20–21). Project thinking presumes a knack for fitting in right away and hitting the ground running. In this, the supply chain embarks on a campaign that differentiates it from earlier versions of location shooting in film-friendly territories.

These preponderances unfold from innovations in 'just-in-time' (JIT) manufacturing, a management process which dynamically regulates a workforce down to precisely what is needed at any given time, investing effort and technology in the calculation of exactly where such savings can be made. Just-in-time is characterized primarily by its goals of zero-inventory and zero capital lying idle, which involves locating what is needed for production in response to demand and at the very last minute. Production services prioritize these sorts of adjustments and corner cuttings, but they are also the victims of it, as are crew members involved more squarely in shooting the film. It is critical to stress here that, unlike film workers, those who test-ran these techniques in the Toyota factories of Japan retained reliably permanent contracts and significant investment from their company.

Rutvica Andrijasevic, Julie Yujie Chen, Melissa Gregg and Marc Steinberg have begun to think about how this ethos is shaping on-demand streaming services, whose modes of production (which dovetail frequently with and employ many of the same crews as supply chain cinema) assume practices familiar from just-in-time assembly (Andrijasevic et al. 2021: 98–99). They unveil how Netflix functions 'on the edge of chaos', leaving all arrangements for production until the eleventh hour so as to save money. Crews for supply chain cinema are routinely assembled according to deliberately truncated contracts. The net results, all in the name of shortening the shoot's length, can be break-neck preparation processes (frequently at the worker's own expense), exceedingly long hours, reduced recuperation periods throughout, and abrupt, holiday-free release when the film wraps. John Caldwell paints a vivid picture of just-in-time filmmaking (although he does not label it as such):

> each new production... functions in a manic, series manner. That is, each shoot is essentially a new corporation that starts up, functions intensively, and closes down in a matter of months... After a production 'wraps,' this burst of labor intensity is followed either by unemployment or a scramble to find new work, or both. (Caldwell 2008: 113)

In countries like the UK, which cannot guarantee decent outdoor shooting conditions for much of the year (unlike Los Angeles or the UAE), this work carries a seasonal weighting, which results in both decidedly more modest annual incomes and particularly frenzied summers.

Caldwell's on-set description relays that supply chain modalities prompt film crews to work not just impermanently, but also at a faster pace. As is almost ever the way, being 'just in time' amounts to cramming the same labour into condensed, break-neck or sleeplessly overworked periods. For certain services, the contracting studio will ask for tenders, playing companies off against each other and, as a consequence, routinely provoke them to vastly over-extend, even bankrupt themselves in the name of honouring their promise and promoting themselves for future consideration. For similar reasons, even those paid a daily rate rarely decline overtime requests. The budgeting rationales that insist on these hours favour reducing the costs of hiring or securing sets and locations rather than affording workers decent breaks between each shift. Industry researchers Michael Curtin and Kevin Sanson confirm that: 'workdays are growing longer, productivity pressures are more intense, and creative autonomy is diminishing. Overall, this has put severe financial, physical, and emotional strain on workers and their families and further threatens the many independent businesses that service the major studios' (Curtin and Sanson 2016a: 2). In this respect, supply chain cinema trespasses (as many sectors do) into the realms of time required to rest, restore and replenish, even to the detriment of current production. The replaceability of workers within the supply chain is likely the heartless fix for such longer-term damage. Much has justifiably been made, for instance, of corporations like Apple's intensity of hardware production cycles and its pressurization of employees beyond legal overtime hours in order to meet release dates (see, for example, Chan et al. 2013: 100). This book takes stock of comparable practices within supply chain cinema and the toll, in fact outright dangers, these methods exact on workers. Here I have been purposefully attenuating the perception of the supply chain as something that is predominantly spatially executed to evaluate its temporal techniques and their fallout. The following section examines what motivates this velocity.

SPEED, LOGISTICS AND FINANCIALIZATION

Big-budget film's lumbering timeline of (very expensive) years between conception and consumption renders movies highly unreliable wares (Cohen 2017: 113; Ganti 2012: 243–247). Expensive mistakes and missteps are par for the course. Contingency plagues planning and budgets (for an excellent discussion of how Egyptian film productions tackle and mitigate against mundane contingency like traffic, see El Khachab, 2021: 120–148). Viewing trends can dissipate during the lengthy process it takes to feed a film along the chain from inception to its various releases. The decidedly more sophisticated and immediate audience taste data feedback loops of streaming services quicken content production and spur traditional big-budget cinema to pick up the pace correspondingly. Understandably, then, the supply chain prioritizes speed to market at the expense of much else and with little less indefatigability than in its recourse to logistics.

Logistics is the management science of keeping things in motion, of saving on time or humanpower so as not to impede the fleet, cost-cutting production and distribution of commodities. It links the chain not only with speed, but also a cold efficiency, ever alert to the potential to exploit and extract. Logistics siphons its own revenue by reducing the time it takes to recoup outlay, to convert surplus value into profit, by hastening production and circulation time, even when stretched around the world, so that products arrive to consumers sooner

(Mezzadra and Neilson 2019: 150). Again, a streaming service arises as perhaps the most tangible moving image example and, indeed, it makes sense to understand platform giants like Netflix and, in particular, Amazon as logistical companies. However, logistics' modus operandi also contributes enormously to principal photography and the competitive advantages that offshore supply chain cinema sites can package. It has always played a crucial role in what it takes to make a big-budget film across different territories (see Steinhart 2019: 91), but, nevertheless, few filmgoers will truly appreciate how vital smooth logistics is to every stage of a film's journey or, indeed, the role it has played in economic globalization.

These days, logistics companies (like their governmental counterpart, the film commission) advertise one-stop shop abilities to service incoming projects in terms of everything from reliable international transportation, customs clearance, security, visas and work permits and equipment sourcing to hiring local crew and other support staff, scouting and locking down locations, and arranging catering and accommodation. In their examination of 'flexible capitalism in the screen media industries', Michael Curtin and Kevin Sanson discern a host of qualities I would also like to attribute to logistics:

> Today, the persistent resocialization and respatialization of production makes for a much more nimble structure, one that can accommodate incidents anywhere in the system, like a policy change or a tragic accident, by rapidly redeploying resources and personnel. It is like an organism capable of interacting with and responding to changes in its environment: suppressing potential threats, seeking new resources, expunging waste material in its wake, and constantly adapting its configuration to suit the circumstances. (Curtin and Sanson 2017: 7)

In so doing, logistics strives to create a frictionless fantasy out of the complexity of conforming and coordinating what and whom supply chain cinema demands on set. Yet no (such) movements happen frictionlessly; many leave workers, citizens and environments scathed and bruised in their wake.

In the making-of video, Mark Somner, the *Force Awakens* unit production manager, extols the logistical capabilities of twofour54 and the Abu Dhabi Film Commission, 'Via them, we've had great contact with the military, who've provided trucks, helicopter support, great support from the Civil Defence, and the Ministry of the Interior, who are working closely with us with regard to the pyrotechnics and the prop weaponry we've brought into the country.' The army's participation discloses, firstly, its expertise in logistics via its central historical (and hardly frictionless) role in developing it for military operations and, secondly, the diversion of public resources the UAE government sanctions in order to satiate big-budget film productions. Their involvement incarnates what Ned Rossiter dubs the 'logistical state', a government that is no mere manager of public assets, but, rather, a negotiating facility for supply chain enterprise (Rossiter 2016: 169–170). The logistics industry also contributes sizeably to the UAE's economy, particularly in Dubai, which is why it features prominently in Chapter 5's analyses of supply chain cinema.

An ever-multiplying raft of logistical and data management software aids this industry, modelling and initiating cost cuts across multiple dimensions of production and distribution, alerting subscribers to the movement of markets and transportation routes, ultimately finessing distances and timeframes so they function in circulatory harmony (Dyer-Witheford 2015: 84; Rossiter 2016: 119–133). Miriam Posner underlines how these tools privilege product demand, conforming everything down to workers' hours to this imperative (Posner 2021: n.p.). Film production management software such as the Movie Magic suite compartmentalizes scripts and forecasts budgets, generating casting breakdowns, call sheets and finance reports, all through artificial intelligence. File transfer systems for the industry ingest, process and dispatch content, deliver intellectual property and intimately searchable data quickly, securely and in real time to wherever it is needed next. Their accent on security abets intellectual property-focused secrecy and non-disclosure rules on such productions, which, in turn, augment dissociation. Such is the tight control on content that 'sides' (the portion of the script to be shot that day) may not even be released to many crew members, rendering their professional preparedness trickier and distinctly more just-in-time.

As a whole, these technologies aim to integrate, in the words of spokesperson for one such company, Tom Ohanian, a 'media creation and distribution supply chain which starts at asset acquisition through to consumer consumption' (Ohanian 2007: 14). Logistical software brings into alignment traditionally siloed phases of a film's production journey as a means of guaranteeing greater potential to oversee, quicken, and economize. Tellingly, though, while they bestow the aerial view, they facilitate more than ever the disaggregation of workers along the supply chain (as exemplified by the sanctity of the sides as intellectual property over crew members' capacities to bring an unknown script to life to the best of their abilities). cineSynch software, for example, enables remote, immediate, high-resolution and annotatable video viewing that allows producers to review and approve material far from the arduousness of on-set conditions. Logistics' maxims are expeditious circulation and trimmed costs, clearly at the expense of most of the humans involved (Chua et al. 2018: 622).

Nick Dyer-Witheford exposes how logistics' 'cybernetic systems… give capital new sources of low-wage labour, via electronically coordinated supply chains, outsourcing systems, and the activation of unpaid virtual [online] work' (Dyer-

Witheford 2015: 37). Although film production is yet to see its labour force Uberized, industry software is a relative of gig economy applications that entirely outsource employee services and is surely moving in that direction. Production coordinators stand as the human agents of film's logistical procedures and their job descriptions increasingly request expertise in supply chain management. Production coordinators absorb any manner of logistical tasks, while, at the same time, organizing the budgets and running of the shoot, overseeing spending, shooting schedules and all the costs from salaries to rentals. Given this conflation of duties, unquestionably their role is not just to diffuse operational complications, but to also bend those on the payroll to the exigencies of the supply chain (including its reduced salaries). When logistical managers and software partner to transform labour into data and precarity into systematization, the end result exceeds pragmatism and practicality and becomes ideological, especially when absorbed (as the following chapters recount) into national policy (see Harney and Moten 2013: 88).

In whose interests? This invigorated, quicker-to-market cinema has attracted a new set of more vulturous investors, ones with little prior interest or holdings in the industry per se. Private equity firms and hedge funds, themselves as agile in where they invest and divest as the supply chain, now increasingly diversify their portfolios of stocks and bonds in this area because it benefits from being decidedly less risky than the stock market, in large part because of how it is floated by soft money from local and national governments (Morawetz et al. 2007: 425–426, 430 & 433; Cohen 2017: 90). Andrew deWaard, one of the few film scholars to involve themselves in the financialization of the movie business, reveals that 'The big [studio] conglomerates still dominate film and television production, but they are mere investment and profit-extraction opportunities for truly powerful [asset management] firms such as BlackRock, Vanguard, Bain Capital, TPG, and Silver Lake, whose watchwords are highly leveraged debt, labor efficiencies, and speculation' (deWaard 2020: 55–56; see also Punathambekar 2013 for additional attention to such operations). While finance capital has always been central to floating the heavy expenses of film production, the previously rather unreliable returns from the industry cordoned the sector as the domain of banks seeking interest, rather than those drawn by portfolio investment.

Supply chain cinema now presents itself as a viable proposition to private equity, which aims to pool capital from multiple investments in search of fast returns, frequently through reducing costs to a minimum and then selling assets onwards for profit, rather than sustaining any given venture for its longer-term potential. The time-limited, project-based structure of the supply chain cinema now chimes well with the liquidity of the finance sector. In addition, the abstraction, digitization and globalization of financial flows enable the spatial redirection of capital in ways that allow for its rapid and commitment-light arrival and flight, key facilitators too of the supply chain model (Harvey 1990: 164). As Vicki Mayer points out, film studios (let alone asset management firms) rarely make the effort to move permanent bases to the regions where they shoot. Instead, they prefer to form a limited liability company through which to take advantage of incentives in a manner that is 'really agile, living fast and dying after the film is done' (Mayer 2017: x). This dispersed geography of exploitation mirrors the principles of investment diversification and supply chain transnationalization alike.

Likewise, hedge funds have exponentially entered the sector. Hedge funds do maintain longer-term ownership of an array of companies, and, in fact, often gear themselves towards forms of vertical integration that would otherwise be vulnerable to legal conflict of interest barriers. Yet their ownership structures are also characterized by the imperative to keep worker costs and rights stripped to a minimum (deWaard 2020: 69). What are the ramifications of this greater financialization of cinema? Michael Curtin explains that, when hedge funds and institutional investors own the majority of the shares in film studios, the industry becomes:

> beholden to 'shareholder value' as the preeminent principle of corporate governance. Rather than seeing their companies as serving a diverse set of stakeholders (e.g., owners, managers, workers, customers, publics, and communities), this new approach contended that corporations should weigh their strategies and administrative priorities based solely on the potential monetary return to investors... [who] have consequently become reference points for decisions about resource allocation and corporate strategy. Indeed, executives constantly cultivate relations with financial analysts who represent the interests of these elite investors to the exclusion of other stakeholders. (Curtin 2020: 95)

Ultimately, with supply chain cinema, the capital garnered by workers' evercompromised labour is not only offshored, but also fed into a sped-up system that gambles with their futures as it darts around the globe (see Chong 2018: 94–95 for its impact on workers in a different sector). The pace impressed by logistical measures upon cinema abets this goal.

Within this scenario, re-investment in the industry, materially or through training a workforce, is routinely sacrificed in the name of dividends for speculative investors. Private equity, in particular, follows a model where companies are bought, restructured into their leanest means of production and then rapidly sold on. Their anonymous investors hold next to no stakes in – in fact are likely entirely oblivious to – the wellbeing of the industry in a manner that might incline them towards nourishing and sustaining the industry's facilities or workers. The restless mobility of offshored manufacturing and even the bankruptcy it can bring does not amount to a set of mistakes; it is planned and strategic, generating profit from instability and indeterminacy. 'Assets' are routinely liquified and traded, squeezed for quick yield, even stripped in that name, cannibalizing what might have received considerable support from public resources. For Nick Dyer-Witheford 'the growth of high-risk derivatives was closely associated with supply-chain-driven globalization' (Dyer-Witheford 2015: 95), enabling, in this sector, a production model that looks up to algorithmic trading across fluctuating currency exchange rates as its inspiration. Without such investments, big-budget cinema might now prove impossible, yet the hazards emboldened by current means and their privileging of short-term profit over foundational and infrastructural development certainly leaves the industry vulnerable in historically new ways. As I have already documented, it is the taxpayer and the employees themselves who shoulder these burdens of more sustained industry maintenance.

We would do well to think of these manoeuvres as a form of resource extraction more acute than was typical of prior capitalist profiteering within earlier moments in cinema history. Sandro Mezzadra and Brett Neilson argue that 'the forms and practices of valorization and exploitation enabled by logistics are no less extractive than those applying to finance', reasoning that the finetuning that logistical management systems typically prioritize, as this chapter has been stressing, override governance standards, outsource responsibility, and opportunistically play off and benefit from difference across the world (Mezzadra and Neilson 2019: 46). Financial accountability remains deliberately obscured as supply chain cinema moves and fluctuates across an 'offshore' land and seascape. Moreover, supply chain cinema preys upon and expropriates not just standard revenues from selling cinematic wares, but also public education and healthcare, debt payments for training, and, as I shall go on to expound, fuller dimensions of the lives of contributors that disrespect prior standards of recompense.

Within this model, Michael Curtin continues, 'financialization mercilessly pressures employees to do more with less, privileging commercial calculation over creative purpose and wringing out cost economies that show little regard for creative sacrifices or safety risks' (Curtin 2020: 96). The chapters to come take stock of these imperatives to work harder, faster, for less pay and less job security. As will emerge in Chapters 2 and 3, the influence the supply chain wields in film education means that the ensuing expendability of workers is increasingly framed as entrepreneurialism, competitiveness and sacrifice for a career calling. Chapters 4 and 5 witness how supply chain cinema and education perpetuate these ideals in the UAE, coupling it with a disposability of workers enshrined in migrant labour policy. Of course, creative workers have long acclimatized to the unreliability of profits from artist endeavours, with financial failures far outweighing easy wealth in these spheres. But newer forms of risk and gamble serve to actualize and accelerate precarious life within a context where workers' material futures increasingly roll into high-speed dividends. As Chapter 3 determines, this includes their configuration through the financialization of debt, which will personally manifest in what they owe for their training (student loans), their homes and even their health, precisely because current models of the film industry shirk such responsibility. Karen Ho's *Liquidated: An Ethnography of Wall Street* details how finance workers pride themselves in an adaptability that matches the constant reconfigurations and conversions of the market (Ho 2009: 243–245). Now closer than ever to this sector, the supply chain encourages film workers to adopt compatible outlooks.

CRAFTING WORKER SUBJECTIVITY

Strategic downsizing, just-in-time organization and the rapid trading of assets plainly accelerates instabilities for these contributors, whose care has been shrugged away as much as possible by the supply chain. Franco 'Bifo' Berardi brings to the fore the injurious abstractions resulting from its calculative imperatives:

> Capital can buy fractals of human time, recombining them through the digital network. Digitalized info-labor can be recombined in a different location, far from the one that produces it. From the standpoint of capital's valorization, the flow is continuous, finding its unity in the produced object. Yet from the cognitive workers' perspective the work done has a fragmentary character: it consists in fractions of cellular time available for productive recombination. Intermittent work cells turn on and off within the large control frame of global production. The distribution of time can thus be separated from the physical and juridical person of the worker. (Berardi 2009: 191)

How are humans persuaded into this uninterrupted flow of production across multiple sites? How does something as complex yet painful come to life to such a degree that its main result is a blockbuster narrative that can slickly and so pleasurably transport its audience around the globe for their delectation? My aims in stressing these means to cinematic ends extend in a number of directions.

Firstly, I am driven to incorporate what we might consider to be 'enviable professions' into our denunciations of the supply chain's injustices by emphasizing the precariousness that 'Bifo' ultimately concludes to be 'the *general form* of social existence' (my emphasis) as the deliberate normalization and extension of insecurity (Berardi 2009: 191). Here I pay heed to Isabell Lorey's cautions against exempting 'specialized groups with critical emancipatory intentions around notions of precarity' (Lorey 2010: n.p.). This division, which presumes and substantiates economic and educational privilege, detracts from our potential to unify in struggle, including on a film set, where a broad spectrum of earners co-habit.

Secondly, cinema work can stand for other types of labour thus offering broader insights. As I elaborate soon, the supply chain has helped roll out a comprehensive model of creative aspiration that bears implications for contributors to this sector as well as others. It encourages a surfeit of qualified workers globally, a reserve army that makes for a buyers' labour market. Many arrive heavily in debt through their educational journey towards qualification, which compromises their standards of job expectations. And film work's elusive pledges of creative fulfilment set in motion holding patterns that suspend aspirants in systemic precarity, often indefinitely (Hesmondhalgh 2016: 36). The governmental accommodation of supply chain cinema meets its deliberate unequal in weak legal protections for these workers.

Film, I argue, as a particularly persuasive and evasive commodity, must be denuded of its glossy sheen in order to divulge its harmful modes of production. Hye Jean Chung's superlative investigation of digital effects work, *Media Heterotopias*, pinpoints how cinema's smooth narrative continuity shores up myths of effortless digitized and deterritorialized production. The resulting smokescreen emerges as:

> a disingenuous ruse that dehistoricizes, deracinates, and manipulates attention away from the inherent violence of ignoring the realities of territorial materiality, conflating specificities of different regions and cultures, and erasing fractures that arise amid cross-cultural interactions. This fetishizing of a seamless integrity conceals the actual bodies and physical sites of labor and idealizes effortless mobility and disembodied flight. (Chung 2021: 18)

We have no 'fair trade' marker or guarantees for cinema in the way we do for, say, cotton or coffee. Yet its glamour does more than envelope the resulting product in illusions that dazzle many from inquiring into how it is actually made. It attracts not only an audience, but also a workforce. The ruthlessness of logistics and the supply chain's self-interested encroachment of borders, obfuscated as frictionless fantasy, incarnates as on-screen illusion, which, in turn, charms incoming employees. The fact remains that people want to become filmmakers much more than many other professions (such as cotton or coffee pickers, probably). Unclouding these current expectations of labour is but a first step towards disputing them.

How is their yearning sculpted into a sizeable group of professionals around the world whose comportment matches the challenging demands of supply chain cinema? How do they willingly adopt its modalities as personal inclination and self-discipline in a fashion that Michel Foucault famously entitles biopower (Foucault 2003: 244)? When the work is categorized as creative, which is often the case within cinema, and when it seems to evolve from the individual and their intellectual, imaginative and affective capacities, rather than more measurable toil, then the boundaries between self-realization and exploitation blur (see Dyer-Witheford and de Peuter 2009: 36–38).

The rest of this book examines in more detail both how workers espouse supply chain cinema's exacting exploitation at their moments of employment and how the education they receive in order to qualify for it unquestioningly inveigles them towards it as necessary forfeit. To prepare the ground for these more involved and situated investigations, the remainder of this chapter introduces how the supply chain manipulates, accelerates and profits from notions of passion and freedom. The supply chain does so in the hope of crafting entrepreneurial workers with superlative abilities in translation (broadly conceived) that immeasurably ease transnational movements from site to site. Higher education's role within the supply chain, I contend, warrants much more scrutiny than it has yet received, including how the sector itself has been tailored into one of privatized, just-in-time precarity. This being the case, the chapter closes with some suggestions about how, following Lorey and Berardi's entreaties not to exclude jobs in the knowledge or creative industries as exceptional, film and its education might unite to stand up to the worst offensives of the supply chain.

To start with the play on passion and its satisfaction. True to genre, the *Star Wars* making-of video, bounces through a litany of declarations of fervid and rewarding dedication from cast and crew. None seem more starry-eyed and wish-fulfilled than the three Emirati interns, the only locals who are actually interviewed for the video. One, who, tellingly, remains unnamed gasps, 'It's a lot of fun. I'm seeing stuff I would have never imagined I would be able to see. It's a once in a lifetime experience,' while another, Abdullah, exclaims, 'I'm having the best experience of my life right now. Amazing people around me. It's mind blowing. It's mind blowing.' This elevation above the graft and dullness of 'typical work' gels well with an industry-pervasive sense of garnering self-worth through skilled craft and exacting standards. Both fuel feelings of gratitude for the opportunity ('an incredible privilege' states Daniel Mindel, *Force Awakens* director of photography) that encourages workers to contribute long uncomplaining hours to the temporal regimes of supply chain cinema. In *Be Creative: Making a Living in the New Culture Industries*, Angela McRobbie (2016) recognizes such strong affinities as both a troubling investment in capitalistic production and an uncritical acceptance of its precarious modalities. Similar confidence in vocational gratification coats academic work. David Hesmondhalgh is quick to note how these promises of self-realization and creative recognition rub off onto humanities students, culminating in an unrealistic oversupply of ready employees for these industries (Hesmondhalgh 2016: 36). In both sectors, the creative agency and respect that this chapter has exposed as distinctly marginal to supply chain cinema nevertheless functions as a promotional mechanism.

High on the wish-list of students enrolling into such courses sits the chance of future employment that skeins together various notions of freedom: autonomy, creative liberty, circumvention of the daily grind. As nebulous a term as it is affecting, freedom can easily become a catch-all for conflicting elements advantageous to the supply chain. Sociologist of work, Richard Sennett, posits that 'Revulsion against bureaucratic routine and pursuit of flexibility has produced new structures of power and control, rather than created the conditions which set us free' (Sennett 1998: 93). This type of freedom has certainly helped usher in JIT-style temporalities (no hours then unsustainable profusions of them at minimum notice), hard work for the suppressed wages of lean production and fewer means of recourse for grievance than in many other industries. There exists no shortage of scholarship that convincingly displays how, when freedom is held aloft in these ways, it frequently means to settle into place not qualities associated with stability (freedom from worry or debt, say), but with free *market* ideals like casualization and the withdrawal of workplace benefits and securities (Gill 2009: 236; Morgan and Nelligan 2018: 148–149).

Chapter 3 in particular untangles the troubling conflation of freedom (or free will) with free labour as a reputed 'foot in the door' of the film industry. In the last couple of decades, the economy at large has normalized unpaid apprenticeship-style training for entrants that can last as long as a year, but with no solid promises of transition into paid employment (see Hesmondhalgh and Baker 2011: 115–116 for fuller data on this expansion). Categorically, what this achieves is a suppression of wage expenditure and rights. Ross Perlin's *Intern Nation* classifies the creative economy's mobilization of unpaid labour as, 'Floods of family-supported interns [who] have brought the bargaining power of young professionals in these fields, minuscule to begin with, close to zero' (Perlin 2011: 169). At the individual level, internships may seem like a worthwhile trade off; systemically and cumulatively, however, they lessen the compulsion towards payment across the board. The *Star Wars* promo shows this in action, spotlighting unpaid interns within a country with no recent history of its citizens foregoing a wage. The growing expectation of unpaid internships as a route into the industry restricts its workforce to those with the means to sustain themselves while working for free. As Perlin elaborates in detail, gender iniquity is augmented by the fact that, across the entire internship landscape in the US, women take up 77 per cent of these unpaid positions. The absence of who cannot afford to accept them in the first place (and Perlin estimates that as many as 50 per cent of all US internships are unpaid or remunerated below minimum wage) render industries like film exclusive class formations by omission (Perlin 2011: 27, 28 & 168–169).

Karl Marx suggests a category that is germane to understanding this context. His notion of *labour power* enfolds the skills and experience required for the job, transformed into a delimited commodity which the worker sells, but whose recompense is then calculated merely according to the hours supplied. When an intern gains their labour power through self-funding, its accrual is thereby downloaded as individual responsibility and cost. Carlo Vercellone lends important insight here into this reduction down into purely the immediate labour of productive activity. He tallies this with a globalized and financialized exploitation of a 'cycle of valorisation ever more autonomous from a social labour process which it no longer subsumes in real terms' (Vercellone 2007: 23). It is now, more than ever, the worker's own duty to pay for their training through university education, rather than learning on the (salaried) job, as the ensuing discussions of the privatization of education, and Chapters 3 and 4, will unveil.

These outgoings frequently condense as debt, through taking out loans to sustain one's daily expenses and as paying one's dues in the hope of future opportunity. This debt falls on the hopeful worker, who owes not just money, but also gratitude to the employer, as the *Star Wars* interns' amazement epitomizes. Financial debt hangs heavy and long-term; it determines choices in the name of repayment (curtailing freedom, in fact) and brings with it modes of discipline and self-conduct (see Lazzarato 2012: 104).

When such education only comes at a cost (be it through university tuition fees or self-funding during an unpaid internship), opportunities in cinema result increasingly from what is known as *human capital*. This concept perpetuates the outlook that skills are an aspect of capital, of monetary value in which we ourselves invest and then own. This century, in countries like the UK, the state has withdrawn its past outlays for higher education, transferring increasingly more of that burden onto the student, now the speculative investor in a future further financialized by debt. The individualization of knowledge meets its match in British universities' policy-prompted turn towards fostering enterprise within curricula. As Chapter 3 lays out, the proposition that such an education better prepares students for competitive, self-employed careers corresponds to what Michel Foucault terms an 'enterprise-unit', wherein a worker transforms into an 'entrepreneur of himself [sic], being for himself his own capital, being for himself his own producer, being for himself the source of earnings' (Foucault 2008: 225

& 226). In the throes of supply chain cinema, to what extent can this be nominated as a liberating pursuit? Through its appeal to freedom and autonomy, supply chain cinema acknowledges how human aspiration is one of its slipperiest and most valuable linking mechanisms.

Just as profoundly (and without seemingly contradicting the pleasures of self-reliance), supply chain cinema also conscribes human sociality into its needs for efficient correlation and synchronization. Human capital and entrepreneurship ready a worker for fragmentation and short-term contracts. But the actual job itself remains, as has been demonstrated by 'project thinking', highly intercommunicative according to complex power dynamics. Michael Curtin affirms that 'big-budget feature production is crucially reliant on location staff that serve as an interface between the global apparatus and local resources. They make the system viable, and quite crucially, profitable,' while Courtney Brannon Donoghue's detailed investigations of transnational film productions reveal them to rely extensively on a fluency across various languages that are also technical and cultural (Curtin 2016: 678; Brannon Donoghue 2017: 89). Both authors thereby affirm Anna Tsing's insistence that 'Translations across sites of difference *are* capitalism: they make it possible for investors to accumulate wealth' (Tsing 2015: 63). Film commissions expressly step up to the plate here, but so too do offshored workers on the individual level.

Language skills nuanced enough to acclimatize the supply chain across divergent work cultures are essential. Film service producer, David Minkowski, defines his job, in an interview with Michael Curtin and Kevin Sanson, as, 'A lot of clarification, whether it was language or different assumptions lost in translation' (Curtin and Sanson 2017: 147). In a globalized context, where the lingua franca of big-budget cinema (including Bollywood's) is largely English, such job-readiness evolves from costly and lengthy educational outgoings for non-native speakers. As will become apparent, this schooling not only reproduces certain relations of production, it also itself derives surplus value (profit) from a training that promises to fulfil dreams of a brighter future. The Emirati interns featured in the making-of video necessarily speak English and become adeptly conversant in an arriving project's ways of doing things, translating them to the sites where they are insiders. Further, Tsing insinuates that such workers more than smooth the passage of the supply chain: they also help excuse its extractive ambitions (Tsing 2015: 64). Their service with a smile endows a pleasing façade to the opening up of their offshored market to these modes of production, something for which they appear to willingly aspire. Beyond mere facilitation, these almost-ambassadorial roles and the education policies that fashion them consume much of Chapter 4.

Rarely recognized as highly skilled, this form of service labour derives from a deep and expensive investment in schooling, often on the part of employees with distinctly less global mobility (but perforce more cosmopolitanism) than those whom they are assisting. Ambitious government efforts underpin these provisions to supply chain cinema from higher education and some brief introductory hints as to how and why is where this chapter now turns.

SUPPLY CHAIN EDUCATION

When a report prepared for the World Bank in 2009 declares that, 'Since intellectual capital and creativity are the most important inputs for the creative industries, investing in their human resources is therefore crucial', what, then, might a country's educational response be (Harabi 2009: 21)? Chapters 3 and 4 tackle that question in detail. In preparation, I now examine how the established ethos of creative training reacts to ever-greater supply chain involvement with the sector.

What we might classify as progressive pedagogy has long welcomed creativity and individuality. Yet, as Stewart Martin posits, the defiantly anti-authoritarian impulses artistic education once nourished now help ease into place a self-entrepreneurial, neoliberal autonomy that, 'needs to be understood in terms of this radical alteration to capitalism's metabolism' (Martin 2008: n.p). Similarly, George Morgan and Pariece Nelligan confirm what has just been noted about entrepreneurship in the classroom: that contemporary curricula routinely shackle creative explorations to modes of learning that prioritize professionalization and self-governance (Morgan and Nelligan 2018: 39).

'Employability' has become a yardstick by which universities are measured globally, including through the many international ranking systems that guide student choice. In countries like the UK, employability has been insistently inserted into courses by government policy frequently side-lining the rebellious esprit that Martin highlights. A human capital approach soars above older ideals of, say, citizenship training. Around the world, more and more universities provide work-based learning opportunities and most position these centrally in how they market their courses. In fact, universities themselves regularly compete to secure such access for their students, all the while saving money by sending students off campus. In this respect, the university does more than actively intervene in the labour market to undercut its salary scales. At the same time, it converts the nebulous translation of study-labour into value with direct benefits to both itself as it accrues tuition fees and to employers (Roggero 2011: 26 & 97; Mayer and Horner 2016: 245). Such manoeuvres exemplify just one small move higher education has made to rapidly reconfigure itself (at least in countries like the UK) as a privatized initiative set adrift from the provisions of the state.

The end result is that students will pay (their course costs as well as their living expenses, often as accumulated debt) to work for free within environments that are highly unlikely to hire them after graduation. Ross Perlin weighs up the consequences when, 'schools are now lending their moral and intellectual authority to illegal and unethical labor arrangements involving their own students...justify[ing] it all with high-minded rhetoric about "situated learning" and "experiential education"' (Perlin 2011: 83). These attitudes, belief systems even, inculcated during higher education, do much to inure the current and would-be worker to the rationalities of the supply chain, to *identify* with it, including its inevitable and systemic future of insecurity and debt. Ultimately, such institutions are populated with students and instructors who have faith in these models, who aspire to embody them, as a necessary route to survival and success. While the desired payoff of work-based learning points in the direction of individual income and satisfaction, the larger net result is an intricate assimilation of attitudes alongside skills that help render any given offshored site of filmmaking globally alluring.

Hand in glove with its moves to support a precarious, entrepreneurial normality for students, the sector has also been remodelling its own workforce similarly. In many parts of the world, people on short-term contracts provide the majority of university instruction. Chapter 3 will point out that, like filmworkers, they contribute many more hours than their contracts stipulate, although with decidedly fewer mechanisms for fair recompense. As with jobs in cinema, popular imagination files academic work as elite and privileged, making it all too easy to overlook how exploitative it can be. It is a narrowing minority who conform to a comfortable moneyed stereotype. Many more barely scrape together a living as they wear themselves down through unrecognized emotional and committed labour. Again, the attachment to vocation can dampen any spirit of agitation just as much as job insecurity discourages complaint. Rosalind Gill, one of the few researchers to consider labour conditions in the arenas of education and culture side-by-side, attends to these correspondences and their analogous technologies of selfhood. For her, the unwillingness by governments, employers and even workers to call these practices out as exploitation, 'leave[s] us without a politicised vocabulary with which to make sense of many features of contemporary labouring – both academic and creative – including exhaustion, chronic stress, shame, anxiety, insecurity, ill health and experiences of intensified surveillance' (Gill 2014: 13). Such professionals frequently subsist on a mosaic of unreliable incomes; they are rarely paid outside of term time, nor can they rest assured that they will be re-employed the following year. Hopefuls put in repeatedly and unsuccessfully for more permanent positions whose application numbers run into the hundreds. In this context, the tendency is, again, to compete, rather than mobilize collectively to change the conditions of labour.

Synchronously, the sector has expanded openings into doctoral programmes, the usual baseline qualification for permanent tenure. With little by way of funding for such study in countries like the UK, PhDs become commodities. Adrianna Kezar, Tom DePaola and Daniel T. Scott conclude that this is no accident: aside from the straight revenue doctoral study might provide a university, PhD candidates routinely teach multiple and large classes at a fraction of the price of a full-time or tenured faculty member (Kezar et al. 2019: 61–62). This labour is framed as training with the implicit promise that it will lead on to more secure employment down the line (so far, so familiar from the internship model in the film industry and elsewhere). Instead, an increase in PhDs and a decrease in permanent openings in the sector creates a supply chain-like pool of floating and replaceable precarious contributors. Kezar et al. continue that, 'human capital waste is built into the production process as a function of neoliberal governance' (Kezar et al. 2019: 26). And it is fuelled by aspirations to fulfil passions and perform unalienated labours congruent to those powering the film industry (see also Gill 2009: 241).

Although it is yet to happen in any profound fashion, there is the same capacity in higher education to 'Uberify' an on-demand and standing reserve academic workforce through logistical media (Beller 2016 presents a dystopian vision of this). That being said, as Marc Bousquet catalogues, the supply chain has still taken hold of education in some decidedly troubling other ways. In Louisville, Kentucky, logistics giant UPS has recruited thousands of low-paid, part-time and non-unionized workers in return for sponsored college education. In a story familiar from those concerning tax incentives, state coffers, not the company, underwrite this deal where, ultimately, few can sustain their studies because of the unsociable hours their work schedules decree (Bousquet 2008: 126–156). Uber itself has partnered with Arizona State and Britain's Open University to subsidize the cost of flexible online learning in return for 'diamond status' and thousands of trips from its drivers. Uber co-owns the latter's platform for microcredentials, FutureLearn. Such ventures accord with Ned Rossiter's apprehensions about 'the smooth-world fantasy of just-in-time services and education commodities delivered within informatized institutional settings and across the world's network of providers and consumers'. For him, these unfold from the encroachment of logistical methods of measure, monitoring and control that include the algorithmic management of research output (also bankable intellectual property) (Rossiter 2016: 32).

As noted earlier, beyond the realms of the digital, the UAE's clusters of privatized universities, largely offshored branches of global university brands, operate within deliberately adjoining free zones to the ones that produce supply chain media. Chapters 4 and 5 elucidate how both sectors avail themselves of free zone-specific architectures and legal provisions tailored to their priorities. In stark, physical form, their proximity points out how education and filmmaking are indeed neighbours along the supply chain.

What can be made of that? As an academic worker writing about conditions shared across film and education – presumably, in the main, for a readership of other academic workers (students and teachers) – one of my core objectives for this book has been to seek out ways in which we might struggle together against the harshest edges of the supply chain. Everywhere I have seen an opportunity along the way, or a vulnerability in the supply chain, I have highlighted it in the coming chapters. Here are some preliminary, more general ideas to that effect.

To start with, a university can insist upon more ethical (and/or paid) liaisons when it negotiates internships, thereby undoing the sector's ambitions to profit from unremunerated labour. The university is a crucial nexus point into which more partisan research and teaching could certainly intervene and materially alter expectations at the level of training. The directive to increase work-related learning and to prepare students for the job market also makes room for a critical education about supply chain cinema's impositions and allows us to consider, for instance, radical refusal and renegotiation, or a rethinking of what 'success' might mean. In this respect, I wish to spotlight the capacities Gigi Roggero ascribes to living knowledge, a corollary to Marxian living labour. Living labour is the work that cannot be recuperated into profit; likewise living knowledge is the excess that cannot be commodified and instead functions within the realms of social cooperation (Roggero 2011: 25–26). What aptitudes does intellectual work hold to push for change, what power to influence or arbitrate, to render conditions visible, to imagine things differently?

Film production studies, as a field of research, arises from an admirable and sustained history of actually talking to workers, particularly about their comportment and its implications, and from a respectful and frequently activist ethnographic perspective (Powdermaker 1951; Caldwell 2008; Mayer et al. 2009; Ganti 2012; Punathambekar 2013; Banks et al. 2016; Mayer 2017; Rossoukh and Caton 2021; El Khachab 2021). In so doing, these scholars frequently study from the ground up, sacrificing the larger economic and political picture for vivid, unique detail (see, for instance, Ganti 2012: 217–236; El Khachab 2021: 53–82). While in 'the field', an anthropologist inclines towards diligent observation without so much wishing to implicate or involve their own sector beyond the requirement of acknowledging positionality. Deliberate aloofness, however, for sure stymies us from recognizing that we are likewise workers caught up in the logics of the supply chain (not studying it from a remove) and that objectivity is, perhaps, just one more mechanism by which the supply chain reduces the friction of its extractive aims. It arguably generates one more product that transforms collected data into intellectual property for individualized gain as human capital or (monetary) value for an expanded knowledge economy (see Colectivo Situaciones 2007: 190; Borio et al. 2007: 163).

Instead, what I propose is something that attends to systemic injustices across the supply chain and how our *interactions* as workers along it might bring us together to stand against its infringements. Methodologically, because of the enormity of the former concern, I have felt the pull towards infrastructures and policies, rather than individuals. However, throughout this book you will hear from film and academic workers (including students), not because I choose to ground my conclusions first and foremost in primary empirical approach of that order, but because several such people have stopped me along the way. They have actively wanted to introduce their experiences as tangible examples of supply chain exploitation, to work through, in conversation, how these larger machinations shape their lives. Amongst these numbers are close friends whose lives I could not help noticing were tough, dangerous and harmful, whose conditions prompted my inquiries in the first place. When we hear from them, I label them as such to dispel any insinuation of neutrality and, because of our closeness, this book gains forthcoming and often humorous insights. The fact that some of them adopted pseudonyms betrays their concerns about speaking out publicly against the industry or at least their non-disclosure agreements. Welcoming in such stories reveals continuities and similarities across diverse geographies culminating in both evidence of homogeneity of ideological operations and, let us hope, the potential for collective struggle.

To think through the significant potential in lessening these distances between academic and cinematic workforces, it serves us all well to explore research traditions that have historically bridged social groupings in the name of political change. I am drawn here to some of the practices set in place as *conricerca* (co-research). This lineage, starting (at least) with Marx in the 1880s, reinvigorated as *operaismo* (workerism) in Italy in the 1960s, has prompted university educators to purposely set out to study working environments alongside those employed there. Study as militant participation arises as a primary goal, standing at odds with the presumed impartiality of most professional academic research. In its ideal constellation, the worker and the researcher become simultaneously informed and empowered by the interaction, united, as Robert Ovetz explicates, 'to uncover capital's weakness, identify tactics that would create leverage to exploit these choke points, strategies that assert and shift power to workers at the point of production or reproduction, and the objective of extracting a series of concessions that makes the workforce ungovernable in order to disrupt the capital accumulation process' (Ovetz 2021a: 8. See also Brophy and Touza 2007: 130; Cant et al. 2021, 175).

Conricerca serves as inspiration rather than method here for reasons that further underscore the slipperiness of the supply chain. *Supply Chain Cinema* does not derive from situated and shared research initiatives conducted on set or location with film professionals. This kind of access, I must underscore, remains notoriously difficult, particularly across two countries and when the researcher's perspective is so clearly critical. The supply chain's fragmentation and casualization of its workforce and the film industry's opportunistic globe-trotting and closed nature (from locked sets to non-disclosure agreements) render sustained endeavours to study it situationally and according to either traditional anthropological or co-research means, decreasingly possible. How much, even, would it cost to journey alongside a multi-million-dollar budget transnational cinema supply chain? These strictures highlight the differences between the settings for classical *operaismo* and now, which, in turn, prove instructive for getting to grips with the shifting shapes of the supply chain.

In earlier worker inquiry projects, the word *operai* basically stood in for assembly-line workers. In recent years, the journal *Notes from Below* has done valuable work to update these methodologies through attention to the gig and platform economies. While *operaismo*'s earlier incarnations were all but premised on a yawning divide between factory toil and the work of research and teaching, *Notes from Below* has insisted on conducting site-based engagement with academic precarity (Woodcock et al. 2018). Taking cues from this newer closer-knit approach provides scope to burrow into the supply chain's interconnectedness that all the while enforces class difference, making for a tighter 'co'/'con' within the co-arrangement. In the case of supply chain cinema, universities produce workers and the industry dictates curriculum. So, with some of the spirit of *conricerca*, this book deliberately speaks to people who criss-cross and coalesce such barriers, with once-student crew members, academics who traverse the practice–theory divide and students-as-workers-(in-waiting).

Employability brings us together. It has altered the structure of film and media departments, which now regularly look to hire practitioner-theorists who straddle both sectors. Similarly, inviting film professionals to class, especially those with imaginative approaches to struggling against injustice, could help expose problems in the workplace if re-routed away from the masterclass or insider tips model. Amidst both fields' crowded schedules, which make voluntary organizing tricky, encounters occasioned by employability provide valuable moments to think together, help each other out and build alliances. Now that the boundaries blur and academia is less squarely at a remove from industry, scholars can begin more openly to think of themselves within – rather than just as researchers of – it. How might these very traversals create momentum for fairer working conditions? And can the enforced interactions between the creative and university sectors become the spaces where we can do our best activist work? The aspiration would be, in the words of Colectivo Situaciones, practitioners of revolutionary, involved research, to establish 'compositions that will endow with *potencia* the projects and elements of alternative sociability' (Colectivo Situaciones 2007: 187). This is no meagre objective, especially within the time restraints of both sectors. Yet at least a shared awareness can grow, nourished by the encounter, hopefully leading towards the development of strategies of protest and refusal.

Recognition of our commonality, ultimately, is a crucial step. Precarity thrives on our disconnectedness, our alienation from each other, a competitiveness that separates us. Even if dreams to join the industry can be guided by false promises, they forge a link that need not entirely conform to the types of bonding the supply chain manipulates to garner its profits. As this chapter has hoped to expose, we share experiences, even if we do not know each other; we are interrelated in ways that can be subverted from the supply chain's ambitions for us. And both film and education carry strong imaginations of and impulsions for a better world situated as public good in contradistinction to a galloping privatization and profiteering. Much of our labour, regardless of supply chain methods, incorporates creative thought and action to this end. We would do well, then, to consider ourselves a creative class amidst precarity whose aspirations cannot be entirely recuperated for profit (as living knowledge) (Roggero 2011: 132–133). Such a manoeuvre requires difficult dissociations, at the same time, from all the operations seeking to split any such common ground. Yet the translational acumen of our workforce – as offshored subcontractors, as educators, as students grappling with new vocabularies and new ideas alike – can not only make our struggles legible to each other, but also work the sameness-in-difference qualities of the supply chain into something decidedly more collective.

2

Hollywood Offshores to British Shores: Riding the Rise of the Creative Economy

A few years back, I received an email from a close friend, a British film industry professional who had dropped out of his usual levels of communication. My prior message had simply read, 'Alive?' Days later than is typical, to excuse his silence, he joked, 'No, I'm an automated bot, a courtesy service from Warner Bros. for the friends and family of those who have sold their souls to us.' Alongside many other British crew members, this friend is regularly hired by the American-headquartered entertainment company (as well as other global media conglomerates) who now shoot the larger part of their movies in the United Kingdom. At the time of the message, he may have been battling through *Paddington 2* (Paul King, 2017) or *Wonder Woman* (Patty Jenkins, 2017). It matters little because the conditions remain consistent: unremittingly long hours sapping the capacity to maintain basic social contact and much more besides. They result from Warner Bros. duplicating a model of supply chain cinema actualized by a battery of variegated yet tightly synchronized government policies, managerial practices, and employee acclimatization whose interconnection this chapter illuminates. My friend's quip insinuates the supply chain's desire, where it can, to prune down human input, here eagerly replacing it with relatives of the logistical software introduced in the previous chapter. At the same time, his invention succeeds as a dystopian joke because of its implausibility. The soul is required, the body to its point of utter exhaustion, the ability to make light and press on nonetheless.

These sacrifices help establish Britain's status as 'the single most efficient onestop shop outside of Los Angeles that you will find in the world', in the eyes of Roy Button OBE, then managing director of Warner Bros. (cited in Jaafar 2008: A20). All the same, why does supply chain cinema flock to the UK and particularly Greater London – a city with one of the planet's highest costs of living – to avail itself predominantly of studio shooting, which could, ostensibly, take place in comparable facilities anywhere in the world? Button, interviewed for a House of Lords report on the industry in 2010, catalogues the draws: tax breaks (with lax impulsions to apportion spending locally), the ease of bringing equipment and workers into and out of the country (a basic logistical advantage to any supply chain), the lubricated mobility of capital through Britain's financial infrastructures, favourable exchange rates (now, all the more so, after Brexit) and an abundance of highly skilled *but freelance* English-speaking crew (House of Lords Select Committee on Communications 2010: 95). This chapter first establishes the broader socio-political measures that have nurtured these qualities. Over the last 25 years or so, the UK has ramped up policy to augment the creative economy, concurrent with broader programmes for casualizing the national workforce, deregulating many sectors, diminishing labour rights and welcoming foreign direct investment. A central factor in Britain's painstaking concoction of a favourable climate for offshored film production is that it bestows lavish tax incentives. These are some of the world's most generous, the kind that, for Button, render it, 'fiscally irresponsible' to shoot in places less accommodating (interviewed in House of Lords Select Committee on Communications 2010: 95). Essential, yes, but not entirely enough. Supply chain cinema also demands smooth and trustworthy operations. The chapter's middle portion examines these as a set of infrastructures and services put in place (often by government) to ease production and lessen its financial burdens. They range from industry-evident ones, such as film commissions, to some less obvious, including health insurance costs, conveniently covered by the country's universal healthcare. As Jeff LaPlante, Universal Pictures' president of production, endorses, 'The crew there is incredibly talented, making it easy to hire locally' (Yossman 2021: 63). Their abilities, this chapter strongly avers in its closing pages, rest not solely on technical proficiency, but a national context for service workers that spurs enthusiasm for and investment in just-in-time manufacturing conditions undertaken by small enterprise units that must be regularly disbanded and reconstituted. A British crew prides itself on being ready for whatever is thrown at them at a moment's notice and on contributing long, arduous and sometimes life-threatening hours. This chapter assesses the many intersecting procedures and practices that render this the case, starting with a necessary documenting of supply chain cinema's presence in the UK.

INDUSTRIAL RECONSTITUTION: FROM BOMBERS TO BLOCKBUSTERS

The United Kingdom consistently figures as one of the world's highest earners of film production spend (Lodderhose 2014: 128). The lion's share (over 80 per cent, and worth £1.55 billion in 2021) derives from overseas interests, almost exclusively offshored Hollywood filmmaking. When high-end television production joins these statistics – and, in the main, the same workers move between the two media – the figure rises to £5.64 billion, with a noticeable escalation in both sectors beyond pre-pandemic levels of spending (Lodderhose 2014: 128; BFI 2018: n.p; Grater 2018: n.p; Yossman 2021: 61–63; Dams 2022: n.p.).[1]

While a fair number of these projects draw on British themes, heritage, built and natural environments, just as many do not. Studios, rather than locations, have proven the destination for such movies as *Pirates of the Caribbean: On Stranger Tides* (Rob Marshall, 2011), *Gravity* (Alfonso Cuarón, 2013), *Guardians of the Galaxy* (James Gunn, 2014), *Jurassic World: Fallen Kingdom* (J. A. Bayona, 2018) and *The Batman* (Matt Reeves, 2022), which bear no narrative connection to the UK or, in certain cases, anything but an entirely fictional cosmos. This being the case, my analysis engrosses itself predominantly with supply chain cinema's thronging to British studios with a particular, although not exclusive, attention to Leavesden Studios, for reasons that will soon become apparent. At the time of writing, the country is experiencing a scramble for available facilities and a hasty development of additional ones. Hollywood blockbusters are solidly booked into London's premium studios, Netflix and Disney have taken out long-term exclusive leases at Shepperton and Pinewood respectively and, so desperate are projects to acquire space, that tales abound of productions renting venues before they even have a cast or crew confirmed (Barraclough 2014: 148; Clarke 2019: 17–18; Yossman 2021: 63). Offshored production nudges out lower budget (British) films as well as the BBC, who struggle to secure suitable crew, space and even necessary resources like generators and trailers at affordable prices (see Clarke 2019:18 and Yossman 2021: 65 for further particulars about this situation). The demand for the competitive advantages of filming in the UK currently outstrips supplies of these resources as well as others, human included (which Chapter 3 will lay out in greater detail).

Sitting pretty above this fray rides Warner Bros. In 2010, Britain's assets and assistance to supply chain cinema appeared so reliable and constant that they bought outright and began to convert Leavesden, their once makeshift studio servicing the *Harry Potter* franchise, into a permanent large-scale base within easy striking distance of London. Warner Bros. had already very much tested the waters by safely spending millions of dollars on this decade-long endeavour, resulting, by that time, in a highly profitable six-part series (Dawtrey and McNary 2012: 1). This period proved the suitable concentration and unique talents of local film workers and a region robustly networked into the global (movie) economy. From transport infrastructure and hotels fit for A-listers to proximity to London's more than a century-old film cluster economy, a site like Leavesden could promise world-class and standardized specifications for top-of-the-line scales of production, meeting the supply chain's simultaneous requirements of competitive exceptionality and interoperability. However, and crucially, before they committed to transforming Leavesden into the first such Hollywood base in the UK since the 1940s, Warner Bros. waited for guarantees from then Culture Secretary, Jeremy Hunt that tax credits would endure (Sabbagh and Sweney 2010: n.p.). This was but the latest of many threats of retraction Hollywood has played to finagle tax and other financial incentives to its advantage. In these ways and a few others, the history of Leavesden's makeover into a physical hub for supply chain cinema exemplifies both film-specific and broader political and economic evolutions that bring us to this moment of frenzied jockeying for the opportunity to offshore to the UK. The studio serves as an axis for this chapter for these reasons.

Leavesden started life as an aircraft factory, hangar and runway, initially developed by the Ministry of Defence for de Havilland and Handley Page to manufacture bombers during the Second World War. Hollywood had long established a presence in Britain by this point, holding a tight (and still unrelenting) rein on its lucrative distribution market. In part impelled by various quota systems that obliged them to manufacture in the UK if they were to sell their own goods there, US film companies set up operational bases, including studio facilities in the country (for a more detailed history, see Goldsmith and O'Regan 2005a: 135–149; McDonald 2008: 220–231; Behlil 2016: 69; and on quotas, Dickinson and Harvey 2005; Magor and Schlesinger 2009: 301). Since the 1920s, Hollywood bears a history, ongoing today, of hiring British crew and investing in UK infrastructure to make films of hybrid provenance. Leavesden's bombers may have helped win the War, but the country lay economically devasted in its wake. To aid recovery, the British Board of Trade stipulated that US companies could recoup their frozen earnings more quickly if they invested in British production (see Steinhart 2019: 31). Making films under these post-War circumstances proved cheaper for Hollywood than in California and, ultimately, Britain has been consistently striving to retain this competitive edge from thereon in. Rolls-Royce, a beacon of British manufacturing, took over Leavesden in 1966, while, a year later, and in contrast to this geography of ownership, Hollywood financed 90 per cent of 'British films' (Magor and Schlesinger 2009: 302). The mid-twentieth century also marked the development of containerization, the logistical standardization of the storage units used for freighting, allowing them to be seamlessly and cheaply transferred between modes of transport. This enabled increasing capacities to convey goods, offshore manufacturing and, in sum, to compound and intensify global supply chain production, as foregrounded here for cinema, but also for heavy industries, increasingly departing the Global North for cheaper prospects elsewhere. After Rolls-Royce closed shop in 1992, Leavesden's scale and clearance made it an attractive temporary studio for its first film production: the James Bond vehicle *Goldeneye* (Martin

Campbell, 1995) (Goldsmith and O'Regan 2003: 61; Goldsmith and O'Regan 2005a: 144; Bingen 2014: 217–218). *Star Wars: Episode I – The Phantom Menace* (George Lucas, 1999) and *Sleepy Hollow* (Tim Burton, 1999) were to follow before Warner Bros. secured use of the site in 2000.

Since their purchase in 2010, Warner Bros. has expanded Leavesden to comprise nineteen soundstages of varying sizes (many built from the ground up), a 102-acre backlot overlooking protected greenbelt land (thereby providing uninterrupted horizons for shooting), one of Europe's largest water tanks, workshops, office buildings, editing rooms, an on-site theatre, a capacious commissary, a gym and, unusually for such a workplace, a childcare centre. To date, Leavesden has begotten significant portions of large-scale endeavours like *Paddington* (Paul King, 2014), *Jason Bourne* (Paul Greengrass, 2016), the *Fantastic Beasts* series (David Yates, 2016–2022), *Justice League* (Jack Snyder, 2017), *The Darkest Hour* (Joe Wright, 2017), *Men in Black: International* (F. Gary Gray, 2019) and *The Witches* (Robert Zemeckis, 2020). While much of its output is understandably Warner Bros. fare (such as *Wonder Woman 1984* (Patty Jenkins, 2020), *The Batman* (Matt Reeves, 2022) and *Aquaman and the Lost Kingdom* (James Wan, 2023)), they also rent out to other companies wishing to benefit from Britain's supply chain potential that are then distributed, for example, by Universal (*Fast & Furious 9* (Justin Lin, 2017)), Paramount (*Mission: Impossible – Fallout* (Christopher McQuarrie, 2018)), Sony (*Spiderman: Far from Home* (Jon Watts, 2019)) and 20th Century Fox (*The Kid Who Would Be King* (Joe Cornish, 2019)).

Beyond just being a studio complex, Leavesden is also home to one of Britain's most trafficked visitor attractions, the Warner Bros. Studio Tour – the Making of Harry Potter, which allows fans to wander 'the real world' of the beloved franchise (its sets, props, costumes and the like) while also discovering how a skilled British workforce (on which Warner Bros. and the supply chain depends) fabricated it.

A carcass of heavy industry repurposed to make cultural goods and pull in tourists: little could be more emblematic of the turning economic tides in Britain over these years. Leavesden evolved from occasional to temporary to permanent studio during the 1997–2010 period of (New) Labour leadership. The Party was quick to establish an economic agenda that played to and aimed to strengthen Britain's creative industries, advancing a raft of policies that would impact both cinema and (as the coming chapter will elucidate) its education (Schlesinger 2007; Petrie 2012; Ramsey and White 2015; McRobbie 2016: 61–62). The country's imaginative flair and panache was to become even more globally marketable and, for this to happen, ever more people must join the sector. Even the Warner Bros. Studio Tour (henceforth 'the Tour') conveys the broader atmosphere stirred up in those times, still prevalent to this day. I draw on the Tour as both an example of this grandstanding and as a source of commentary on the industry from its workers, whom it liberally cites. Matthew Freeman, a media scholar who has analyzed the Tour, observes how it maintains a balance between 'behind-the-scenes' and 'into-the-scenes', an interplay that I wish to argue both advertises British creative exceptionalism and entices visitors into this economy (Freeman 2019: 126). Copious signage explains each filmmaking department's role and takes pains to acknowledge workers whose roles equivalent attractions rarely honour. We repeatedly hear quotes from and descriptions of the work completed by, for instance, set decorators, the construction team and those involved in hair and makeup; Stuart Craig, the production designer for the series, is mentioned more frequently than any of the individual films' directors. To elevate their contributions with the help of the franchise's theme, the language of magic recurs (Brannon Donoghue 2017: 106–108 also notes this). The audio commentary heralds the set building as 'real-world wizardry', cinematographer Roger Pratt (cited on a display board) refers to 'the images that we conjure up'. Bewitchment renders the realities of supply chain labour by turn mesmerizing or invisible. Most of all, though, ticket buyers are encouraged not simply to marvel at the cinematic sorcery, but to appreciate how, latent within British ordinariness (the kind architecturally expressed by some of the film sets on view, such as the humdrum British cul-de-sac where Harry Potter lives), the nation, like Harry Potter, might also possess extraordinary faculties. The fastidious how-to descriptions open out to numerous hands-on, immersive exhibits, full of 'you too can' spirit.

In these ways, the Tour falls into line with Prime Minister Tony Blair's 1997 call for 'a second industrial revolution... defined by creativity' through which the country's historical reputation as 'the workshop of the world' would be re-established through knowledge, information and design (cited without precise date in Blair et al. 2001: 174). Once a factory, now a workshop, with all the latter's implications of smaller scale units of production. The British labour-force was to constitute itself as a collection of modest, sometimes single-person and self-employed companies available for hire as freelancers on short-term projects such as a movie or any supply chain portion thereof. Industries like film, which had long since dismantled those elements of the production line that guaranteed permanent contracts, helped set the trend. In fact, as Jack Newsinger charts through careful attention to government statistics, the number of small and medium independent film production companies more than quadrupled under Labour, rising from a near-negligible figure to constituting almost half of the sector's workforce, with 33 per cent over the national average of them registered as self-employed (Newsinger 2012: 137). The allure of creative industries like cinema helped ease into place what George Morgan and Pariece Nelligan identify as an *'implicit contract between capital and labour'*, whereby creativity is promised as freedom, as satisfaction, as release from the mundanity of other work when, in actual fact, I argue, the bargain ushers in exactly the sorts of flexibility and self-reliance that are crucial to the lean and just-in-time modalities of the supply chain (Morgan and Nelligan 2018: 22, emphasis in original).

In 2019, the United Kingdom registered one of the world's largest percentages of creative-sector contributions to gross domestic product, amounting to £115.9 billion in gross value added to the national economy, more than aerospace, automotives, life sciences and oil and gas sectors combined (United Nations 2008: 29–30; Creative UK 2021). Not-for-profit industry body Creative UK signals that around two million people were by then employed in the creative sector with those figures rising at three times the UK average, making for double the numbers operating as freelancers than in the wider economy (Creative UK 2021).

As part of this shift, the individual much more than the collective arises as the dominant imaginary, something the Tour keenly, and unusually for such an attraction, perpetuates as well. One of the rooms along the way stores a wand box assigned to every credited cast and crew member, applauding the 'more than 4,000 talented, passionate and dedicated people who worked on the *Harry Potter* motion pictures'. What this does not acknowledge is that the franchise will have devolved significant responsibilities to these small and casualized entrepreneurial units. US legislation (which guides much of the offshored film practices in the UK) determines that an employer should not train or pay union dues for independent contractors, reinforcing the human capital model and encumbering the worker with those costs (Randle 2011: 151). Labourers in industrial regimes could rely on a supply of tools; now film crews must largely bear the cost of their own equipment (including licensed software), which they typically then rent to the production. Ben, a sound mixer, explains:

> We're in charge of our own kit. It's your responsibility, it's your liability. They'll always ask for personal liability insurance on your kit now. You've got to store it, you've got to deal with it, you've got to make sure it's all working, because it does require continuous maintenance. You're constantly buying new stuff. Now I've got about £100,000 worth of gear.

These expectations, in tow with sweeping casualization undergirded by government backing, fashion a business climate that unshackles the industry and the state itself from certain responsibilities that make it highly supply chain-friendly. Incrementally, workers begin to expect a lot less, including from the state, according to a trajectory that authors like Isabell Lorey convincingly contend helps shepherd in a broader neoliberal project to dismantle national social security systems (Lorey 2010: n.p.).

Phil Ramsey and Andrew White are not alone in contending that Labour's hyping of and support for the creative industries meant to buttress their 'decision not to reverse the long-term decline in manufacturing industries to which, through its traditional supporters and links with the trades unions, it [the Labour Party] still had a nominal attachment' (Ramsey and White 2015: 79). As physical scars of this transition, abandoned industrial spaces like Leavesden, Cardington (once an airship hanger) and Longcross (a former tank-testing facility) were converted into sound stages to meet increasing demand. Such buildings had been gutted by forty years of not only economic, but also anti-union policy, the rights of the workforce retrofitted in tandem. As suggested by my friend's comment about selling his soul and having no time for basic social life or leisure, the labour protections furnished by the UK's traditional manufacturing unions certainly, and by design, I argue, do not extend nearly as far into the creative industries. When a freelance film worker scrambles from one project to the next (which itself consumes considerable efforts in self-promotion), they relinquish not only the salary stability familiar from the former industrial model, but also the durable institutional communities, including comprehensive unionization, that helped sustain and push for workers' privileges. The British entertainment industry unions are now substantially weaker than their US counterparts, a not insignificant attraction for offshored film projects. British crews are left less reliant on the state, less unified against its infractions and thus certainly more competitive as a limber and self-reliant workforce for the global supply chain. The next part of the chapter digs deeper into other ways in which the government has actively built mechanisms to encourage external investment in (better labelled the exploitation of) this wing of the UK creative economy.

'A NATURAL DESTINATION FOR INTERNATIONAL INVESTMENT' OR THE MANOEUVRES OF A LOGISTICAL STATE?

How are these the machinations of what Ned Rossiter classifies as the 'logistical state': national capacities (people, spaces, infrastructure, legislation and fiscal policy) modelled to the needs of supranational marketplaces, vaunted as particular, unparalleled, and consequently competitive via this very patterning (Rossiter 2016: 169–170)?

Various government-affiliated trade and advocacy organs for the film industry, such as the UK Film Council (active between 2000 and 2010) and now the British Film Commission, have taken particular pains to attract Hollywood offshoring, including through an office presence in Los Angeles and a board that advocates for a commercial rather than patrimonial or protectionist attitude towards what British crews might manufacture (see Magor and Schlesinger

2009: 308; House of Lords Select Committee on Communications 2010: 96; Doyle et al. 2015: 52 & 145). Warner Bros.' permanent presence at Leavesden realizes a dream initiated at the turn of this century as part and parcel of the government's creation of the UK Film Council, whose first chairman, the movie director Alan Parker, urged the country away from 'parochial British films' to instead strive to become 'a natural destination for international investment... a natural supplier of skills and services to the global film market' (Parker 2002: 8–9). In a later interview conducted in 2013, Parker stipulated that:

> We've had two industries from the very beginning and it's not a bad thing... You have inward investment which relies upon our tax incentives to encourage films, mostly from the United States – very large budget films that fill our studios, and most importantly, create an incredibly qualified workforce of technicians... And you have the indigenous industry, which is the one that cannot survive... without government subsidy of some kind. (interviewed in Doyle et al. 2015: 56)

More than anything, the Harry Potter franchise, which created the momentum for Warner Bros.' permanent occupancy of Leavesden, muddles any hard and fast understanding of what might register as 'Britishness' in ways that carve inroads for the globalized supply chain. Reliant on international financing, directors such as Chris Columbus and Alfonso Cuarón and, of course, a Hollywood studio, a British intellectual property comes to life through the labour of British craft, including through an esteemed cast steeped in respected dramatic heritages. Yet to what extent are these aptitudes, long understood as the motor for Britain's own export commodities, instead being sold to overseas tender within a supply chain formation that now guzzles the finite resources for which local production also vies?

The Tour itself builds a bridge between these two configurations of labour. *Variety* journalist Adam Dawtrey reviews the experience as not 'so much a theme park, as an exhibit paying homage to the craftspeople who built the franchise. Its purpose is not to create illusions but to strip them away and reveal the skill behind them.' To his mind, 'There's no better advertisement for what the British film industry can achieve than the Warner Bros. Studio Tour' (Dawtrey 2012: 11). His assessment hints that the attraction functions as a calling card at the same time as a celebration. Every label exults the expertise of the predominantly British technical teams, the workers who have created the sets, costumes, prosthetics, scaled models, makeup, props and rigs. Overwhelmingly, the Tour trumpets the (standardized) 'difference' that Anna Tsing flags as crucial to viable market placement, matchless against any other film-friendly site.

All told, the Tour and the actual movie production carried out at sites like Leavesden embody Parker's demarcation of British crews as supplying competitive technical services to an outside market arriving with its own vision, thus normalizing an international division of creative labour. Courtney Brannon Donoghue concludes that the Tour's reiterative insistence of all of these workers' staunch involvement in the franchise 'in turn reinforces, promotes, and spins WB's presence in the UK' (Brannon Donoghue 2017: 108). And, simultaneously, the government's dogged promotion of the creative economy finds validation in a site that tourists from near and far visit in order to revere its achievements.

Such policy, however, does not stop at stage-managing a workforce. While Parker barely masks his dismissiveness of government subsidy for homegrown cinema, he remains open and supportive towards tax incentives as a primary means of acquiescing and appealing to incoming productions. In 2005, Chuck Roven, *Batman Begins* producer, summed up how, 'The crews are great, the facilities are great. But shooting in the U.K. without the tax benefit makes it the most expensive place to shoot in the world' (cited in Hofmann and Goodfellow 2005: A4). His appraisal underscores these measures as the crucial fulcrum to the border-crossings of the supply chain, which now finds it 'fiscally irresponsible' (to repeat Roy Button) not to chart courses according to such affordances. A producer whom Susan Christopherson interviewed for her research admits that, 'Many projects are now budgeted with specific incentives in mind before a director is hired' (Christopherson 2011: 184). Generous financial relief has remained consistent in the UK since 2006 and is considered largely responsible for the surge in inward investment, which rose from 63 per cent of total production spend in 2000 to 81 per cent in 2011, to demand outstripping supply as this book went to press (Doyle et al. 2015: 137). Allowances shapeshift according to policy and who is in power, but, indicatively, in 2022, film companies could apply for cash rebates of up to 25 per cent on UK expenditure as long as at least 10 per cent of the film's total outgoings landed in the country. 'Off-the-shelf' enterprises set up on behalf of an international parent operation are explicitly welcomed (British Film Commission 2022a). In addition, the Enterprise Investment Scheme exchanges tax breaks of 30 per cent and deferral of capital gains tax on other assets for those purchasing shares in 'knowledge-intensive' ventures, including film projects (see HM Revenue & Customs 2016; Cohen 2017: 43). Certainly, other countries offer even larger rebates: all the more reason to boast British technical prowess, and, as the final pages of this chapter will prove, a workforce willing to push itself to insufferable limits.

Ethical issues arise from these fiscal policies. Although it is nigh impossible to calculate their costs to the British taxpayer, Norbert Morawetz, Jane Hardy, Colin Haslam and Keith Randle estimate that 2003's £1.16 billion production activity revenues set the Treasury back around £2 billion (Morawetz et al. 2007: 438). Questions then emerge as to whether handouts to successful multinational entertainment corporations or rich individuals and equity fund intermediaries who defer tax payment through the Enterprise Investment Scheme might be the best use of public money. Jack Newsinger proposes that, 'Tax relief is, then, by far the largest single subsidy to film made by the UK government and is designed solely to provide incentives to Hollywood studios' (Newsinger 2012: 136). Rather than investing in other aspects of state or citizenry support, rather, even, than concentrating on more squarely national cultural expression that might stand up well to Hollywood fare, these measures, I contend, amount to purposeful engineering of a supply chain service industry. Orchestrated by the logistical state, they undercut the costs of production elsewhere, all under-written by the British tax payer. These moves fuel a competitive rivalry for (rather than autonomy from) Hollywood's attention as new countries and regions each year join the incentives game, increasingly affirming the tax break as a necessary price for advertising one's capabilities to supply chain cinema. On-the-ground US film worker, Calvin Starnes (interviewed by Michael Curtin and Kevin Sanson), blatantly calls such allowances *bribes*, continuing that:

> after these temporary communities are built on incentives or subsidies, the state legislature could determine the tax incentives aren't beneficial, which they aren't, and shut off that money and production would just leave. You would then have all this infrastructure gathering dust and people without jobs who invested in a career that no longer exists. (interviewed in Curtin and Sanson 2017: 109)

If tax laws were to change on a political whim, already precarious British crews would suffer near-instant repercussions to their livelihoods.

Dishearteningly, applicants have roundly abused these schemes on a number of levels, from double-dipping to claiming more tax relief than was ever invested (see Morawetz et al. 2007: 433 & 436–437; Szalai 2014; Doyle et al. 2015: 58; Johnson 2017; Goodley et al. 2021). When these profits are largely repatriated elsewhere, they attest to a proposition Chapter 1 put forward: that offshored movie production and financial offshoring frequently intermesh. Investigative journalist Nicolas Shaxson reveals the enormity and ubiquity of the latter:

> The offshore world is all around us. Over half of world trade passes, at least on paper, through tax havens. Over half of all bank assets, and a third of foreign direct investment by multinational corporations, are rooted offshore... Tax havens don't just offer an escape from tax. They also provide wealthy and powerful elites with secrecy and all manner of ways to shrug off the laws and duties that come along with living in and obtaining benefits from society – taxes, prudent financial regulation, criminal laws, inheritance rules, and many others. (Shaxson 2012: 11)

Quite clearly, individual and corporate manipulation of tax schemes transpire to be under-examined dimensions of how supply chain cinema both routes its journey around regulation and garners its profits. Shaxson uncovers how corporations, rather than criminalized individuals, bestow offshored tax shelters with the majority of their business (Shaxson 2012: 29). To give some historical flavour to that predisposition, in the early twentieth century, Warner Bros. fled the East Coast of the USA to California to escape licensing fees due to the Motion Picture Patents Company. A hundred years later, it still declares a loss on its high-grossing *Harry Potter* series, thanks to cloudy accounting processes that obscure expenditures and bypass taxation and royalties, through methods known, tellingly, as 'Hollywood book-keeping'. As an intriguing sidenote, within the Panama Papers (hundreds of thousands of leaked offshore client-attorney documents), various of the whistle-blown tax dodgers and money launderers were assigned code names from the Harry Potter universe, accountancy sleights of hands equating with the story-lines' magical themes.

From the government's perspective, job creation, both direct and indirect, in support of film projects, is the stated gain. However, while British citizens certainly profit, there are simultaneously levels of exploitation and extraction siphoned through not just tax breaks, but also universal healthcare. When a US company shoots in the UK, it avails itself of significant health insurance savings, thanks to coverage from the National Health Service (NHS) (for how this has similarly happened in Australia, see Breen 2005: 80). A friend's recent experience epitomizes these manoeuvres. While working at a remote location on another blockbuster franchise, he sustained a serious injury that saw him helicoptered to the nearest large hospital where he underwent surgery, then physiotherapy for months after. All of this was free on the NHS. His short-term contract meant that he was only paid for the following few days and, even though the company admit liability, ongoing legal negotiations (eighteen months and counting) have yet to see him compensated for loss of earnings due to his inability to stand (which is essential for his job) for the rest of that busy summer. Thankfully, his legal expenses are covered by his union subscriptions; those who aren't members typically have to launch proceedings on a 'no win, no fee' basis. His case points to how, at the same time as lowering costs and likely augmenting profits, what the UK provides in terms of state healthcare in parallel to state promotion of casualized labour helps exonerate foreign companies from duties of care.

Beyond these direct subsidies to production (and, evidently, well beyond), the UK government, like other equivalents around the world in search of supply chain cinema traffic, sets in motion what Ben Goldsmith and Tom O'Regan categorize as *measures* (Goldsmith and O'Regan 2005a: 42). By adopting this term, Goldsmith and O'Regan borrow its semantic weight as calculated steps taken by government to achieve quantifiable industry goals, often as a corrective to avert misfortune. Writing back in 1998, the state-mandated Film Policy Review Group proposed that 'Government and industry must continue to work together, so that each party can lever up the value of the other's contribution', although in almost the same breath as 'we need to create an environment that is attractive to foreign investors' (Film Policy Review Group 1998: 1 & 5). In 2022, the remit for this primarily falls to the British Film Commission, tasked with drawing in international production, promoting the country's infrastructure and lobbying for an ongoing film-friendliness of policy (British Film Commission 2022d). In harmony with a handful of regional and devolved-national bodies, the BFC strives to attract production spend by providing bespoke, around-the-clock assistance with studio facilities, locations, and crew, including arranging visas and shooting permits, and by lending a hand in negotiating the tax credit system (see, for example, Creative England 2022; Screen Scotland 2021a). Many of these agencies also supply additional financial support if they see local economic benefits to a project, with Scotland's Production Growth Fund, for example, furnishing up to £3 million (British Film Commission 2022b; British Film Commission 2022c).

Largely, though, film commissions facilitate. They ensure interoperability to big-budget cinema's highest specifications, fiscal and logistical. While a world-standard and standardized studio like Leavesden incarnates this in infrastructural, architectural and technological terms, the specific exigencies of smooth supply chain production rely just as much on workers' skills and attitudes.

MEASURES PERSONIFIED: SERVICING INTEROPERABILITY

For Anna Tsing, the creation and sustenance of a world-traversing supply chain depends on sites offering up not simply competitive distinction, but also conspicuous proficiencies in steadying and quickening its movements (Tsing 2009: 150). As this section unveils, the latter quality hones the former in how it creates a secondary tier of less-regarded service workers locally, bringing to life discrepancies (in pay scale at the very least) between colleagues of different nationalities. What, then, comprises this work?

As introduced in Chapter 1, crews who guarantee interoperability expend enormous effort on various types of translation. Translation becomes the labour of conformity and stands as often under-acknowledged additional labour in the name of profit for a multinational whose journeys search out lower salaries for such specialized work. In *Hollywood Made in China*, Aynne Kokas emphasizes how 'Cross-cultural competence is a requirement for most assistants on film co-productions. Indeed, cross-cultural knowledge can take precedence over a filmmaking background' (Kokas 2017: 150). Kokas is one of a steadily growing number of scholars who foreground the roles that local production and location managers play in smoothing over any of the (film) cultural differences that might slow the tempo of supply chain production (Kokas 2017: 140–154; Szczepanik 2016; Sanson 2018; Sayfo 2020). Kokas also recognizes these efforts as a form of translation and even compares the many local employees to compradors (historically apt for her context of Sino–US projects), given that, to a considerable degree, they take on the roles of trade negotiators (Kokas 2017: 112–113). The necessary service work to arrange travel and accommodation, say, involves constant assessment of needs, capacities and expectations across geographic and cultural borders. While supply chain standardization means a British crew will be usefully familiar with, for instance, how a shot might be set up according to Hollywood norms, they will still have to acclimatize to all manner of other practices of the arriving team. Kokas gives the example of adjusting to dining etiquette (Kokas 2017: 136). Even in supposed 'down time' a crew must fit in, not seem obtrusive or perplexing if this might disrupt the work of the international team: the unrecognized labour of learning to use a fork in a particular manner. Certain sites hold a competitive advantage here with Britain clearly faring well by sharing its official language with the US. Cultural, linguistic and even culinary proximity ease the movement to this site in the first place and help interconnect complexly dispersed projects already in motion. The fewer overseers and mediators in excess of the crew required, the lower the costs of production. These capacities blend into rather than contradict the qualities of expertise and pride in craft extolled by the Tour. A tension between the two fortifies how, for Anna Tsing, 'performances of cultural identity through which suppliers show their agility and efficiency', together incarnate a form of 'management' (Tsing 2009: 171).

When each becomes indistinguishable from the other, translation morphs into measures. Within the daily working habitus of all crew members, the demand for fast-paced and immediate comprehensibility according to the arriving team's ways of saying and doing things entails stepping up to a guileful compound of the latter's standards as well as all manner of new impositions. Examples might include when a film commission helps transform a rural location (such as Puzzlewood in Gloucestershire) into a fantastical setting (Takodana forest scenes in *Star Wars: The Force Awakens*) by arranging a temporary infrastructure that can bear the weight of a significant influx of people and equipment. It could also be how British trade bodies and unions like PACT (the Producers Alliance for Cinema and Television) and BECTU (the Broadcasting, Entertainment, Communications and Theatre Union) almost never challenge the prominence of major international studio projects that dominate over their members' own indigenous productions, instead concentrating on retaining wage rates within the former's established inclinations (Davenport 2006: 255). British creative exceptionalism and polite deference in these contexts boosts deft hosting abilities, each manifesting as a cultural attribute, which, in turn, displaces these activities further from how they might register as exploitation, precisely because they penetrate personal regard and outlook so thoroughly.

Noting the necessarily persistent nature of such efforts, geographer Allen J. Scott observes how the spatial concentrations of the film industry are 'also active hubs of social reproduction in which crucial cultural competencies are maintained and circulated' (Scott 2000: 33). Their reach extends considerably further, I would claim: in Chapters 3 and 4, I illustrate how expensive prior educational investments mean to indemnify these fluencies and normalizations long before anyone arrives on set. In the UK, this calls for an all-encompassing espousal of, as Ben describes it, 'What I understand to be the American culture of film, rather than them adapting to British modes of working'. He clarifies:

> They like to work in a very flexible way... If you're in studio, for example, the whole day could just be shot on two big techno-cranes, so the camera could, in seconds, go anywhere and do anything at any point in time. Although there will be a plan, that plan can quickly go out the window. The expectation is that they can throw anything at you, making the parameters as wide as they can... You have to be covering far more eventualities. You can have stuff dropped on you at very short notice.

Just-in-time modalities transpose here into creative possibility for directors, instantiating steep hierarchies along the way. As Ben explains:

> To keep all the possible plates spinning and cover all permutations of what might happen requires an awful load more work on the part of the crew. It also means that, once production have got the infrastructure in place to make anything happen, then they don't have to think about it so much or the director can say, 'well I don't have to plan in this way'.

He concludes current practices to pamper an elitist creed of 'you can have whatever you want, you just have to pay for it'. Does not all of this match up to Stefano Harney and Fred Moten's reflection that contemporary workers are compelled 'to move without friction, to adapt without question, to translate without pause, to desire without purpose, to connect without interruption' (Harney and Moten 2013: 87)? The two authors explicitly impute these impositions to the influence of logistics, the major force driving supply chains. Logistics' gains from brisk and uninterrupted flow finds its form in this shooting style. Ben associates it, in part, with how 'they don't particularly want to rest the actors, they want to keep them in the moment. There's an efficiency to it, you can get through things very quickly.' These techniques seem something of a translation, too, of the manufacturing processes of the 'pull' economy that logistics has enabled and which find more footing in video streaming services: a variant of demand-driven production that, in the words of Miriam Posner, 'means that suppliers must be prepared for a high degree of volatility' (Posner 2021: n.p.).

With British crew now so adept at these practices, Ben registers a decreasing need for supply chain cinema to bring over international (largely Hollywood) personnel, thereby saving substantially on flights, accommodation, expense claims and US union-pegged wages. The logistical honing of skill amidst the restless choreography of people, objects and places subsequently affirms their interchangeability. As a worker designs themselves to fit in, they simultaneously assume their replaceability within a competitive global market.

Logistics is a science of extraction as well as coordination. Mike Gasher, who has studied Hollywood offshoring to British Columbia, Canada, strikes a correlation with the exploitation of natural resources for which that province is more historically famous. To his mind, old patterns repeat: labour for an outside enterprise (once colonial logging companies, now Hollywood) creates a commodity then sold back to local consumers, but with little tribute or suitable share of the profits paid out (Gasher 2002: 142). Natural resources equip supply chain cinema with its quickly built and demolished sets (timber in particular) as well as its spectacular settings. While locations may be recognizable, a showcase even (as any local film commission or tourist board would hope), logistics simultaneously renders them what Hye Jean Chung terms (after Foucault) 'media heterotopias'. Chung's study brings to light the multiple and overlapping sites that make up any given place we see on screen, especially the effaced offshore workshops where digital imagery is composited (Chung 2021: 41). Her attention to hierarchies of creativity, labour rights and salary remind us to question the standing of (workers at) studios like Leavesden, their particularities erased by the spectatorial contract of the globetrotting narratives, like *Mission: Impossible – Fallout* and *Fast & Furious 9*, that they service.

And, similarly, to ask fundamental questions about the mobility of these workers, both geographical and social. When international projects move in, they will soon leave without taking many locals along with them to the next site. As Petr Szczepanik and Omar Sayfo divulge in their investigations of service crews in, respectively, the Czech Republic and Hungary, fulfilling though translational negotiations may prove, equal peer status is nigh impossible and professional upward mobility unlikely (Szczepanik 2016: 99; Sayfo 2020). These workers will 'stay put' in a number of senses, advancing a bordered geography of exclusion that protects certain workers' privileges at the expense of others.

The boundaries encircling the British economy make its crews traditionally more affordable than their American equivalents. Not the cheapest crews in the world, however. Supply chain cinema's forays into the UK for the incredibly human labour-intensive form of manufacture that is principal photography depends upon, as I have expounded, an aggregation of tax incentives, governmental measures, skills and fluencies, alongside relative affordability. Any consideration of aptitudes, however, must also embrace how these workforces are constituted and the limits to which they are willing to strive, both of which policy has done much to engineer. I progress now to British film recruitment processes as one of these particularly lucrative measures.

This book has already detailed the advantages to the supply chain of precarious labour formations as well as the active governmental determination to augment them that colours recent British history. The savings from project-based labour, though, require hiring protocols that unfailingly keep pace with just-in-time production methods while betraying the job security that anchored earlier versions of these techniques in Japanese automotive factories. Employment practices within the privatized and entrepreneurial sector of supply chain cinema streamline away many familiar steps and, in so doing, bypass legal and ethical protections that are routine within other industries. Companies rarely advertise or apply equal opportunities principles. Instead, networking, word-of-mouth and, most particularly, prior experience and trust form the basis of an appointment. Jessica, a trainee, details her journey into now-regular participation in the camera department by exactly these means. After more than a year of fruitlessly sending off CVs, a fortunate set of circumstances, recommendations, hard work, aptitude and compatibility allows her to humorously conclude, 'It's almost as if I'll never do an interview again.' This is because selection regularly devolves to local department heads to constitute the rest of their team, most typically from colleagues with whom they have worked for some time (Blair 2001: 152 & 167; Blair et al. 2001: 180–1; Nachum and Keeble 2003b: 465). Jobs do not last long, maybe even only a day or two, exponentially multiplying the rate at which contracts need to be generated, thus further inciting these kinds of corner-cutting.

In terms of scale, the fragmentation of labour down into short portions and small, sometimes individual human units does more than simply enhance the supply chain's nimbleness. Each group or single person assumes responsibility for not only their own success and reputation (making for a highly diligent crew as a whole), but also, as noted above, often their own equipment costs, which, in turn, reduces certain overheads. Moreover, while a crew member may join a department whose head probably put them forward for the job, individuals themselves negotiate their own wage and certain other terms and conditions.

This discombobulation leaves the worker and the sector extremely vulnerable to rights discrepancies and with very little of the bargaining power that unionized labour can preserve through scale and consistency. Tethering these creative industries norms to the 'individualized outlook' they inure, Angela McRobbie posits that, 'Maybe there can be no workplace politics when there is no workplace, where work is multi-sited' (McRobbie 2016: 23). The supply chain's need to recomposite itself quickly and with agility can only benefit from such loose protections.

If film workers want to earn a living in this environment, they must sustain the excellent personal connections, multi-layered interdependence, loyalty and trustworthiness vital to cohering 'project thinking' along the chain, despite the sudden and changeable just-in-time disposition of these jobs. Interestingly, when the Harry Potter Studio Tour relents on valorising individual achievement, it describes the team as 'a large extended family... skilled in a number of disciplines that all reached an exceptional standard'. Conservative social normativity naturalizes efforts in cooperation and collaboration as something seemingly beyond the wage relation and very much estranged from trade union solidarities. Ironically, as the final pages of this chapter will attest, the scheduling demands placed on British crew dramatically depreciate close bonds with flesh and blood relatives, substituting them for those with colleagues instead. And here, like in many families, unacknowledged emotional labour must be expended to sustain likeability within acute hierarchy, be that amidst units, across the international divide or in deference to those more squarely deemed as 'creative' and essential, like directors or stars. Cultural and social difference complicates the situation all the more when job retention or loss figures as an unambiguous threat amidst fierce (global) competition.

Expeditious hiring procedures and long, pressurized working hours frequently favour like-for-like, whether that involves engaging whom one already knows, a candidate's capacity to seem culturally recognizable to the employer, or even their acclimatized cosmopolitanisms that ease operation within an international team. I discuss these conventions with Serena, who hopes to break into the industry. After four years of volunteering for a small company, her boss invites her to apply for a temporary job, informally inferring that, 'we'll sort it for you'. Weeks pass without her hearing back and then, when she inquires, they tell her the post has gone to someone else, someone whose social media clearly betrays a prior friendship with the employer. The company informs her that the new hire has more experience, but, for Serena, 'let's be honest, she was pals with you and she went for a coffee a bit more than I did'.

'Familiarity' and 'camaraderie' advance from one's context, racialized and gendered at the very least. No such qualities occur neutrally or even cheaply; with scarcely a nod to meritocracy, all these criteria participate in the reproduction of a social and economic status quo (Randle 2015: 330–343). The industry's hiring mechanisms, by intending to retain certain types useful to the efficiencies of supply chain production, thus concurrently bolster a *class* of worker. For instance, first jobs often derive from family connections, increasingly after an unpaid or poorly paid internship (a topic for the following chapter), well beyond the reach of those who cannot rely on, say, family support to live within expensive striking distance of studios like Leavesden. A BFI (British Film Institute) study concludes that this self-perpetuating conservatism 'creates institutional barriers whereby those outside of these networks are not aware of opportunities in the screen industries and struggle to begin, sustain and advance their careers' (BFI 2017: 19). Serena, who is a migrant to the UK, benefits from no such backing. When a potential employer shows interest in meeting up with her, he offers narrow availability windows that clash with the schedule set by the restaurant in which she works. When she asks whether he can be more flexible, fearing that she might get fired for skipping a shift, he bluntly declares, 'that's not my problem'. That the UK film industry remains unrepresentatively white and exclusionary of those unable to coast through income-free periods (BFI 2017: 18) mirrors the gatekeeping of how Britons appear on screen and the supply chain's wholesale peddling of upper-class tradition, still redolent in *Harry Potter*'s boarding school mise-en-scene, with its Gothic and chivalric aesthetics.

Dispelling this detrimental image should also involve attending to who is hired to manufacture such movies in the name of supply chain efficacy. The ability to jump when just-in-time manufacturing says so relies on a categorical independence from social responsibilities or care duties, which are apportioned with much greater regularity to women and racialized workers (Randle 2011: 151–152). Serena once put in for a job that would involve eighty unspecified days of work across nearly an entire year, £120 paid out for each of those days after the fact. Or, in her words, 'Whenever we need you, you have to be there, no matter what and we're paying you nothing.' The reason the company gave her for rejecting her application: 'I didn't show willingness to leave my full-time employment. How do you expect me to leave? It could be months without you calling me for a job.' She recognizes that others would move in with their parents to cushion this seemingly crucial first step into the industry: 'I just don't have that option'.

Relatedly, but at the other end of the temporal spectrum, and as Chapter 1 introduced, supply chain cinema also demands unrelenting periods at work, practically unthinkable to primary care-givers. In closing, Chapter 2 now examines this culture, how it has come about, why it is so valuable to supply chain cinema and the harm it exerts.

'CRAZY HOURS NON-STOP'

Describing her job for a BECTU survey of more than four hundred UK film and television professionals, production coordinator Karen Rodrigues, holding perhaps the most logistically affiliated role on set, recounts details common to most British crews:

> In my job, I can be at work, or travelling to and from it for 16, 18, sometimes even 21 hours a day. These hours aren't the exception – they're the rule. All the pressure we have to deal with and we assume we can just work these crazy hours non-stop without decompressing and processing everything that happens to us? I asked a co-ordinator friend if she would hire me if I told her I wanted to have one-hour lunch break and she said no. Another co-ordinator friend said he would disapprove if I decided to take an hour lunch away from my desk and probably wouldn't hire me again. I don't think any of my colleagues have a proper break during our 16-hour working day. At best, we sit at our desk while eating lunch and replying to emails. There's no HR department here either. No one seems to have given any thought to the impact this practice has on our lives and mental wellbeing. I remember when the early, unexpected death of a location manager was reported, the news reports quoted him – in one of his final comments to his colleagues – saying: 'Being a location manager is very lonely. It is one of the loneliest jobs on a film. There is no HR, there is no structure'. (interviewed in Evans and Green 2017: 13)

Writing back in 2001, Helen Blair, Susan Grey and Keith Randle recorded a 12.1-hour average working day for the British film industry, not including travel time, which is significant for reaching out-of-town studios like Leavesden (Blair et al. 2001: 178). By 2017, Gerry Morrissey, Head of BECTU, confirmed that location-based prep-and-wrap departments (such as location managers, assistant directors, hair, makeup and costume) were routinely expected to put in eighteen hours (cited in Evans and Green 2017: 3). Jessica explains how unaccounted for hours build up, especially on location, 'We're filming in stately homes... so, often it's an hour's drive to work... then you've got long periods of prep and de-rig because of the location being difficult to access.' Ben agrees, 'The contract says, "We're basically buying you for sixty hours a week and within that week we can allocate that time whenever we want." You've really got no say in that. They can also call you in for time off the clock... You're continuously going over[-time] most days.' All told, an eighty-hour week is far from uncommon (unlike in some other European countries, such as Italy and France, although not in the US), meaning that, as standard practice, film workers sign contracts that opt out of the legal regulations that keep UK maximum working hours per week down to 48. Ben reinforces how supply chain cinema's primary 'imperative is to get as much done in the shortest time possible. The shortest number of days possible.' Logistical coordination of schedules like these maximizes savings on resources, trimming down rental expenditure on equipment, studios, locations or crew accommodation, if they are shooting away from base. The quicker the film to market, supply chain wisdom upholds, the sooner outlays and profits, particularly for the newer and more inconstant investors from the financial sector, can be recouped. British crews generally accept lower wages than their US colleagues (especially when the pound is weak against the dollar), but they are not the cheapest in the world. It is their relationship to the working day and night, amplified by their allegiance to skill and service, that particularly attracts supply chain cinema.

Its own shrine to this way of working, the Tour's descriptions of painstaking labour in the name of meticulous detail, divulge the human sentiment that stimulates it. For instance, while other films rely on digital backdrops, *Harry Potter*'s were hand-painted and often up to 183 metres long. Justifying the superlative end results, a sign relays, 'Although more labour-intensive, requiring hundreds of hours of effort, painting by hand provides more control over the texture, details, colour and shading, and results in a more natural blend between the backdrop and the foreground elements.' A pronouncement like this traces its lineage to British historical esteem for artisanship propagated by nineteenth-century figures like William Morris and John Ruskin, who politicized, even helped moralize this process in opposition to the country's pioneering of industrialized mass production. Overwhelmingly, the means by which creativity is presented throughout the Tour toasts the team's resourceful perseverance and stresses their resulting sense of achievement. Construction manager Paul Hayes (who also appears in Chapter 1's making-of video example) relates that, 'Every day was a different challenge, but everything the art department came up with, we achieved. It was just brilliant.' Banished is any sense of distance or alienation, the kind so classically accredited to industrial processes. Instead, this labour falls more squarely into a category that labour sociologist Richard Sennett calls 'craftsmanship', wherein skill and dedication bring personal investment and fulfilment in tow with such breath-taking outcomes. Rewarding enough to occupy gruellingly long hours that would rarely be tolerated in other sectors.

Paul Evans and Jonathan Green, the authors of *Eyes Half Shut*, the aforementioned report for BECTU, register that a 'martyr culture' persists in these workplaces, where no one wants to be seen as the first to leave (Evans and Green 2017: 6). Jessica points out how acute this becomes for women assuming jobs such as hers that have traditionally been occupied by men and which therefore carry additional pressures to 'prove yourself'. She continues, 'There's definitely a massive culture in certain departments of never taking days off. Someone who's very old school wouldn't look kindly on someone taking a day for whatever reason.' *Who Needs Sleep?* (2006), the title of veteran political filmmaker Haskell Wexler's campaigning documentary against the evolution and implications of the extended working day in the US film industry, draws attention to crew bravado about stamina. Jonathan Crary's examination of 24/7 culture reminds us that, 'Sleep is the only remaining barrier, the only enduring "natural condition" that capitalism cannot eliminate', although supply chain cinema clearly pushes hard at that boundary (Crary 2013: 74).

Even the Tour's hyperbolic signage discloses glimpses of regular futility when sequences derived from colossal effort hit the figurative cutting room floor. The transformation of the Great Hall for the Yule Ball took ninety decorators over a month. However, stories of wastage emerge as commonplace, 'More than 15,000 of these glowing orbs were created to fill the Hall of Prophesy set in *Harry Potter and the Order of the Phoenix*, before director David Yates ultimately decided to recreate the entire set as a computer-generated environment.' Extravagance in the name of perfection ascends as the overriding narrative, with more than a hint of sacrifice for the greater good to belie the exploitation engendered.

Unsurprisingly, what lingers untold by the Tour is that such expectations bear considerable consequences. First, and to press on with the urgent need grasp all this as a mechanism that bars entry to the industry: certain demographics are less predisposed to these job expectations from the outset, thus further kindling inequality of access to film careers. Although the national workforce is constituted by 47 per cent women and 11 per cent people with disabilities, the statistics stand at just 40 per cent and 9 per cent in the supposedly liberal sphere of the screen industries, in large part because accommodations to their needs and responsibilities have not been made with respect to working hours (BFI 2017: 18). Data from the BECTU survey bring to light the near impossibility of refusing extra hours with 18 per cent of participants professing that they had 'no choice at all' in real terms when it came to their legal right to turn down overtime (Evans and Green 2017: 6). Ben agrees that refusing overtime is 'not really going to wash'. Jessica details a fairly routine such extension of the working day, requested in order to shoot out an actor due to promptly fly back to the US (lean production by another name), 'When we came in in the morning, we knew they were going to ask for an hour of OT [overtime] before the day had even begun because they needed to get as much time as possible with this actor. You go in thinking, "oh, I have no evening left now, I'm just going to go home and go straight to bed."' She tells me, 'I've done jobs where I feel that OT is just not written on the call sheet [the industry term for the daily schedule, sent out in advance].' The repercussions for promotions and pay gaps borne by the supply chain's denial of this option, particularly acute during the Covid-19 lockdowns, when women took on disproportionate childcare and home-schooling (and were also therefore consistently passed over for contracts), will resonate for years.

Then there are the outright dangers involved for those who are available for long hours. One British crew member I interviewed mentioned the common practice of having to slap your face driving home afterwards in order to remain awake. Brent Hershman, a US second assistant camera operator, died because he fell asleep at the wheel after putting in a nineteen-hour day. These conditions have caused serious or deadly accidents for those handling heavy equipment on shoots, with Michael Curtin and Kevin Sanson acknowledging the impossibility of accounting for every instance across the globalized industry (Curtin and Sanson 2016a: 4. See also *Who Needs Sleep?* 2006; Caldwell 2008: 184–185). Eighty per cent of the BECTU survey participants admitted to mistakes attributable to fatigue, with more than nine out of ten disclosing that they felt unsafe at work or travelling to or from it through tiredness (Evans and Green 2017: 5 & 7). Jessica relays the knock-on effects, personal and interpersonal. For her, these conditions lead to a forgetfulness that means, 'I have to focus a lot harder and work a lot harder to perform at the level I'd like to', but also that these hours 'just make people irritable. It isn't good for your team spirit... which I also think can be unsafe because people start having a go at each other and sometimes I think that's an issue as well for mental health.' Ben ascribes these rigours to logistical importunities: 'Big Hollywood productions are far more intense atmospheres to work in. They're generally a lot more stressful. The demands on you are far higher and there's far greater expectation that everything is going to run smoothly.'

The impact creeps beyond set and into quality of life: the long-term physical consequences of diminished sleep and damage to social relations. In *Capital Volume 1*, Karl Marx rhetorically asks 'How far may the working day be extended beyond the amount of labour-time necessary for the reproduction of labour-power itself' (Marx 1990: 375)? Jessica proffers some concrete responses concerning the insubstantial attention to recuperation for a job that is 'mentally and physically taxing, with a lot of physical work and your body does need that time to heal'. This complicates still further, 'because you don't have days off during the week, so it's quite hard to go to the doctor, or go to the dentist, or pick up your prescription, and things like that'. Additionally, in a landscape of increasingly privatized health provision and fewer prospects of sick pay, employer responsibilities recede as self-care, even doctrines of self-help, less robustly plug the gap (see Lorey 2015: 89–90).

Crary blames over-exertion for 'a suspension of living that does not disclose the human cost required to sustain its effectiveness' (Crary 2013: 9). Aforementioned US grip, Calvin Starnes, offers a common insight from within supply chain cinema's voracious schedules:

You're overworked. You're exhausted. Your health declines. Your family life declines. Your entire quality of life declines... They will finish at eight in the morning on a Saturday, only to have to be back at six or seven in the morning on a Monday. Your Saturday is fucked because you can't function. Sunday you're barely back to normal, and then you're heading to work on Monday. And they're paying you less money than you deserve. (interviewed in Curtin and Sanson 2017: 104)

Marx, whose own incitements helped precipitate successful struggles to shorten the working day, corroborates how reduced rest, 'usurps the time for growth, development, and healthy maintenance of the body', not to mention relaxation and intellectual development (Marx 1990: 375). Social and familial relationships suffer undeniably, as do future plans (Evans and Green 2017: 6). Jessica lists, as any crew member equally could, the friends and family slighted because you seem to privilege work over them, the missed moments with children as they grow up, the over-burdening of partners with often solo care duties, the broken relationships, the plane rides home over the weekends off (if they are assigned) to attend to these basic dimensions of social life. With so many productions flocking to the UK, its workers can find themselves uncharacteristically working this intensely back-to-back for periods now of years punctuated with barely a few weeks off. Ben reminds me of how the aforementioned team loyalty around hiring can mitigate against holidays between jobs: 'You're obliged to go with your people' or else potentially forfeit future contracts via that head of department who will need to turn to someone else in the interim, who might later replace you.

Calvin Starnes remonstrates that unit production managers and line producers find such practices inhumane and inefficient, but that they hold little sway against 'the overlords who control the purse strings' (Curtin and Sanson 2017: 104). Again, Marx's words ring true: 'Capital asks no questions for the length of life of labour-power', nor does such life concern capital beyond its capacity to expand itself (Marx 1990: 376). Extending a shoot by a day during the planning stage alarms a producer more than a raft of overtime payments during it. *Who Needs Sleep?* concurs, pointing out how far financiers currently stand from the industry. A now-common practice that a number of film workers related to me becomes almost symbolic of this distance: production will send in a food truck to boost morale during a run of six-day weeks without evaluating how many crew members simply cannot step off set, scarcely to go to bathroom and certainly not for the time it takes to eat some pizza. Ben informs me that, 'I regularly spend most of my working day with one of my bodily functions unrequited.' Financiers and planners' detachment makes it increasingly simpler for them to abstract labour into balance sheets and away from the long-term health of crews, who are, in any case, highly casualized and next to anonymous compared to the salaried staff of yesteryear's studio systems.

Just as these calculations stretch hours, they also compact them in terms of expectations. Less so in the principal photography stage, but certainly for workers in pre- and post-production, fixed bidding has become a staple, squeezing outsourced efforts to punishing deadlines. Diligent, responsible workers who gain job satisfaction from the quality of their output frequently surrender leisure and social time to getting these jobs near-unfeasibly finished on time. Chapter 1 gave the example of how just-in-time practices privilege intellectual property security to the extent that crews are not given 'sides' in order to adequately ready themselves in advance for their day's duties. When Marx rails against how the nineteenth-century capitalist 'haggles over the meal-times, where possible incorporating them into the production process itself', he could just as easily be decrying the British film industry's now-standard continuous working days or nights (Marx 1990: 376). The industry category 'continuous working' means not officially stopping for food but instead relying on a running buffet, its nourishment typically crammed into spare moments while standing, in order that production can march on, uninterrupted by basic physical needs. Trainees are now regularly assigned the supplementary task of fetching this meal when the rest of their team cannot leave set to help themselves. Even though this might amount to an entire twelve-plus-hour day without a break, crew members like Jessica actually prefer such schedules because it means they can at least get home earlier.

The UK's agile protocols for working during the Covid pandemic testify to the country's propulsion towards these priorities as wedded to just-in-time competitiveness. The government forwarded £500 million worth of Covid insurance to production companies and waived the necessity for incoming international cast and crew to quarantine, thus, logistically, saving considerable time and expense. In the name of a swifter return to production, and when many sectors were still closed or banished to home-working, health precautions were bent for the film industry. As a consequence, crews were obliged to work under conditions of uncertainty, rigorous testing, wearing uncomfortable protective equipment for lengthy periods (Barraclough 2020; Barraclough et al. 2020). Typically for the supply chain, its workers absorb any added stress involved in its fluid interlinkage, often competitively grateful for the opportunity.

It proves increasingly tricky for workers to challenge time-based hardships. The global range of potential sites of production and their competition with each other increase any prospective activist's vulnerability. Anna Tsing terms the perilous expansions in rates of production ensuing from the threat of capital migrating 'the riotous diversity of nonscalability' (Tsing 2015: 63). While her analyses sit nowhere close to cinema, the UK, nor any such middle-class or creative industry professions, her conclusions demand our attention. The supply chain holds less interest in protecting and sustaining a workforce when it is replaceable. The copious interviews with industry and union personnel conducted for *Who Needs Sleep?* reveal the obstacles to contesting these conditions or their narrowed employment demographics from uncertain, freelance positions that concurrently rely on affability and perseverance. *Who Needs Sleep?* also demonstrates how union leaders hesitate to back reasonable campaigns for a maximum working day of twelve and even fourteen hours, given the flight threat of the supply chain. Indeed, the relative strength of the Hollywood unions, which have historically maintained something of a closed shop on big-budget productions, advantages more malleable crews in the UK (where no such force of membership prevails). More so the United Arab Emirates, where, as will become apparent in the last two chapters, the international zones of production have legislatively outlawed unionization (for a more in-depth comparison of British and American film unions, see Blair et al. 2003: 623).

Nevertheless, in the UK, PACT and BECTU have partnered to make certain petitions about temporal conditions in the form of the *Agreement – Terms Applicable to Major Motion Pictures*, which pertains to films of budgets over £30 million (the cost of very few British movies, but most supply chain cinema). The Agreement stipulates: standard working days (running up to twelve hours, depending on the department and break allocations) and weeks (55 hours over five days); overtime rates and work guarantees for sixth and seventh days; and turnaround time-off allowances to account for any transfer between day and night work (PACT/BECTU 2021: 1–2, 4 & 6). Sadly, closer inspection of this document concedes to language of hesitation and capitulation like 'Producers should endeavour' and 'should wherever possible' (PACT/BECTU 2021: 6). Rather than reducing working hours on principle, the Agreement prioritizes financial compensation. Similar to opting out of state-determined maximum hours, the bottom line appears to be that crews forego decent working conditions in return for increased wages (or food truck treats), a rapprochement that, in the end, affiliates with supply chain pressures (to return to Ben's phrasing: 'you can have whatever you want, you just have to pay for it'), rather than protections from national legislation. When I asked friends in the industry what would make their jobs more manageable, they all agree with Ben's summary: 'In a nutshell, I would say shorter hours. By far.'

It would be wrong, however, to assume an equivalent degradation of all standards. Standardization can, in fact, make things better. Wages are typically higher on offshored productions, catering is of better quality, in large part because these are the expectations of arriving overseas colleagues (Sayfo 2020 finds the same to be true in Hungary). As I complete this monograph, business is flourishing, with several new studio complexes under development to meet the demand. Finally, the unprecedented *choice* of jobs available to experienced workers allows them certain leverage in terms of pay and even other provisions (Barraclough 2016: 63). It remains to be seen whether these negotiations will continue to be largely conducted at the individual level or whether organized labour can institute meaningful change, ever wary of the supply chain's geographical volatility. In studio spaces themselves, improvements have materialized in the form, for example, of Leavesden's first-of-its-kind childcare unit, which broadens the scope of who might be able now to work in the industry, even if such services predominantly ease, rather than alter, the difficulties generated by long working hours.

The unusual surfeit of opportunity has also promulgated a skills shortage. The industry recognizes the imperative to train more workers and, as such, the next chapter examines their education, paying particular mind to how it impels future crews to uphold the central pillars of the supply chain ethos, as detailed in this one, within their workplace comportment.

NOTE

1   The presence of multinational producers of high-end television in the UK in the early 2020s cannot go unacknowledged. As noted, they contribute more to the British economy than big-budget cinema. Streamer giants such as Amazon and Netflix employ thousands of British crew members across multiple productions, taking advantage of the same tax incentives that will be discussed in this chapter. Given the increasing vertical integration of these corporations (which now make as well as distribute audio-visual content), not to mention the more accurate feedback loops they sustain concerning consumer tastes, I would argue that they are even more supply chain-inclined than big-budget cinema. Ultimately, they bear the capacity to further rationalize the journey to market, exacting ever-new means of just-in-time manufacturing as they do so. These practices are worthy of a comprehensive study in their own right; a digression into this field in the current context could barely do justice to the production techniques at work in contemporary high-end television.

3

Training Creative Wizardry: UK Supply Chain Filmmaking Education

Leavesden-shot *Harry Potter and the Goblet of Fire* (Mike Newell, 2005) contains a short, but germane encounter that does not feature in the original book. Barty Crouch Jr, disguised as one Professor Moody (Brendan Gleeson), confronts his estranged father with, 'Bartemius! Not trying to lure Potter into one of the Ministry's summer internships, are we? Last boy who went into the Department of Mysteries never came out.' Here he darkly alludes to how his own parent had imprisoned him in Azkaban. The joke succeeds because work experience that is arranged through educational institutions is now so commonplace. And because, for many, the process feels like a torturous betrayal of one generation by another. The Harry Potter series, of course, is largely set in a school and, as the previous chapter noted, the studio tour that celebrates it adopts an overwhelmingly instructional tone. The franchise's success in mythologizing a particular ideal of traditional (and elite) British education is consolidated by its cast (some of the country's best-trained actors) and its highly skilled crew.

As Chapter 2 concluded, film business in the twenty-first century, even post-pandemic, has rocketed, courtesy of numerous measures to attract supply chain production. The UK finds itself in the rare position of an under-supply of capable, ready-to-hire film workers and a resounding imperative from government agencies to train more. This chapter investigates these junctions between formal education and the industry. The casualized and freelance shape of the latter has led to it largely relinquishing its potential or desire to invest in training (through apprenticeships and the like). Higher education, notably paid for by the student, not an employer, has assumed that role. Now industry, supported by government, presses for courses that impart the standards (technical and attitudinal) required for cinema's supply chain to operate without hiccup. In so doing, they contest many precepts critical higher education holds dear. The sheer extent of the supply chain comes to light as it reaches deep into how workers are trained to comply with its priorities. The upcoming pages therefore explore how UK film and media education at universities becomes an armature tasked with such preparation. I shall concentrate, primarily, on broad outlooks and disciplining mechanisms, rather than the nuts and bolts of, for instance, set lighting or particular software.

Here I concur with Angela McRobbie, one of the foremost scholars to connect these dots, that degrees increasingly animate students to 'adjust themselves to the idea of enterprise culture' (McRobbie 2016: 11). More specifically, this chapter investigates how 'employability', with an ever-escalating emphasis on 'work-readiness', entrepreneurship, competition and networking, helps usher in and normalize the culture of unpaid, underpaid and dangerously long hours explored in the last. The sector's teachers endure comparable conditions at the same time as they are asked to promote them within an increasingly defunded context that endorses a human capital paradigm floated on student debt. In drawing to a close, then, this chapter seeks ways to confront and disassemble the supply chain's injustices at the meeting points of these two sectors.

SUPPLYING THE SUPPLY CHAIN

Government estimates predicted the potential to earn an additional £1.43–2.02 billion in film and high-end television spend by 2025, on top of 2021's £5.64 billion (ScreenSkills et al. 2022: 2). The only snag: the need for an additional 15–21,000 new full-time crew members to satisfy capacity (ScreenSkills et al. 2022: 2). In something of a surprise turn, an industry typified by much aspiration and little in the way of success stories now scrambles for workers. Adrian Wootton, Chief Executive of the British Film Commission and Film London, admitted, 'We do have a skills shortage. We have managed to crew everything, but we are getting a huge amount of demand. We're coping, but we need to do more than cope' (Barraclough 2016: 63). Around £289.3 million would be invested to hurriedly train more (ScreenSkills et al. 2022: 3; BFI 2022). Skills gap reviews and forecasts, commissioned by the Department for Digital, Culture, Media & Sport, pinpoint a particular urgency for the sorts of service roles supply chain cinema commands, such as production coordinators, location managers and assistants, and unit managers (BFI 2022; ScreenSkills 2022e; ScreenSkills et al. 2022: 5). Like never before, the industry is pursuing ways to not just populate its supply chain, but also shape its workforce in advance. Having all but by design stepped away from this responsibility, it now relies on established providers from higher education, who have trained at least 68 per cent of the current workforce (Paterson 2014: 137).

No wonder, when the supply chain marshals an 'industry' constituted in large part by a ceaselessly reconfiguring patchwork of small self-contained units according to lean and just-in-time constitutions that have jettisoned many such long-term investments. In years gone by, Hollywood's Fordist persuasion made for extensive on-the-job brass-tacks training; concurrently, the planned economies of the socialist states pipelined their film school graduates into guaranteed jobs. Nowadays, casualization plagues in-situ learning, provoking an unpredictability in workers' journeys towards more senior roles. A clapper loader, say, might progress throughout their career to eventually become a director of photography, but only along channels troubled by the unmonitored informalities catalogued in the previous chapter (such as the industry's tendencies towards maintaining socially compatible teams and hiring according to family connections and personal recommendations, rather than through interviews).

Permanent studio facilities involve themselves in training to a certain degree. Leavesden, for example, offers apprenticeships in a few scant areas, such as set lighting and plumbing (Warner Bros. Studios Leavesden 2022). Netflix and Amazon have committed to apprenticeships via television productions, rather than films and, similarly, the long-running show *Outlander* supports a flourishing trainee initiative in collaboration with Screen Scotland and ScreenSkills (Yossman 2021: 65; Screen Scotland 2021b). BECTU, the union representing production workers, provides a range of free or discounted courses to its members, predominantly short-range (such as the Creative Industries Safety Passport), targeted towards freelancers (for instance, a two-hour copyright awareness Zoom course) or responding to immediate and smaller scale shortages (like hair and makeup for BAME performers). The chief player in this landscape is ScreenSkills, an industry-led body sustained by public funds. Screenskills runs its own portfolio of short online courses, a careers service, a mentoring network, a broad range of apprenticeships around the county, job sharing matches (largely in television) and a trainee finder programme (ScreenSkills 2022a; ScreenSkills 2022b; ScreenSkills 2022g). However, it is its capacity as a broker between industry and education providers that preoccupies this chapter in the main.

While universities have happily enrolled increasing numbers of aspiring filmmakers over the years, they have not traditionally understood themselves to function in the service of industry, let alone its more supply chain-oriented proclivities. As Duncan Petrie and Rod Stoneman's detailed *Educating Film-makers* charts, film schools have customarily upheld a conservatoire model, typically funded by governmental coffers, that might feed directly into national production. Nevertheless, they have regularly fostered inclinations towards unfettered artistry. Elsewhere, Petrie charts how, from the 1990s, the UK's two most prominent film schools, the National Film and Television School and the London Film School, sculpted their curricula into degrees in order to take advantage of more fulsome subsidy via HEFCE (the Higher Education Funding Council for England). In 1992, a swathe of polytechnics gained university status, adapting their more practice-based approaches to film and media training to also meet a degree structure (Petrie 2012: 359). Synchronously, and not at all unrelatedly, ScreenSkills' former incarnations saw their funding reduced, prompting them to lean more heavily on universities to train future film industry personnel (Petrie 2012: 371–372). The degree thus became a predominant qualification at the same time as the government began to withdraw funding for higher education, demand and then increase tuition fees.

In the wake of less forethought or involvement from industry or state, it was not long before a 2010 House of Lords report could regret that, 'University courses are not delivering the skills required', amplifying the deficit of 'set-ready' workers the following decade (House of Lords Select Committee on Communications 2010: 7). Accustomed to prolonged dismissiveness towards (even historic stigmatization of) the 'usefulness' of a degree, university teachers might remonstrate that study within the arts and humanities was never designed to lead into a straightforward job qualification (even though, as this chapter will soon particularize, they increasingly promise as much).

At this moment, ScreenSkills steps in, tasked with closing the distance between higher education and industry, although rarely on equal terms. Launched first as Skillset (later Creative Skillset) in the 1990s, the industry-led body's mandate is to inaugurate and coordinate training, including through prescriptive accreditation mechanisms that tighten this portion of the supply chain considerably (for a detailed evaluation of ScreenSkills' history and priorities for higher education, see Petrie 2012: 358). As its chief interaction with the university sector, ScreenSkills ratifies qualifications and those fit to award them, a hallmarking process for which courses nominate themselves. If their application is successful, accreditation advertises both graduates to industry and courses to prospective students, narrowed to the parameters of job prospects. The process adheres to a system of standardization and easy recognition familiar from supply chain modularization, rendered literal by an insistence on proficiency with industry-standard equipment and technique.

'Are you industry relevant?' the ScreenSkills Select leaflet to educational institutions bluntly challenges on its second page (ScreenSkills n.d.b: 2). Answering affirmatively according to ScreenSkills' specifications turns out to be a costly endeavour for institutions that have weathered plummeting state subsidy. Although supported by public monies via the BFI, the National Lottery and Arts Council England, ScreenSkills charges administrative fees of £2,999 for each application, plus an annual re-endorsement fee of £980 (ScreenSkills 2022d). Much more expensive, though, are their stipulations that students must work with 'professional facilities and resources that replicate current industry practice... [and receive] sufficient dedicated access to supervision and technical support' (ScreenSkills n.d.a: 4 & 8). In so doing, they couple a preference for industry needs with a deflection of their costs onto the student and university in an untenable manner. Jessica, introduced in Chapter 2, graduated from one such postgraduate programme. Counter to ScreenSkills' ambitions, she repeatedly finds what she learnt to be conspicuously outmoded in the eyes of her colleagues. She reasons that 'technology, especially in the technical disciplines, advances so fast that it's quite hard to be teaching you what's actually happening on set at uni'. How beholden to short-termism is the acquisition of prescriptive technical skills that could well outdate quickly? That such things can only be properly grasped in situ suggests how ScreenSkills' pedagogical priorities may be otherwise motivated.

A series of policy decisions impelling higher education towards a more skills-based approach embolden ScreenSkills towards expediting what 2012's influential Wilson Review, an independent report commissioned by the Department for Business, Innovation & Skills, termed the 'business–university collaboration' (Wilson 2012: 2). In parallel spirit to Chapter 2's giving voice to film professionals, the pages to come compile plentiful commentary from university faculty, whose analyses stem empirically from teaching within this context. In the eyes of Yael Friedman and Steve Whitford, two academics who deliver a ScreenSkills-accredited course at the University of Portsmouth, this relationship unequivocally places universities 'at the service of the economy and industry' with the objective to '"produce" graduates who would possess the skills to contribute to Britain's growing post-industrial knowledge economy' (Friedman and Whitford 2018: n.p.). In order for any such course to pass ScreenSkills' rigorous and regular evaluation process, they must meet criteria that notably include (first and foremost) 'an industry focus', 'strong engagement with employers' and evidence that they are (and I wish to flag this particularly in relation to the current climate) 'addressing current sector skills gaps and shortages in curriculum design' (ScreenSkills 2022c). Duncan Petrie summarizes the resulting emphases as 'a very singular, highly contestable and ultimately reductive vision of film and its wider purpose and role in society' (Petrie 2012: 369; for further critique of university-creative industries alliances, see Oakley 2013; Noonan 2015; Ramsey and White 2015; Friedman and Whitford 2018).

Friedman and Whitford also identify an objective of realigning 'the British film industry as a hub of skills and services catering for the global film market' (Friedman and Whitford 2018: n.p.). The insistence on technical fluency converged to international norms eases the movement of offshored projects into the country's film economy. Indeed, the Wilson Review, which politically licences ScreenSkills' agenda, repeatedly enforces that, 'Universities are an integral part of the skills and innovation supply chain to business' (Wilson 2012: ii). This is no mere figurative turn of phrase. The Wilson Review's conceptualization of a lengthened and multi-dimensional supply chain adamantly integrates higher education, insisting that its more formal inclusion 'can only be secured through close collaboration, partnership and understanding between business and universities' (Wilson 2012: ii).

On the ground, these interactions amount to 'an active participation by employers' (another Wilson Review recommendation) (Wilson 2012: 30). Rebecca Boden and Maria Nedeva identify a shift from a time when universities forged connections beyond their walls according to shared ethos. For them, 'a functional attribute' has recently supplanted this ideal, one that concurrently permits government, 'through technologies of audit, accountability and performance measurement', to determine and manage the precise nature of universities' external relations (Boden and Nedeva 2010: 41). Film academics have been kept peripheral to policy decisions and even to ScreenSkills' constitution, while suffering disconcerting levels of intervention. ScreenSkills' application guidelines remind prospective courses that 'Curriculum design should have regular input from the industry' and that there must be 'industry assessment of student work' (ScreenSkills n.d.a: 7). Phil Ramsey and Andrew White justifiably remonstrate that, with these actions, industry partners become 'the final arbiters of what the involved universities should be teaching', marginalizing other ideals of liberal, critical, or politicized education (Ramsey and White 2015: 87–88). Moreover, ScreenSkills proclaims that 'project work *should not undermine commercial business opportunities*' (my emphasis), this imperative all but ruling out non-conformity to capitalist manufacture and accumulation (ScreenSkills n.d.a: 7). We find ourselves far, at this point, from the image of the art or film school that foments rebellion, where, to the mind of Dick Ross (an experienced tutor at institutions like the NFTS, the Royal College of Art and NYU), 'To try something and fail is better than to deliver to Sir something that is perfectly light, perfectly sharp, but just crap in terms of content' (interviewed in Boorman et al. 2002: 44). Kate Oakley attributes teaching staff's compliance with such directives to a concurrent casualization of increasing numbers of workers within the sector, contract renewal remaining a central concern that disinclines educators from more disruptive actions (Oakley 2013: 39). When these colleagues parachute in to deliver often pre-ordained syllabi, the institution affords them little critical engagement with the wider curriculum or scope to involve themselves in on-campus political organizing, including through unions.

Explicitly recognizing (and implicitly encouraging) the dwindling of secure forms of employment across the board, the Wilson Review urges universities to practically guide 'students [to] understand the opportunities that are available in the SME sector or in self-employment' while refining and monitoring their 'employability, enterprise and entrepreneurial skills' (Wilson 2012: 3 & 2). Success in these terms was to be used in recruitment and to determine how universities would be evaluated. ScreenSkills was already well positioned to operate within this milieu, in fact the Wilson Review holds it up as an exemplary sector skills council (SSC), representing an industry extolled for its composition as a network of small independent companies (Wilson 2012: 42–43). ScreenSkills requests that entrepreneurship features prominently in its endorsed programmes, abiding by the Wilson Review's encouragement that it be 'celebrated, rewarded and promoted' (ScreenSkills n.d.a: 6; Wilson 2012: 14).

THE EMPLOYABLE ENTREPRENEUR

What sort of 'enterprise' can retain its essence of self-determination while also accommodating a seemingly contradictory obedience to standardization? One, I would argue, that hinges, on 'employability'. Note the Wilson Review's naturalizing coalescence of the two terms. To refresh some observations from Chapter 1: national policies and international university ranking systems alike now place employability centre stage, reaffirming a human capital approach to higher education, with the goal set as student-consumers walking out of degrees into jobs. ScreenSkills' promise of 'set-ready' graduates acquainted with the industry's techniques and technologies bears this out.

This is but a portion of what employability encompasses and grasping its ramifications necessitates attuning to enterprise's place in British universities. First and foremost, it is government-mandated, substantiating Gigi Roggero's allegation that academics increasingly operate as 'state-subsidized entrepreneurs' (Roggero 2011: 62). His focus falls on how academics are obliged to hunt for grants to bankroll their own salaries as intellectual property relations encroach upon the sector. Increasingly, in the UK, funding bodies also favour a tightening of orbits between industry and researchers, pressure that certainly reinforces and magnifies the agendas with which this chapter grapples. Caitriona Noonan catalogues how this entrepreneurial ethos beds down in increasing curricular pressure for students 'to network, self-promote and develop social capital, along with demonstrating flexibility, self-governance and an absolute willingness to contribute' (Noonan 2013: 141). As well as soaking in the directive to implant entrepreneurialism into what they teach, British universities have absorbed its spirit into how they vie against each other to advertise their programmes. Their range of golden ticket enticements dangle bright futures through rhetoric of employability at the same time as they pledge to nurture personal vision.

George Morgan and Pariece Nelligan qualify the latter as: 'your fate depends primarily on your inner drive, your ability to mobilise a questing creative individualism' (Morgan and Nelligan 2018: 37). These characteristics lie at the heart of how such programmes frame entrepreneurialism. Even the customary degree structure that assesses students independently, including for group work, regularizes this. More specifically, film (and especially ScreenSkills) education congregates around workshops, masterclasses and professional advice sessions whose narratives insist upon chutzpah and initiative as the entrepreneurial keys to (far-from-guaranteed) lucky breaks (Banks 2019: 73 confirms this emphasis in US courses too). So much for imparting the crucial industry requirement of seamless teamwork. Repeating these means to happy endings clearly obscures what the previous chapter revealed: that race, gender, class and income more forcefully determine who gets 'a foot in the door' (see McCarthy 2011: 303; Littler 2018: 93; Banks 2019: 78–79 for how higher education upholds class privilege). This version of entrepreneurialism conveniently absolves the state and industry from initiating more thorough systemic change at the level of inclusive entry points or working conditions. It also corresponds to the supply chain's ready disconnection from any such ethical duties when they entail deeper investment. Furthermore, for scholars like Angela McRobbie, entrepreneurialism fosters a resilience amidst casualization, as well as a decreased reliance on organized labour, workplace protections, collectivity and public sector provision, all deliberately engineered *by the state itself* (McRobbie 2016: 67). The end results both benefit a smaller state and deftly advertise the country over rivals as fruitful for the transnational supply chain cinema's undercutting of local safety nets and benefits. After all, the supply chain also yokes standardization to self-motivation and self-sufficiency.

These surfacing as the contours of the landscape, Sophie Hope and Joanna Figiel fittingly inquire, 'How does education service employers when so many graduates, especially in the creative industries, are self-employed' (Hope and Figiel 2015: 362)? Would it be a step too far to construe employability as a comforting assurance to incoming university students of a chimerical stable working future? One that simultaneously cloaks the acclimatization for harsher actual labour market conditions as entrepreneurialism? The end results cunningly balance expectations of security, certain standardizations that fulfil that need (and, more so, the supply chain's) and a considerably more penetrating adaptation of this portion of the workforce to precarity.

Even in a policy-massaged climate of abundant opportunity, precarity still functions as both a glistening inducement to supply chain efficiencies and a powerful mode of discipline. Pressing further, Franco 'Bifo' Berardi identifies it as, 'not a particular element of the social relation, but the dark core of the capitalist production in the sphere of the global network where a flow of fragmented recombinant info-labor continuously circulates. Precariousness is the transformative element of the whole cycle of production. Nobody is shielded from it' (Berardi 2009: 191). Bifo's definition stresses ubiquity. The embourgeoisement insinuated by a (now-costly) university degree provides little shelter against it.

Uncertainty has swelled with the rise of impermanent work in both Britain's creative and educational economies.

HESA (the Higher Education Statistics Agency) points out that the sector is Britain's second most casualized after hospitality, with 50.9 per cent of academic staff on insecure contracts, not including the more than 82,000 who are paid by the hour. A significant proportion of these are doctoral students, girded by similarly fading promises of 'employability' via degree qualification (Fazackerley 2013; Gill 2014: 18–19; UCU 2019). Racialized social groups figure higher in these statistics both in relation to white academics and to their numbers in the general population, with, for example, black academics finding themselves 50 per cent more likely to be employed on zero hours contracts (UCU 2021: 3 & 25). Forty-six per cent of universities hire their teachers in this way, which can only be described as a just-in-time, on-demand modality familiar from other reaches of the supply chain and the gig and platform economies more broadly. In all such contexts, the sheer time and effort involved in getting up to speed undermines the capacity to plan, let alone to pause for thought to query rights infringements or to collectivize (see Hall 2016 and Kezar et al. 2019 for excellent analyses of how we might think of academia as a gig economy or an 'Uberized' sector). According to a survey of 3,802 non-permanent higher education staff, 61 per cent had held two or more jobs over a twelve-month period, 71 per cent reported fragile mental health and almost 60 per cent were struggling to make ends meet (UCU 2019: 4; UCU 2021).

One in seven British academics in 2016 earned less than the National Insurance lower earnings limit of £500 a month, so how come many more of them persist without even this level of income (UCU 2016: 7)? In a corollary of the exploitation of passionate vocational fulfilment detailed in Chapter 2, academic workers sacrifice themselves to long hours, low pay, and health hardships in the name of a process or product (teaching or research) they lionize as gratifying. In her politicized unravelling of her own catchy moniker DWYL (do what you love), Miya Tokumitsu unmasks how creative jobs (a category in which I enfold film and higher education work), pose as:

> not something one does for compensation, but an act of self-love. If profit doesn't happen to follow, it is because the worker's passion and determination were insufficient. Its real achievement is making workers believe their labor serves the self and not the marketplace. (Tokumitsu 2014: n.p.)

The absorption of failure as personal inadequacy recurs. In a world where entrepreneurialism keeps us on our toes, self-disciplined and at a distance from state welfare provision, DWYL, Tokumitsu posits, arouses an artificial sense of privilege, aloof from grunt workers. It dazzles us from seeing ourselves amongst those ranks, let alone aligning across sectors. When fulfilment, success or stability do not arrive in the immediate, we incline towards neither challenge nor flight, but, rather, a doubling down that thereby accedes to further exploitation. Lauren Berlant's notion of 'cruel optimism' hits this mark: 'when something you desire is actually an obstacle to your flourishing' (Berlant 2011: 1). Rosalind Gill, who has studied this situation empirically, attributes some of this willingness to 'the dominance of an individualistic register – a tendency to account for ordinary experiences in the academy through discourses of excoriating self-blame, privatized guilt, intense anxiety, and shame' (Gill 2017: 207). Gill's collaborative writing with Ngaire Donaghue proposes, furthermore, that these processes of internalization find a potent enabler in 'hope labour', which hangs in uncomplainingly in the present, trusting in rewards later down the line (Gill and Donaghue 2016: 93).

Weighing up this dire situation from within the discipline of Cinema and Media Studies explicitly, Charles Burnetts rails against how 'the contingent labour problem' is still relegated as 'incidental to its modes of discourse', including, I argue relatedly, how its workforce remains largely complicit (by design and through fear) with advancing the casualization mandate under its guises of employability and entrepreneurialism in their classrooms (Burnetts 2016: n.p.). More so, just as employability sacrifices salary and hours to false idols of permanence, it bears considerable responsibility for enshrining low or no pay and long hours, now endemic to the film industry, as valuable and value-generating activities.

UN(DER)PAID AND OVERWORKED

In the process of writing this book, I receive a message from a friend with credits on several of the Harry Potter films, a good few others shot at Leavesden and many more supply chain productions routed through the UK and other countries. He is picking up casual day work on a video for ScreenSkills, also the agency (under their former name) who set him off in the industry as a trainee. He describes it as 'some weird Russian doll of making a film for potential interns with the crew being actors playing themselves but not being paid as actors'. He rightly intuits that the blurred lines between cut-rate remuneration and the project's topic of un- or barely paid labour corresponds entirely with my broader analysis of supply chain cinema training.

Internships now seem such essential CV milestones on the road to multiple careers that it is hard to remember how new they are to the landscape. Back in 2010, Kayte Lawton and Dom Potter estimated that 280,800 organizations in the UK offered around a quarter of a million internship places over the course of just one summer (Lawton and Potter 2010: 6). The Milburn Report (a 2012 government-commissioned investigation of social mobility) specifies that 'The practice in much of the media industry is more akin to treating interns as free labour' and that, of all the professions, this one was deemed 'the worst offender' when it came to interns' rights (Milburn et al. 2012: 5). BECTU admits that the 'film and TV industry relies hugely on precariously employed runners, trainees and junior department members. They are often expected to live in London, have a car at their disposal and work very long days – regularly breaking the legal 11-hour "daily turnaround"' (BECTU 2017: 2). Serena remonstrates point blank that she 'can't afford to take on these jobs', a set-up she directly calls out as classist. She recounts a meeting with a producer who insists no one can join the industry without first spending time as an unpaid runner. When she explains that she does not have a car or a British driving licence, which, as BECTU highlights, are all but necessary for this role, let alone the family backing to work for free, the only solution he can drum up is, 'well, you just have to save up for it'. She earns £280 a week, if she is lucky. Such sizable donations of low or unpaid labour require support and resources evidently not at the disposal of many people wishing to join the industry. And numerous aspirants, in the first place, secure their internships through family or social connections, making a mockery of meritocracy (Milburn et al. 2012: 53), especially for someone like Serena, whose relatives do not even live in the UK. In some small way, the industry connections made possible through internships might fracture such nepotism, if only they were affordable and accessible options in the first place.

Neil Percival and David Hesmondhalgh's extensive survey-derived research found that 94 per cent of film workers had undertaken unpaid work, including internships, accepting it as an inevitable paying of one's dues (Percival and Hesmondhalgh 2014: 194 & 197). Such is the perceived significance of this career rung that, during term time, universities have increasingly incorporated them into their formal curricula, encouraged by education policy, including the Wilson Review, which advocates for their inclusion in every undergraduate programme (Wilson 2012: 5. See also the academic analysis of this situation by Berger et al. 2013; Lee 2013). Universities now expend considerable energies procuring suitable placements for a growing student population in response to demand and, more cynically, because on-the-job learning usually turns out to be cheaper to run than a taught course. Depending on the programme, these might last a couple of weeks, a whole term, or even the entire academic year. Some derive from prolonged relationships between the university and the employer, others the students themselves must arrange, while many necessitate a competitive application process. I would venture that, given all the moving pieces that must be puzzled together to provide placements for each cohort, academic staff find it difficult to fully or regularly vet what happens within these contexts. Nonetheless, similar to ScreenSkills validation, proximity to industry (presumed to be a surer gateway to employability) can act as a lure onto a degree course. An entry-level employee now pays for their own training, which may well include shelling out tuition fees to work gratis in the industry.

On one hand, this chapter insists on grouping together work experience orchestrated by a university and less formalized types of internships as associated components of a broader culture of unremunerated labour. On the other, I need to stress how legal rights diverge across this spectrum. Under UK law, an intern must receive at least National Minimum Wage unless their labour fits the detailed criteria for volunteering (which counteract the principles of individualized human capital at the very least). Or if conducted as part of a further or higher education course (see BECTU 2022 for the legal obligations required of different types of work experience). This proviso therefore exposes universities as primary feeders of free labour to industry, validating the practice as pedagogy.

Why the wholescale willingness to sign up in the first place? In his approachable, entry-level manual *Internship & Volunteer Opportunities for TV and Movie Buffs*, Adam Furgang answers this question with:

> They can be the ticket to your future. What you do and learn in internships or volunteer opportunities counts as pure experience. You're not subject to layoffs or budget cuts, and people in the field are getting to know you. That's great news if you want to continue to work in the field in the future. (Furgang 2013: 7–8)

Notwithstanding the bleakly positive spin on unsalaried workers sidestepping being fired, Furgang's description encompasses the tentative and suspending disposition endemic to internships. First, it must be emphasized that internships seldom lead to full-time employment. Speaking for many who arrange such encounters, Mara Einstein relates, 'I rarely saw a student receive a job offer after completing an internship. This is so unusual I can count the number of job offers on one hand, and this is not because the students were unprepared or underqualified' (Einstein 2015: 480). Percival and Hesmondhalgh concur, while David Lee's research uncovers how familial connections play a much more fundamental role in whether one moves onwards into a solid job (Percival and Hesmondhalgh 2014: 190; Lee 2013: 202–203).

After analyzing diaries kept by students on placements within foreign film productions in the Czech Republic, Petr Szczepanik distinguishes 'deferred career gratification' as an incentive behind his interlocutors striving wholeheartedly to appear indispensable (Szczepanik 2014: 59). Serena, similarly, feels 'I have to do these voluntary jobs with the hope that one day one might become even a freelance contract.' The perception of precarity as a short, difficult sprint gains traction from narratives of entrepreneurial success. Interns also frequently reframe unreliable hiring prospects as, instead, a means of accumulating social capital (meeting the right people) and human capital (valuable learning opportunities to be treated as an *investment*) that will logically convert, sometime soon, into surplus worthy of a salary. Michelle Rodino-Colocino and Stephanie N. Beberick's interviews with interns demonstrate that the majority have convinced themselves that they are lucky even to have landed these roles, rarely ever experiencing 'their internship labour as labour and as exploitation' (Rodino-Colocino and Beberick 2015: 491). No wonder this might be received as good fortune if the notion of topping up one's own human capital reservoir presides. Jessica rationalizes, 'I did a lot for free because I was just trying to build up a skill level and I felt I couldn't charge because I wasn't confident I could provide what people wanted.' This outlook modestly undermines the value of such labour.

These postponements and re-inscriptions remain troubling not only because they rely on undependable assurances, but also for the ways in which they obfuscate that students are *already* workers, in this capacity and frequently in others. When a student juggles a part-time job simultaneous to study and uncompensated work experience, they often relegate the former as a staging post en route somewhere 'better', perhaps disregarding their potential for promotion in the process. When a family member chips in to support this multifarious existence in pursuit of a brighter future, they may well be compromising their own present comfort.

All the while, the student is working *qua* student. Study labour generates a good deal, and not just labour power (the Marxian terminology for the skills and experience we bring to a job, whose hours are not directly exchangeable for an immediate payment) (Marx 1891: 5) including for the state and the supply chain. The insurrectionary US pamphlet for the Wages for Students movement of the 1970s demands the rights, respect and financial support provided by a salary as acknowledgement for what students contribute in multiple forms and timeframes. Their rhetoric would not seem fanciful in countries that provide living expense grants, as was the case in the UK until the 1990s, and free or subsidized tuition. If it does, then it demarcates how far removed we are from Marx's reminder that 'All surplus value [from even compensated labour], whatever particular form (profit, interest, or rent) it may subsequently crystallize into, is in substance the materialization of unpaid labour-time' (Marx 1990: 672). Starting with these premises makes it easier to spot how training can justifiably claim payment and all the more so when work experience blurs with what would be defined simply as work if carried out by a non-student (Lawton and Potter 2010: 9 explain how the majority of work experience covers duties that legally justify a salary). In reality, the casualized preponderance of contemporary labour has found new, expanded forms in the means by which many companies collage together a re-composed team of sequential interns who fulfil the same role, unpaid and according to a principle similar to supply chain modularity. To give some scale, in the US in 2005, journalist Anya Kamenetz calculated, conservatively, that internships fed nearly $124 million annually to corporate coffers (Kamenetz 2006: A19). Beyond this clear advantage to capital, the rise in unremunerated labour (frequently facilitated by debt, as I introduced in Chapter 1) exerts downward pressure on wages more generally (Kamenetz 2006: A19; Perlin 2011: 62; Standing 2011: 76; Oakley 2013: 40).

Interns also suffer extremely restricted access to rights (including legal recourse against racial or sexual discrimination) precisely because they remain outside the wage relation (Perlin 2011: 64; Steyerl 2012: 109). The fact that various interns have won victories in court (including the famous case against infractions inflicted during the making of the film *Black Swan* (Darren Aronofsky, 2010)) speaks more to the tenacity and resources of certain individuals than the success of organized struggles for all. More quietly, it also announces how narrowed the demographics remain for those who can afford to work for free in film and then, after that, as longer-term paid workers within the industry (see Perlin 2011: 161; Roggero 2011: 152; Oakley 2013: 35 for investigations of the broader restrictions upheld by unpaid work experience). Will the skills gap, so anomalous for the global film industry, generate headwind for change here? I suspect that unpaid work will persist as a more firmly entrenched ethos within supply chain cinema, etched deep, as I have illustrated, into its workers' self-regard.

It finds form, also (and as Chapter 2 examined), in the long hours film workers input, uncompensated in multiple ways, including financial. These habits take seed in education, again nominating its utility to and absorption into supply chain production. When I arrived in my former job in a university-based film school, I was surprised to learn that the building remained open 24/7. It did not take me long (not least because I was working beyond a traditional schedule as well) to realize that it was in use at all hours by production students sleeplessly beavering to finish their projects. The same students would gradually disappear from film studies classes in order to devote themselves to their practice. In this respect, encouraged by their teachers as much as their own drive and impression of the industry, they were already mirroring commercial production's culture of long hours romanticized as artistic dedication.

Likewise, Lisa Kelly and Katherine M. Champion, who have conducted fieldwork amongst the trainees on the *Outlander* placement scheme mentioned briefly above, register how it inculcates taxing temporalities:

In our early visits there was an air of excitement and high levels of energy exhibited when speaking to the trainees. However, later in the shoot we turned up to see a row of people perched outside on the kerb with their faces in their hands staring into space as they tried to catch a few minutes of respite. (Champion and Kelly 2017: n.p.)

Despite a concurrent shortage of crews (a very reason for its existence), the *Outlander* scheme impresses a gruellingly exploitative regimen. Clearly, the supply chain must instil this as a norm as early as pre-employment and during education in order to avoid any gains in workers' struggles for more reasonable hours.

Even during a learning stage, the supply chain's schedules advantage the strong and resilient, those with few outside caring responsibilities. BECTU attributes the shockingly low number of women in key creative positions in cinema to this state of affairs, all the more bafflingly persistent within the 2020s' capacity shortage. As Ben, the sound mixer from the previous chapter reminds us, 'There is this idea that films can only be made when you're working for twelve hours [per day], that you just have to do it that way… You don't. At Ealing [the British studio particularly successful in the mid-twentieth century], they worked eight-hour days.' Although film education exhibits pretty much a fifty-fifty gender split in enrolment, the union's research concludes that 'long family-unfriendly hours means only 15.8% of first assistant directors, 9.8% of camera department and 14% of TV drama directors are female' (BECTU 2017: 1). Later down the line, the surrender of all available time to 'the project' hinders crews from breaking away to update their skills, aggravating the current gap and the sustainability of the established workforce.

It is arguably easier to normalize these behaviours within a sector – higher education – that itself has channelled dedication and 'indulging' one's passions (such as by following a unique research trajectory, say) into excessive commitment to overworking, all too frequently to breaking point. UCU (the University and College Union), which represents academic faculty in the UK, discerns from a survey of over 13,000 members that those in the profession donate on average more than two unpaid days per week, with the figure rising to four additional unpaid days per week for those on zero hours, hourly paid and term-time only contracts (UCU 2022a: 26 & 29). As in the film industry, supply chain higher education sucks free labour from casualized workers through their very precarity (their need to be re-hired) and their commitment to doing their best for their students. As resources have been stripped from the sector, as it has privatized and entered into leaner and leaner modes of production, managers have simultaneously increased student numbers and, with them, administrative and support duties without adequate budgeting (see Gill 2014: 20; Gill and Donaghue 2016: 93). To better understand how British higher education fortifies both its own and cinema's supply chain modalities, a firmer grasp of its current capitalistic formation is required. I shift here to the wider plane of (creative) higher education, notwithstanding a few brief zooms to close-ups on how this context precisely impacts the study of filmmaking. The broader view feels more apt for the upcoming analysis of commodification, financialization and debt, which bear down much more pervasively on the population. And, besides, the film industry very much welcomes graduates from other degree programmes.

HIGHER EDUCATION COMMODIFIED AND FINANCIALIZED

It would be erroneous to suppose that British higher education (if ever it were so possible to homogenize) either fully contested or lagged behind the drive for knowledge and creative economies that cleared the path for supply chain cinema. In many ways, it served as their incubator. In the 1990s, the same decade as creativity's refurbishment, transnational organs like the OECD (Organisation for Economic Co-operation and Development) and the World Bank began dedicating tremendous energy to promoting the idea of university education as a commodity that could also be harnessed for economic growth (Ward 2012: 142–144). Sympathetic reports and white papers in countries like the UK soon ensued, followed by policy action introducing tuition fees for citizens in 1998, measures which the devolved Scottish government, unlike other countries in the UK, has refused. Since then, fee caps have crept up, most dramatically with the triple hike to £9,000 in 2010. The maintenance grant is now a distant memory of the previous century, replaced by escalating personal debts for most students simply in order to subsist while studying. If the screen industries were already largely the preserve of a certain social class, then the cost of an education next-to-expected for entry into a sector plagued with insecurity and no or low-pay, renders entry even more of a risk, even more unreachable. Ironically, during the years when *Harry Potter and the Chamber of Secrets* (Chris Columbus, 2002) spoke against restricting education to 'pure breed' elites, equivalent real-world struggles were being vanquished.

By the 2010s, Guy Standing's book *The Precariat: The New Dangerous Class* could describe higher education as:

> brashly depicted as an industry, as a source of profits and export earnings, a zone of competitiveness, with countries, universities and schools ranked by performance indicators. It is hard to parody what is happening. Administrators have taken over schools and universities, imposing a 'business model' geared to the market. (Standing 2011: 68)

Likewise, Stefan Collini accuses the government of 'helping to turn some first-rate universities into third-rate companies' (Collini 2017: 154). Interestingly, Harry Potter now plays a role in marketing higher education as a commodity. In my current university's gift shop, alongside the usual (and increasingly more American-style) branded merchandise, sits a display of Harry Potter items. I ask a shop worker if they are popular. He replies that they appeal largely to the international students, a steady number of whom enjoy taking photos amidst the neo-Gothic architecture of the campus buildings dressed as characters from the franchise. A university that 'looks like Hogwarts' exerts not insignificant magnetism within this marketplace.

Annual charts such as the QS and the Times Higher Education World University Rankings more prevalently guide student applications. All endow prestige with proportional respect to the supposedly measurable qualities of 'graduate prospects', 'employment outcomes' and even 'employer reputation'. Employability, intensified through policy, thereby also participates in the commodification of degrees. ScreenSkills steps into this logic, asserting how its accreditation (ultimately its branding potential) 'signposts prospective students', 'supporting your student recruitment' and 'helping you stand out from the crowd' (ScreenSkills 2022f). The broader social patterning of pedagogical emphases, strong-armed by industry and government, as discussed earlier, conveniently doubles as an item for sale. 'Employability' can evidently mean any number of things (Thornham and O'Sullivan 2004: 722–724 trace some of its shifting meanings across time within British media education). At present, what it amounts to within the idioms of British universities' promotional and success-focused rhetoric squares precarious, entrepreneurial, under-regulated and time-draining supply chain modes of (movie) production, often vocational, utilitarian and uncritical in the extreme, with a petition to their value as human capital.

Such training stridently pitches itself as competitive advantage. Considered more defensively, education-consumers regard it as future-proofing against rapacious precarity. Following creative labour scholar-activists Sophie Hope and Joanna Figiel, however, I would like to examine some of the ways in which these assumptions about education and internships alike slipstream human capital accrual into broader intensifications of financialization (also holding increasing sway in film industry ownership structures). Students cannot assuredly predict reliable returns on their internship or educational outlays. Hope and Figiel determine what is happening here to be less of an investment and more students *speculating* on something closer to their own stock, low in value at that moment, but hopefully paying dividends in the future (Hope and Figiel 2015: 369). As with financial markets, there are no guarantees and high probability of externally provoked volatility. Any such perceived assets cannot be safely retained for later advantage. No film student, for instance, should rely on current notions of skill, as Jessica has made clear, let alone stability in fiscal policy that would keep supply chain cinema close by as a dependable employer. When radical educator Paulo Freire initiated the concept of 'banking' to describe a mode of teaching where information is merely deposited into students without engaging their creativity (as is the tendency within certain enclaves of employability training), he doubtless had not envisioned his metaphor's contemporary implications (Freire 2005: 72). Nor, perhaps, that these financialized craftings of the self-as-future-worker nest, without question, within another financialized context and temporality: that of debt.

In England, 95 per cent of eligible students take up a government-administered loan, which, for the 2022–23 intake of undergraduates, averaged at around £46,000 (although lower for other nations in the UK and nowhere near as high as those burdening arriving university-educated US crew). They will typically also rack up thousands more in personal debt to pay for high rent, other costs of living, as well as, perhaps, the outgoings incurred during that necessary unpaid internship or to put in place expensive requirements for it, like a driving licence and use of a car (Bolton 2022: 12 & 17). Student debt is most eloquently described by those pressured into signing up for it. Here is a small section of the *Student Handjob* pamphlet (a play on words on the handbooks typically given out at the beginning of a course) and produced during the 2011 uprisings against fee hikes:

> The university-factory sells you a degree at the price of the future. The debt now involved in study will take decades of future labour to repay... This is a new feudalism for educated young workers, as the future itself is colonised by financial capitalism. When a degree will just about obtain work in a supermarket, nightclub, care-home or casual labouring, workers must surrender 40 years of earnings in order to work for a piece of paper that is now simply a work permit and a piece of cursory cultural capital... The government doesn't expect this debt to be repaid either, but expects all tax-payers to remain in debt, like itself, and therefore bound to financial institutions, who have caused the economic crisis which is everyday capitalism. (*The Student Handjob* 2011: 19)

This overview astutely extends its framing of debt beyond personal confines to instead view debt's global dimensions. Supranational bodies like the World Bank and the International Monetary Fund have enticed countries rich and poor towards state and public debt. The terms of their loans customarily mandate drastically reduced welfare systems and the privatization of public resources, including university education, but also sectors that support affordable study, like local authority housing. Accordingly, individuals without prior assets (savings, an owned home and so forth), like migrants or low earners, dwell more at the mercy of loan culture. Few will take the gamble of borrowing in order to enter film higher education, followed by unreliably remunerated (first) jobs in the field. Few, too, seek to join the crowded labour markets of academia determined, as they largely now are in the UK, by commodified doctoral preparation rather than government-funded studentships. Universities' escalation of fees to replace state support becomes viable because of the availability of credit through a profit-making sector.

As Annie McLanahan points out, the terms of students' loans mean, long-term, that they are 'agreeing to become the embodied collateral of the collateralized debt obligation' (McLanahan 2011: 65). Hence the clambering for employability, the wariness about impractical, abstract or anti-establishment topics or modes of study that refuse to pledge safe earnings. Unquestionably, this future resides very much in the present. Gigi Roggero pithily summarizes the venture of academic training as 'risk upstream' followed by 'capture downstream' (Roggero 2011: 62). Through 'capture', he implies all that a debt might compel of us. Certainly, the visceral fear of impecuniousness that debt instils drives people faster and more indubitably towards wage exploitation, including the thankless 'unskilled' jobs upheld alongside full-time study and often well beyond it. Including the 'teaching only' contracts for academics. Including the day work on corporate videos (for ScreenSkills or other employers) that clash with many film workers' politics. A future promised away thus contradicts the vista of choice higher education purports to provide in terms of both income and where I would like to move next: freedom.

Roggero's sense of 'capture' takes cues from Maurizio Lazzarato, one of debt's most comprehensive theorists, who argues how debt accelerates exactly the same sorts of disciplining to the regimes of capital that Tsing imputes to the supply chain. Debt constrains its subject not so much:

> to reimburse in actual money but rather in conduct, attitudes, ways of behaving, plans, subjective commitments, the time devoted to finding a job, the time used for conforming oneself to the criteria dictated by the market and business, etc. . . . In other words, debt reconfigures biopolitical power by demanding a production of subjectivity. (Lazzarato 2012: 104)

Through debt, risk is absorbed right into the emotional and financial life of the student. While I recoil at Nick Dyer-Witheford's classification of debt-servicing jobs as 'indentured servitude' (especially when more forceful incarnations of coerced labour receive attention in the coming chapters), what Lazzarato identifies as 'the power of debt on subjectivity (guilt and responsibility)' persists. As both a persuasive and enduring disciplining mechanism, it allows 'capitalism to bridge the gap between present and future' (Lazzarato 2012: 46). In the industries of film and education, the financial reality that disposes a graduate to take on 'whatever' job co-exists with the illusion of an almost morally inflected indebtedness for the unique opportunity of work. New entrants, as this chapter has demonstrated, fruitlessly pursue 'lucky breaks' (again the language of gambling) comprehensively inscribed as 'paying one's dues' (the language of debt).

Debt's manoeuvres into personal responsibility have evacuated it of much of its social and political lineage. A wealth of theorists of debt are keen that we re-invest it with its collective and thereby associatively collectivizing qualities. Stefano Harney and Fred Moten underscore how 'Credit is a means of privatization and debt a means of socialisation' (Harney and Moten 2013: 61. See also McLanahan 2011: 58; Lazzarato 2012: 157–158). What strength can those of us who together hold trillions of dollars of debt wield against the forces – private and state – that mortgage our futures while pillaging our common assets? In closing, this chapter weighs up the potential for unity in not just shared debt, but also, relatedly, shared experiences of the supply chain.

LINKING OTHERWISE

I don't doubt that anyone from either profession will have reached this point in the book with a sense of collective identification. As an academic, I too convince myself into intensive work schedules like film workers do – ones that I am similarly persuaded to tolerate through an engineering of my 'passion' and 'commitment'. I too could joke about needing a courtesy bot to sustain my friendships or ask myself the question, 'Alive?'

While jam-packed schedules crowd out the time or energy to agitate for change, scope surely exists to align through our proximity. Paradoxically, the industry's urgency about skilling up a larger workforce and the university's employability crusades bring us together. Certainly, the principles driving these collaborations aim towards a tighter and more efficient supply chain, for commodified education just as much as for cinema. But is there latitude to turn the sheer interconnected length and transversality of the supply chain against itself? Can networking be metamorphosized from its current individualistic or nepotistic preponderance into a more radical solidarity, where meeting points become points of exchange and strategizing in the name of collective transformation?

Organizing of this nature can only reinforce prior gains. Students have long militated against privatization, of which the razor-sharp insight and transformative inventiveness of *Wages for Students* and the *Student Handjob* cited above are just two examples and the mass demonstrations, civil disobedience and occupations in protest of aforementioned tuition fee hikes in 2010 another. BECTU and UCU benefit from the resources to conduct the research that has built the foundations for this chapter and the last. UCU has been on intermittent strike since 2018 challenging corporate profiteering from the reduction of members' pensions, and, by declared association, welfare provision and secure futures more broadly.

All the same, the current structure of both sectors complicates union organizing, as well as a more general collectivity. In the film industry, unreliable salaries and casualization across the board have reduced membership and strike action. Each movie project's contracting of a different composition of crew members, for example, very much discombobulates workplace mobilization. Academics tend towards lone, often competitive research ventures; they predominantly study contexts with a presumed objectivity that can inhibit them from horizontal political organizing. As registered above, the mainstreaming of employability stymies criticality and the threat of a contract not being renewed discourages militancy. And so to pause for a minute to recognize myself more stable than most: an academic with a reliable enough job. Here wondering what distinct skills and tactics colleagues can offer each other against the very forces of transnationalized, competitive capitalism that deliberately reduce our numbers, along with these sectors' wages, conditions, and securities.

From within the academy, crucial first moves would include scrupulously plotting out the devastation we see done in our own quarters according to what can only be described as lean and just-in-time supply chain paradigms. No such study should linger as either an abstraction, or a rarefied item of intellectual property (bolstering its writer's own employability) when we have access to what might be attained in the classroom. Can students' actual training, so crucial to and dominated by supply chain cinema, so explicitly commodified and individualized, offer occasions for renegotiation, even outright refusal? As this chapter has illustrated, universities are deeply implicated in reproducing and propagating systems of biopolitical preparation for capital's abuses, feeding precarious or unpaid workers into industry as well as our own labour pools. How can we really have our students' best interests at heart when we ready them to be the ones who 'make it', imagine them as the exception rather than the rule, fail to show them practices that refuse such competition?

In the UK (and regularly working beyond its borders), a collective by the name of the Precarious Workers Brigade has directly intended to intervene in this way. Their actions stand as just one example of many. I draw on them now predominantly because, as a member myself, I feel I can convey their operations with a certain precision.

Among many other objectives, the Precarious Workers Brigade has strived to transfigure the current curricular requirements for employability from within the university itself. The group comprises salaried academics who benefit from the elbow room to address such concerns in their daily praxis. I have not yet been disabused of the idea that many of us still enjoy privileges in exploring critical, even revolutionary perspectives and actions in how we bring our syllabi to life. Employability, however, is regularly handed over to either career advisors detached from the daily unfurling of critical scholarship, or colleagues in the most casualized and vulnerable positions within their departments and consequently in serious need of shared materials to lessen their own heavy workloads. As such, the Precarious Workers Brigade also convene workshops in universities and other spaces (hopefully undoing the typical expert-consultant visitor relationship) and have published the free-to-download *Training for Exploitation?: Politicising Employability and Reclaiming Education*, a tool kit for those requested to oversee such professionalization. Stressing the unevenness of access to employment, disabusing the promise that such training safeguards against joblessness, and uncovering the lack of 'neutrality' of the attributes ascribed to being 'employable', the resources collected within include bibliographies and statistics that support the critique of the current engineering of the labour force. Drawing on a host of radical pedagogies, *Training for Exploitation?* provides ready-made possible templates and exercises that range from manifesto writing, forum theatre, and photo romance creation to how to devise open letters and 'ethical internship' contracts. These activities invite students to question their positions as labourers, past, present, and future. Clearly, then, there exist many resistant activities that can still take place under the umbrella of professionalization.

Let us at least divert from teaching that hallows stories of individual success through hierarchized master classes, tips on how to triumph at the expense of others or how to confect a unique and highly socially weighted 'lucky break'. We can certainly place legal rights and duties, as well as mechanisms for standing up to contemporary prejudice and privilege more prominently. Can we find industry partners more equal, rather than those seeking to command higher education to supply chain needs?

The internship and the work placement leave themselves susceptible to hijacking of this persuasion. Whatever the individualistic-capitalistic ideals that nourish the pressure to undertake such unpaid labour, these periods observing and simulating a desired job certainly afford eye-opening insights into real conditions. But why subject anyone to this first hand when we already have enough information to want to challenge or modify the impulse to dispatch students out into these jobs, when most students already have enough lived experience of workplace exploitation? At the very least, a university's sustained provision of students' usually unpaid labour to particular companies should pave the way for insisting on the augmentation of certain rights typically inaccessible to interns. However, rather than replicating a practice that predominantly leads only to criticality, what is the scope for transforming these opportunities for communicating both shared injustices and strategies for transformation between the two sectors? How might students returning from these placements isolate what needs to be changed about supply chain cinema, guided by their own insights in collaboration with those of their experienced mentors therein?

Here I revisit Chapter 1's summoning of *conricerca*, co- or militant research. *Conricerca* derives from deep alliances between community members, who need not all be researchers in the textbook sense, working together to realize profound and situated change. It refuses the extractive impulse that contours conventional academic research, familiar also from a human capital approach to work experience. The needs and priorities of all those involved expressly motivates militant research, their numbers overlapping in this particular situation because of analogous circumstances and, in the case of trainees, the binding of present to hypothetical future employment. Ironically, as the global supply chain and its governmental agents close the gap between academy and industry for their own ends, the resulting proximity renders *conricerca* more possible. The supply chain has forced us to learn each other's languages, through which we might now converse and invent better idioms and praxes. Our encounters together, not just the work placements, internships, but also guest visits to professionalization seminars, the growing trend in universities to hire practitioner-theorists (admittedly often to save money), offer sustained capacity for co-research and collective struggle. From *The Working Class Goes to Heaven* (Elio Petri, 1971) to *La Commune* (Peter Watkins, 2000) to *Out on the Street* (Jasmina Metwaly and Philip Rizk, 2015), there have long existed filmmakers who exemplify such embedded engagement. Likewise, there are many academics who encourage community-centred student media-making, using the film-industry's tools to unearth injustices other than its own. Might we draw on these accumulated strengths to also address in multiple forms and from manifold yet overlapping perspectives, for instance, casualization or the compulsion to work taxingly long hours?

Rather than peddling 'professionalization', these congregations bear the potential to undo that very notion and its biopolitical lockstep with the supply chain's demands. Vicki Mayer puts forward a generative query from which to launch: 'When does the pedagogy of an alternative media studies move students from an academic model based on creative labour and into a creative activism based on plural voices and an alternative politics for media' (Mayer 2019, 10)? In collectively writing *Training for Exploitation?* it became imperative to search out and then disseminate solid alternatives to these ways of working. Academics' courses and publications can introduce and even model workers' co-operatives, alternative (cultural) economies, mutual support networks, affinity groups and examples of the commons that present other means of sustenance through creativity beyond these sharp edges of capitalism (Precarious Workers Brigade 2017: 76–85). Here, in the heart of training, where worker subjectivity is fashioned, ideas become material, as the supply chain knows only too well.

The supply chain has hitherto vaunted British training and currently requires an influx of those who have passed through it. It may capitulate to this leverage; it may choose to reroute around it. In either case, utopian templates might also travel with an eye to its speed and adaptability. As the next two chapters emphasize, the translation of ideas and practices from place to place is something offshored film production explicitly demands (including through higher education). How might we exert these aptitudes against its abuses?

4

Greasing the Wheels of Transnational Film Production: The United Arab Emirates' Post-Oil Vision for Education

'Dubai understands business and the need to deliver results. That's how this city has emerged to become a globally recognized finance, trade and business hub... because of the can-do spirit that infuses the city. The same can be true for your production' (Dubai Film and TV Commission n.d.a: 1). Thus fanfares the Dubai Film and TV Commission. In neighbouring Abu Dhabi – a different emirate, but the same country (an emirate is a principality of sorts) – even the Covid-19 pandemic could not halt production. 'Mission Possible' became the watchword for the strict protocols and tight coordination that protected *Dead Reckoning – Part One*, the latest (and, given the situation, perhaps rather clumsily titled) episode of the franchise, returning to the UAE for its third time (Vivarelli 2021b: n.p.). Other ambitious projects availing themselves of the UAE's 'can-do spirit' this millennium include *The Kingdom* (Peter Berg, 2007), *Wall Street: Money Never Sleeps* (Oliver Stone, 2010), *The Bourne Legacy* (Tony Gilroy, 2012), *Furious 7* (James Wan, 2015), *Star Trek Beyond* (Justin Lin, 2016), *Independence Day: Resurgence* (Roland Emmerich, 2016), *Sonic the Hedgehog* (Jeff Fowler, 2019) and *Dune* (Denis Villeneuve, 2021). The ever-growing number of Bollywood and Chinese productions comprise *Dabangg* (Abhinav Kashyap, 2010), *Happy New Year* (Farah Khan, 2014), *Welcome Back* (Anees Bazmee, 2015), *Housefull 3* (Sajid and Farhad Samji, 2016), *Airlift* (Raja Krishna Menon, 2016), *Ki & Ka* (R. Balki, 2016), *Kung Fu Yoga* (Stanley Tong, 2017), *Race 3* (Remo D'Souza, 2018), *Bharat* (Ali Abbas Zafar, 2019), *Vanguard* (Stanley Tong, 2019), *Bunty Aur Babli 2* (Varun V. Sharma, 2021) and *Pathaan* (Siddharth Anand, 2023). As in the UK, the UAE's capacities emanate from an intricate compact of public and private involvement. The logistical state that loans its army to *Star Wars – The Force Awakens* also engineers an education system that will administer to the supply chain a diverse array of contributors, most of them precarious in the extreme.

Retaining the focus of the previous chapter, the current one dedicates its energies to supply chain education, suspending scrutiny of offshored filmmaking until the next. It does so because the UAE put higher education, along with other crucial infrastructure, in place first. Fulfilling a campaign to kick-start a post-oil economy, steered by policies like the Abu Dhabi Economic Vision 2030, the country committed to swelling its creative and knowledge sectors. Over a couple of decades, a raft of future-facing governmental measures and this same 'can-do spirit' conjured a busy cultural landscape from one with little in the way of filmmaking or universities beforehand.

Chapter 4 therefore commences with an investigation of these policies and their motivations, how education would escalate creative output and arise as a lucrative economy all its own. It concentrates, as does Chapter 5, on two of the UAE's seven emirates, Abu Dhabi and Dubai, the temporary homes to most film productions so far. While a federal constitutional monarchy, with legislative, executive and judicial matters administered at that level, each emirate retains a certain autonomy over matters of education and (film) industrial policy. These governments recognize the need to prepare larger numbers of suitably skilled creative workers and, to aid this mission, have welcomed in branch campuses of multiple foreign, English-medium universities. Higher education of this order does not simply prepare a workforce predisposed towards the supply chain. It becomes itself a globalized product, offshored and franchised, its own supply chain. The central sections of this chapter dissect how, through multicultural liberal arts pedagogy, these institutions hone a workforce suitable for the creative economy. Modes of comportment, notions of expressivity, entrepreneurship, linguistic dexterity, translational aptitudes and hierarchized diversity bequeath their recipients the capacities to steady the supply chain's passage between its geographically and culturally atomized sites. As ever, easy compatibility and competitive difference remain the key selling points. This chapter attends to the latter by scrutinizing the UAE's (creative) labour market, fine-tuned like hardly any other to the just-in-time precepts of supply chain production. Its composition, almost entirely migrant in character, renders its workers more immediately disposable and its students willing to pay to gain temporary residence. Urban planning also keenly attunes to the supply chain. In closing, the chapter investigates the physical spaces of this education, identical in type to those where films get made: the sector-specific free zone. Free zones, as I elucidate over this chapter and the next, stand aloof from legislation governing the country proper. They market to the supply chain the elasticity it dictates, less fettered by local law and convention. The state, however, inaugurates all such exceptions, so that is where I now begin.

INSOURCING FOR OFFSHORING: BUILDING A KNOWLEDGE AND CREATIVE ECONOMY

As offices of the government expressly tasked with attracting international business, film commissions both straightforwardly and revealingly communicate what they believe to be their territory's merits. Dubai's wants to make it known that, 'with over 200 nationalities in the city, numerous neighbourhoods are available that reflect the distinctive character of the ethnic expatriate community that lives here, so they can stand in for Asian, European or other international locations' (Dubai Film and TV Commission n.d.a: 2). Geographical stand-ins have become staple lures for supply chain cinema itineraries. For decades, Toronto has played New York or Chicago in a glut of productions. The UAE doubles for Saudi Arabia in *The Kingdom*, Karachi in *The Bourne Legacy*, Kabul in *War Machine* (David Michôd, 2017). But it can do more than look like other desert countries, the ones where it might be dangerous or expensive to insure a film crew. It can play India or even Europe, precisely because of the size of their expatriate communities. *6 Underground* (Michael Bay, 2019) managed to transform Abu Dhabi into Afghanistan, California, Uzbekistan, Las Vegas and Hong Kong (as well as the fictional Central Asian republic of Turgistan) no less. If they appear on screen in these productions, non-citizen inhabitants must both help substitute a home where maybe they cannot even live right now and embody a social diversity in and for a country that opportunistically refuses to fully absorb them as anything much other than economic agents.

Well before the UAE gave much of a thought to the knowledge and creative economies, it composed a population where migrants in their millions far outnumbered citizens, adding up to nearly 90 per cent of the population, almost none of whom enjoy the luxury of settled status. Like other oil-rich neighbours, the UAE's resource wealth surpasses the capacity of its few citizens to exploit and diversify it. Border scholar Harsha Walia labels their solution '*neoliberal insourcing*' (Walia 2021: 139, emphasis in original). Neoliberal, to her mind, because of how staunchly the state choreographs migration to economic ambitions alone, although with the qualification that, while capitalistic, a privatized free market this is not (for a rigorous and persuasive argument about how markedly modern these approaches are, see Vora 2013: 15 & 179). By far the majority of migrants arrive only when contracted by sponsors for particular jobs or a run of equivalents. In 2019, the introduction of the golden visa alleviated a select few from needing this prerequisite, with those eligible counting real estate investors, doctorate holders and certain specialists in a variety of desired fields that include arts and culture (but only with a recommendation letter from a government office). Skilled media creatives can also apply for freelancer visas, a more recent addition discussed in fuller detail in the following chapter. Much to the supply chain's delight, whatever their visa, migrants' salaries are calibrated to their home country's costs of living. Muhammad, a Palestinian filmmaker whom I talked to at length about his experience in the UAE's media industries, confirms that he would always be paid significantly less than American or European film crew colleagues carrying out exactly the same job. Without the permits these positions underwrite, most migrants have no legal recourse to remain; even the golden visa must be renewed after its five- or ten-year expiry date and will not lead to citizenship. A flexible (read: 'disposable') just-in-time workforce, then, barred access to most of the welfare affordances and political rights dispensed by a typical state, abides and greatly appeals to both the budgeting priorities of the supply chain and the lean state agendas that ideologically nurture it. Lining up unswervingly with this agenda, Linda Low, a policy advisor for the Abu Dhabi government, sums up this profiting from precarity as, 'A virtue... made of a necessity via a manpower plan' (Low 2012: 60).

Low here narrowly deems the 'necessity' to be the UAE's. She elides the often devastated economic and geopolitical contexts from which certain migrants flee, the essential remittance they send back. Tom, a Lebanese student at New York University Abu Dhabi, questions (knowing the answer) the preponderance of Lebanese, Syrians and Palestinians working in the media in the UAE with 'is it because there's nowhere else to go?' Even as a highly educated worker, 'you just have to find a job, you just have to eat'. Anthropologist Xiang Biao lays bare how the Indian state of Andhra Pradesh has diverted its agricultural surplus into private education geared towards preparing citizens to work overseas (Xiang 2007: 28–29 & 31). Harsha Walia aptly describes the situation: 'This is a bifurcation and segmentation of the global labor force, made precarious through bordering practices' (Walia 2021: 6–7). The border wide open for *Star Wars*, but safeguarding the low salaries, unyielding transience and resultingly dutiful work ethics of many who helped make it. Borders sculpt divergent mobilities like these and, with them, not just exclusion, but also 'differential inclusion' (to borrow Sandro Mezzadra and Brett Neilson's apposite term), an extractive mechanism absolutely foundational to contemporary capitalism (Mezzadra and Neilson 2013a: 159–160; see also Tsing 2009: 158).

Little spotlights these discrepancies, this coining of a rigid class system, more acutely than the state's munificence towards its own citizens. To them, it bestows secure jobs, subsidies for education, housing, healthcare and a host of other generous handouts. Even if only to citizens, oil wealth is rarely so widely distributed in other parts of the world. The film industry wrestles to recruit Emirati nationals precisely because they enjoy uncomplicated access to secure public sector jobs and expect better employment conditions than the long hours and unreliable incomes supply chain cinema offers (Yunis and Picherit-Duthler 2011: 126). At the other end of this spectrum, sometimes in near carceral conditions, dwell migrant construction workers, who justifiably provoke the most critique from labour activists. Responsible for building not only the branch university campuses, but also the temporary film sets and the permanent media-centred free zones, they may have been hoodwinked into paying illegal recruitment fees, had their passports confiscated on arrival, suffered unpaid wages or lower incomes than promised or intimidation if they raised grievances; they predominantly live in cramped and unhygienic conditions and work punishing and dangerous hours (seventy-plus per week), including compulsory over-time (Human Rights Watch 2015a: 12). Their toil materializes social division as urban design: the satellite labour camps, the luxury hotels hosting Tom Cruise, Daisy Ridley or Timothée Chalamet when they arrive for a shoot, the functionally gated communities that structure co-mingling predominantly through service and servility.

Let's first examine the willing into place of some of the more middle-class migrants imagined to inhabit this last type of development. Local policy, like the Abu Dhabi Economic Vision 2030, explicitly means to 'attract the most talented media professionals with... high living standards and superb quality of life' (Government of Abu Dhabi 2008: 118). Scholars of the UAE have, more often than not, interpreted such declarations as appealing to the migrant-as-consumer (for instance, Vora, 2015a: 175–176; AlShebabi, 2015: 111). Certainly, the country's new cultural quarters, film festivals, art biennales, illustrious museums (such as the Louvre Abu Dhabi) and other global calibre cultural institutions and events fashion 'superb quality of life' according to the acknowledged leisure preferences of a creative class. Yet these environments are also, of course, productive workplaces, strategic to calculated economic plans. Anticipating yearly regional growth of 25 per cent from the media (Government of Abu Dhabi 2008: 118), the country speculatively invests oil wealth in a particular type of human capital, somewhat more renewable. I cautiously temper renewability here through the previous chapters' insights into the supply chain's destructive exploitation of film workers, rendered replaceable through precarity and modularity.

All the same, I concede to the UAE's appreciation of higher education's abilities within professional and social reproduction. The landing page for Media degrees at the University of Wollongong in Dubai could not make the objectives of government any clearer:

> Sheikh Mohammed Bin Rashid Al Maktoum, Vice President and Prime Minister of the UAE and Ruler of Dubai, launched the Dubai Creative Economy Strategy which aims to transform the emirate into a global hub for creative industries and double the industries' GDP contribution to 5% of Dubai's economy by 2025. The new strategy welcomes creative individuals and companies from around the world and provides an environment to transform their dreams and aspirations. (University of Wollongong in Dubai n.d.b)

To aid this objective, in less than a couple of decades, multiple universities like Wollongong have broken ground in the UAE as part of many large-scale, long-range infrastructure projects for which the country is renowned (for a sense of previous projects, such as the dredging of the Dubai Creek and the building of the port and airport, see Kanna 2011: 38). RIT, Murdoch, Curtin, Birmingham City, De Montford, Bath Spa, Herriot-Watt... The plethora of private universities, branches of established overseas institutions in the main, enrol a good number of internationals hoping for a foothold in the country, thanks to various forms of post-education stay-on visas, the most prized being the golden visa, available to a top tier of high-achieving graduates. The majority of the students hail from migrant populations already settled (though rarely permanently so) within the UAE. These cohorts linger on residence permits otherwise set to expire upon adulthood. Higher education extends that tenure a little (for the price of tuition fees) and jobs upon graduation still further. This trajectory shores up a fragile existence dependent on rolling sponsorship in a country that may be the only place they have known as home, but which provides no other means for them to remain. The public universities, on the other hand, are practically free to attend and remain the preserve of Emirati nationals.

New York University Abu Dhabi (henceforth NYUAD), exceptionally, mingles the two populations, providing, until recently, full and highly competitive scholarships that included tuition, accommodation, travel and more for all its students, nationals and internationals alike. Now these are need-tested, although anecdotal information suggests they remain for anyone with a family income lower than USD $100,000 per annum. In 2021, NYUAD attracted over 17,300 applications for around five hundred places at an acceptance rate of approximately 3 per cent; its required SATs scores as high as US Ivy League schools (NYU Abu Dhabi, 2021a; Foderaro 2010: A24).

Back in 2011, UAE-based film educators Alia Yunis and Gaelle Picherit-Duthler queried whether the high-achieving, competitively selected NYUAD students would actually remain within the country, given that only a minority of them are Emirati (Yunis and Picherit-Duthler 2011: 134). The 2021 NYUAD graduate outcome numbers now claim, across the board, that 60 per cent stay on in the UAE (NYU Abu Dhabi, 2021b) and Alia Yunis, now based at NYUAD, tells me all of the most recent graduating class for Film are still there. For many from the Global Majority, the UAE represents not just opportunity, but also a gleaming beacon of non-western modernity incarnate, a territory that permits them entry when North America and Europe refuses, and all the less racist for it. Notwithstanding, the UAE still persists in the imagination as something of a temporary place, where one gains experience and money, then leaves. While a supple supply chain relishes transience, a country investing substantially in its workforce looks for a solid, enduring skills base whose impermanence it can then control according to its own whims. In this, it gains from others' losses: from the second, even third generation expatriate bourgeoisie to whom it has denied permanent residence, from instability elsewhere (some of the students, educators and film workers who talked to me about their experiences in the UAE are Palestinian, Venezuelan or Lebanese). Yet a comment from Tom registers a shift that these investments in the knowledge and creative economies elicit: 'Had I remained in Lebanon, I would probably have become a chemical engineer.' His reflection testifies to how NYUAD has opened him to the possibilities of the arts and humanities against the grain of more respected and seemingly reliable career trajectories.

For the UAE to gain from Tom's change in outlook, indeed from all this investment in the creative economy, it must sustain some extraordinary balancing acts. Can it manage the tensions between imported education systems, the expectations, norms and traditions of their incredibly diverse student populations and the policy aspirations that govern their structure, funding and regulation? Adroitness with exactly these types of negotiations simultaneously readies a worker fit for offshored filmmaking, as later portions of this chapter reveal. Yet, universities do not simply help fulfil these expectations of foreign direct investment through curricula tailored to the supply chain's skills needs. Commodified curricula themselves directly propagate such revenue.

SUPPLY CHAIN EDUCATION

Before we arrive along the supply chain at the attributes that education contributes to competitive production, then, let's hang back, as Chapter 3 did, to take stock of its earlier moments of profit accrual. Make no mistake, universities can be big business, thanks to various global policies and transnational agreements that have roundly transfigured higher education into a tradable service with the potential for franchising and offshoring (Knight 2011: 224; Ross 2009: 190). In the Gulf as a whole, private education was worth around US$15 billion in 2014 (Hanieh 2018: 215). Branch campuses have mushroomed around the world, spawned, predominantly and in order of prevalence, from US, Australian, British, French and Indian home institutions. For places like the UK and Australia, this expansion correlates with significant reductions in state support for the sector, prompting a search for rewarding markets overseas.

Collectively around seventy in number, they bestow the UAE with the largest constellation of foreign branch campuses of any country in the world and in a region – the Middle East – that also counts the highest concentration of such institutions (Becker 2009: 7; Knight 2011: 229 & 225). As with offshored film production, the climb has been steep and recent. While, regionally, Egypt may boast a claim to inaugurating the world's first university (Al-Azhar in AD 970), the more sparsely populated areas of the Gulf did not benefit from home-grown universities until much later. The independent country by its current name of the UAE formed in 1971 with indigenous universities following on towards the end of that decade. Australia's University of Wollongong arrived in 1993 and, since then, growth has continued apace filling newly built and expanding free zones such as Dubai International Academic City (Wilkins 2011: 75–76), with the likes of Middlesex, Amity and Wollongong teaching Film and/or Media strands. Most only advertise a handful of cherry-picked degree programmes that they think will deliver profit; these are not comprehensive universities in the typical sense. Instead, they advance an elastic, even just-in-time vision of higher education. By 2010, Gari Donn and Yahya Al Manthri registered that these Emirates-based institutions enrolled over 35,000 students; eleven years later, that number had more than doubled, a significant leap for such a small country (Donn and Al Manthri 2010: 41; Shukla 2021).

The incentives that, for example, Dubai's International Academic City free zone furnishes its overseas educational investors – tax exemption, foreign ownership and repatriation of profits – amplify the operations of a logistical state, public funds boosting global capitalist extraction. So far, so familiar from earlier chapters. Education now features in the top five most lucrative export services for the US, New Zealand and Australia (Ross 2009: 196). Transnational bodies like the World Trade Organization abet these moves by aggressively designating education as a commodity, rather than a protected right. In the process, the UAE gleans a skilled workforce as well as the diverse revenues funnelled from hosting a university community, rental income perhaps the foremost.

Tellingly, branch campuses provoke significant anxiety 'back home'. Academics and journalists alike fear everything from the degradation of standards and values to the suppression of various freedoms of speech, gender equality and sexual practice, which they also worry might tarnish the university's repute (see, for example: Lewin 2008: 14; Daley 2011: A25; Sorkin 2014: 5 for journalistic responses of this persuasion, as well as Vora 2015b: 21 for a scholarly critique of these reactions). In her report on the phenomenon, Rosa F. J. Becker claims that Yale pulled out of an Abu Dhabi deal, concerned that their brand had more to lose than gain from the expansion (Becker 2009: 12). *Commentary* journalist Abe Greenwald dubbed NYUAD a 'frightening love-child of Western multicultural lunacy and Arab oil money' (quoted in Sorkin 2014: 5). Andrew Ross, one of the most vociferous antagonists of the NYUAD project, New York campus-based faculty himself, predicts a turn towards the harshest practices of offshoring, where savings on labour costs could lead to remote instruction and curriculum design outsourced to lower-income wings of the sector, such as casualized teachers on affiliated campuses (Ross 2009: 202–203). These sound like past alarms about 'runaway' production, in cinema and other spheres. Certainly, Ross' suspicions are not unfounded. These universities turn out to substantially surrender the regulation and remuneration of migrant worker contracts to local sponsors (as Chapter 5 further delineates), forsaking responsibility for insuring rights equivalent to those of the originating campus or Emirati law alike. I stress here cross-border culpability via a practice common along the extent of the supply chain. Any racialized accusation of illiberalism or conservatism critics might hurl at branch campuses in the UAE bely their highly adaptive character, modern and lissom, bending quickly and easily to the needs of the global supply chain, assuring a class system that can be rapidly dissolved or reconstituted. They sprout not from a permissive 'Western multicultural lunacy', as Greenwald prejudicially dreads, but a variant that presses on with the economic exploitation of difference.

All told, the branch campus format reminds us more indubitably, and in the words of anthropologist Tom Looser, 'that capital has really been tied to the nation-state for only a brief time, and is now aggregating into quite different configurations'. For him, more fundamentally, these universities comprise 'practices and dispositions that are driving and redefining "global" structure' (Looser 2012: 99). Scholars have long migrated for and to provide schooling; for centuries, regional pillars of learning like Al-Azhar University have assembled a community from many corners of the world. However, our new consolidations of global consciousness and communion modulate according to the contemporary prominence of offshoring. Nearly two decades ago, the students studying for UK degrees outside that country surpassed in numbers those within (Wilkins 2011: 73).

When Jerry Zaslove announces that 'the university has been remade on the Wal-Mart model, so that everything is available in any size or quantity, and with no centre', he proclaims, primarily, its consumer availability (including a UK degree for sale outside that jurisdiction, perhaps) without much concern for that retailer's dependence on supply chain manufacturing (Zaslove 2007: 98). He intends an analogy, but higher education palpably exists in actual supply chain form. Borderless accreditation presides, course syllabi conform and modularity abounds so that students and faculty might move from campus to campus (although, as along any supply chain, with unequal ease). Programmes like Film and New Media Practice at NYUAD, hallmarked by an established, internationally respected university, aim to enhance, through their distinguished reputation, the prospects and mobility of graduates through the educational supply chain and into jobs. The advantages to the student body resonate: they attain recognizably global qualifications from known international universities.

Even earlier educational stages both fortify supply chain standardizations and extend its length. Two NYUAD undergraduate friends, Pamela and Emilia, inform me of recognized feeders to their university, prestigious international schools like the multi-continent-spanning UWC (United World Colleges) group. Of all the many standards and standardizations UWC and NYUAD share, instruction in English holds firmest. What prior incomes and investments underpin viable applications for NYUAD's free or heavily subsidized education? To what extent does the university manifestly maintain the borders and blockages upon which a supply chain also flourishes in order to perpetuate competition, compromise and capitulation within a workforce? Retaining a legacy of more than a century's worth of regional tertiary teaching (for instance at the American University in Beirut), the UAE also elects to deliver the majority of their public universities' programmes in English. It grasps that, for the moment at any rate, most supply chains forge their links in this language and therefore has pervasively normalized English as the working language across the country, in so doing, expediting horizontal connections between cinema's supply chain and others. Multi-sited movie manufacturing has long insisted upon the ability to work in English. Film historians of early post-Second World War forays from Hollywood to Europe emphasize just how many translators were initially required on set and how, over time, multilingual local crew diminished this necessity (Steinhart 2019: 106–111). The supply chain could thus save time and money thanks to prior education. While in Abu Dhabi, I met with Shaima, who had interned on *Star Wars* and featured in the making-of promo video. She reflected on how one of her peers was not well respected by the international crew, nor could they take full advantage of the experience, precisely because they barely spoke English. The same obstacles would arise for anyone working on Hindi and other Indian-language shoots taking place in the UAE, where, as in India itself, the lingua franca is also more often than not English (Ganti 2016: 119).

These characteristics instantiate education as both a supply chain on its own and the motor for others. Universities can sell degrees as commodities and lodge specific qualities in the student-as-consumer, confecting a *subject*, a worker, suitably adjusted to offshored filmmaking. As in the UK, branch campuses' curricula, alongside other activities associated with university life, establish and re-enforce certain relations of production, again, flexible, service-oriented, contract-based and insecure. Everyone I talked to who had undertaken such schooling and who now works in supply chain cinema (in the UAE, as well as other countries) repeatedly flagged up how their typically liberal arts educations proved all but essential to their roles in gelling transitory, multi-sited, transnational or offshored film.

In what follows, I identify some of the resulting dispositions: the championing of a self-starting, self-reliant temperament; readiness for supply chain-sensitive teamwork and participation; deft interoperable translation skills; and acceptance and perpetuation of a strategically delimited form of diversity. All this, usually, for a lower salary than their colleagues coming in from elsewhere.

THE LIBERAL ARTS INDIVIDUAL: ENTREPRENEUR, LEADER, TEAM PLAYER

The 'world-class' degrees on sale in the UAE purportedly advance their graduates' career mobility, but through what type of *content*? ScreenSkills would recoil at the paucity of nuts-and-bolts filmmaking appearing in UAE degree programmes (for an excellent summary of the offerings available in 2010 and their emphases, see Yunis and Picherit-Duthler 2011). NYUAD, like a handful of the other branch campuses, offers a Bachelor of Arts with a specialization in Film and New Media, but, in short, nowhere is there to be found a rigorous movie industry-readying training. Instead, NYUAD especially administers the type interdisciplinary liberal arts curricula whose breadth conveniently anticipates unpredictable, flexible and entrepreneurial futures. Technical capacity alone cannot skyrocket a creative or knowledge economy and perhaps the governments maintain less interest in filling those particular roles anyway. The decisive ingredient becomes a particular set of *attitudes*, behaviours that the liberal arts approaches advertised by these universities might more reliably fashion.

Michael Lightfoot avers that, 'Openness and freedom of expression have always been central to much of the discourse about the knowledge economy' (Lightfoot, 2011: 4). Such priorities are presumed to blossom within liberal arts education and the Abu Dhabi government's extensive support (material and political) of the NYU expansion to its shores aligns with these ideals. Local law has enshrined academic freedom, exceptionally, in the contracts between the government and the foreign university; NYUAD is conditionally sanctioned to circumvent national curricular parameters in the service of these aims, falling anomalously under the watch of not the education, but the tourism and culture department.

A sentence from the promotional literature of the NYUAD Film and New Media Major, fairly typical of comparable programmes around the world, highlights how this course of study, 'prepares students for a lifetime of creative and critical thinking and rigorous analysis of media' (NYU Abu Dhabi n.d.: n.p.). Such pedagogy, premised on freedom of expression, eschews regional legacies of learning, rooted in Islam, that encourage the imbibing of knowledge through rote recitation and recall. While the latter techniques can advantage a thorough mastery of the current, necessary skills and standardizations demanded by supply chain production, their value might only persist in the short-term before new developments supersede these competences, leaving a workforce lacking. Many readers of this book will perhaps consider an emphasis on critical thinking an innate good, in so doing, naturalizing, maybe even assimilating, the social and economic stance it galvanizes. Criticality of this order favours capacities to adapt, to position oneself – as an individualized self – situationally. In small classes, student-centred learning and debate counters a teacher- or textbook-disseminated body of knowledge with their implications of conformity to established norms. Tom notices how teaching at NYUAD 'assumes a certain kind of individuality' premised on self-expression that, while unrestrained and inclusive is also competitive. Pamela determines the environment 'much more individualistic' than her previous school and Tom even references Foucault's theories of self-discipline to describe the atmosphere. These methods more efficaciously prepare students, I contend, for the vicissitudes of both market fluctuations and the unknown multiplicity of possible offshored projects to which future workers might effectively contribute. They also neatly affiliate with the Abu Dhabi Economic Vision's desires to coax a less dependent workforce more inclined towards the freelance models, as Chapter 5 discerns, that power the Emirates' media free zones.

Already customary within contemporary creative labour, for political scientist Verónica Gago, such mindsets also dominate in how a migrant, including for study, frequently becomes 'an investor in himself or herself' (Gago 2017: 110). When seated together within liberal arts education, with this accent on self-enrichment, the resulting belief in human-capital-as-resource can certainly diminish, by sleight of hand, a solid sense of education as public good. Given its generous government subvention, NYUAD proves the exception in form, if not its function, while the private branch campuses established themselves through a decidedly more entrepreneurial spirit. As in the UK, this shift in what education means and how it sustains itself bleeds through into policy stipulations and course content. The Abu Dhabi Economic Vision 2030 lays out how 'Universities and colleges are working closer with the private sector to design appropriate courses to match Nationals' skills sets with the needs of business and enterprise' (Government of Abu Dhabi 2008: 75). And the BA in Film at Middlesex University Dubai even includes a compulsory 30-credit course entitled 'Film Entrepreneurship', which emphasizes employability in a fashion reminiscent of the British imperatives that dominate at its London campus, including through ScreenSkills endorsement. Entrepreneurship and the liberal arts ethos that fosters individuals who stand coherently for themselves and on their own two feet often also stress the value of 'leadership qualities', which, in turn, may not gel with, for instance (and as I will unravel through examples), established Emirati concepts of community or social position. Neha Vora, an anthropologist who has conducted in-depth fieldwork at comparable branch campuses in nearby Qatar, distinguishes a distinctly Eurocentric inflection of leadership that disadvantages students who might neither subscribe to nor show up with much prior experience of these behaviours (Vora 2019: 76).

At the same time (and meant not to contradict), specific patterns for collaborating and cooperating prevail, assets that appreciably overlap with supply chain cinema's etiquettes and priorities for interaction. Beginning-of-year orientation and extracurricular activities that provide the everyday texture of globalized liberal arts education help settle such practices into daily life and frequently emphasize all-but-essential evidence of team-building (a must for future CVs). While the commuter campuses of most UAE universities impede a fuller involvement in such goings-on, NYUAD's residential one, along with its small class sizes (considerably smaller than at the New York campus itself), clubs, field trips and after-class events optimize the social confidence required for networking. Tom remarks upon how NYUAD classes similarly give precedence to a confident, individualistic and possessive purchase on learning and creativity, which is all the while (indeed intimately intwined with), in his words, a 'transactional' attitude. Not everyone starts or finishes on a level footing. Neha Vora points out how Qatari students found that contending with a supposedly inclusive sense of on-campus participation alienated them on a number of levels that set them at a disadvantage (Vora 2019: 53). Tom, reflecting on the liberal arts compulsion to talk in class, underscored how 'While, for me, this is a great, great way to engage, for many people, it's culturally unacceptable. It's not like they're shy. It's just not how we do things, for whatever reason and so how do you negotiate that?' Advocating for one's ideas muddles into advocating for oneself, a stance that here figures as privilege and employment skill at once, something to be muscularly reproduced.

Tom conveys to me the amenability of professors, who also largely live on-site or cycle through on visiting residential fellowships, to communing with students (their ratio sitting at a luxurious 9:1), which hones an assured conviviality with older and authority figures. Conversely, Shaima (educated at Zayed University, a public institution) recalls that her initial nervousness about approaching senior colleagues on the *Star Wars* shoot hampered her prospects in a way that a more socially entitled NYUAD graduate might not recognize. The story of Shaima, who has since transitioned into a successful career producing children's content for Abu Dhabi Media, proves how universalized behavioural standards and expectations preclude broad access to the industry as it currently stands. When she was encouraged to apply for the *Star Wars* internship, she was living at home with her family, whom she knew would not approve of her travelling by herself across country at odd hours or mixing so freely with strangers for the sake of a job. The clandestine shrouding of the project's intellectual property in comprehensive non-disclosure agreements provided her with a loophole. She could simply inform her parents that she was heading off to work with trusted twofour54, the free zone coordinating the shoot, and where she had become a stalwart member of their Creative Lab community of young Emirati aspirants. Not so many people in similar situations would find their way around such obstacles. Maitha, another former intern via twofour54, extolls on their website how, 'I also got to develop my personality. It became stronger due to the fact that I worked in a new mixed environment, which was something new to me' (twofour54 Abu Dhabi n.d.b). For both women, having gone through a public, rather than a branch campus higher education, the free zone palliated their passage, although it holds considerably less capacity to do so. Ahmed Kanna's anthropological investigations substantiate how the Dubai knowledge and creative economy free zones pivot into place a more liberal version of, in particular, women's working subjectivity (Kanna 2010: 112–113). With all these universities save NYUAD housed in similar free zones, their activities, in this respect, dedicated to profiting from liberal exception, end up remarkably analogous.

Tom muses on the fact that course grades frequently correlate to these boldly discursive and socially strident characteristics and that US-trained faculty often seem oblivious to nuancing their approaches in order to accommodate a variety of social norms. He concludes, simulating a faculty perspective: 'are we really preparing them for a *western* global world?' Here he concludes similarly to Gayatri Spivak, who remarks: 'It is no secret that liberal multiculturalism is determined by the demands of contemporary transnational capitalisms' (Spivak 2012: 142). I argue now that schooling which cherishes diversity provides expertise that melds this assimilation into a particular type of creative work culture. Within it, translational articulacy emerges as fundamental to stabilizing the supply chain's excursions into sites like these.

TRANSLATING DIVERSITY

In their analyses of media clusters like the Emirates' dedicated free zones, Charlie Karlsson and Robert G. Picard observe plurality of expression to be vital for their efficacious functioning (Karlsson and Picard 2011a: 16). The examples above, however, betray that presumptions in the name of liberalism whittle the contours and limits of diversity into sometimes barely even tolerance. The supply chain bends diversity to its needs, tasking its service crews to traverse and mediate it.

The UAE, and particularly Dubai, registers as one of the most diverse places on the planet. The majority migrant population makes for a profoundly multicultural and multilingual environment, even for those who do their best to confine themselves to expatriate enclaves. Yet, prior to university (and even during), young people living in the UAE are, to one extent or another, primarily educated in a segregated fashion. Emiratis can attend free Arabic-medium public schools (although the wealthier prefer private ones) and migrants typically enrol their children somewhere that follows their 'home' curriculum (an Indian or German school, say) or an endorsed international one. Life-long inhabitants of the UAE sometimes only properly meet members of other communities when they start university.

Branch campuses deliver co-educational instruction, unlike the predominantly single-sex public universities. Overall, considerably more women than men enter tertiary education in the UAE and the country ranks higher than the USA in terms of gender parity in educational attainment according to the World Economic Forum's 2022 *Global Gender Gap Report* (World Economic Forum 2022: 348 & 15). For every (often white Global Northern) academic who rails against a lack of political and academic freedoms, there are likely ever so many more people in the sector who delight in the radically diminished racism they experience on campuses like these (Vora 2019: 129). All the NYUAD students with whom I talked appreciated how 'culturally literate' (to use Tom's words) they had grown by being there. The experience intensifies at NYUAD, which, being a residential rather than a commuter campus, consolidates the negotiation of diversity as a pervasive and ongoing lived experience. In their entirety, these characteristics advertise the UAE to incomers from the knowledge and creative economies; they serve well the graduate who needs to leap straight into such continued negotiations of difference with an international film crew (Ballon 2019: 170).

But how much give and take is entailed? In his study of Czech film crews working on international productions, Petr Szczepanik observes that the most adept and employable expressed propensities for 'behaving like Americans' (Szczepanik 2016: 99). Muhammad corroborates how the onus to adjust to these presumed norms falls to local crew. He relays how such expectations spill over into the more social, even after hours, elements of the job, stressing the advantage of his English-medium and Global Northern education. Through this schooling, he has amassed cultural reference points, TV shows to discuss, say, a shared sense of humour, and a familiar-seeming self-presentation untroubled by what they might read as 'outwardly Muslim'. After a while, white co-workers would admit 'I don't think of you as Arab', an inclusivity that speaks volumes, but all the same refuses to remuneratively reward the accrued social capital and ongoing emotional and cultural labour of 'passing'.

Such efforts help bind a discombobulated supply chain. Does somewhere like NYUAD implicitly train students in this direction and might this be a desired outcome of Abu Dhabi state investment in them? Both Shaima and Tom remark that, precisely because the campus is residential, it somewhat cocoons its own particular manifestation of diversity. The university cannot run advanced classes in, for example, the literature of the region because so few students come with the requisite levels of Arabic (including those for whom it might geographically appear to be a mother tongue, but whose formal learning has taken place in English). Vora observes that branch campuses embody a contradiction that both embraces the multicultural and must arbitrate it through a 'supposedly blind universal humanism' ultimately reliant on US precepts (Vora 2019: 56).

Tensions like these are deliberate and lie at the very heart of supply chain cinema, not least in its vehement preservation of racialized divisions of labour. A liberal arts configuration of world citizenry best adapted to its methods asks for more than just 'behaving like Americans'. To better get to grips with all these implications, I turn in detail now to the scholarship of anthropologist, Aihwa Ong. I am drawn, in particular, to a concept that she variously dubs flexible or graduated citizenship. For certain, only through these modifying adjectives can an approach to such a status hold water in a territory like that UAE, which hosts many stateless people and almost never endows citizenship. With that proviso centre stage, let's continue. For Ong, 'graduated sovereignty is the effect of market-driven strategies that are not congruent with the national space itself but that are biopolitically and spatially attuned to the workings of global markets', complexly embedded through, amongst other processes, higher education (Ong 2006: 96). In their transnationalism, flexible citizens are still choreographed by and to the advantage of nation-states, still at the mercy of borders, yet they frequently prioritize means of accumulation through which they can enjoy mobility at the expense of what stable, traditional citizenship might deliver (Ong 1999: 6). Clearly, the UAE incarnates and even engineers flexible (through which to intuit temporary and non-)citizenship, especially in its branch campuses, media free zones and offshored film shoots (see Kanna 2010: 114; Kanna 2011: 151). Ong's work brings forth cosmopolitanism as a means of establishing a 'transnational linkage of sites' and this much we have seen too through the binding capabilities of liberal arts curricula (Ong 2006: 88). What would it mean to absorb this into Ben Goldsmith, Susan Ward and Tom O'Regan's reflection that Hollywood's offshore sites can only succeed if they adhere to globalized standardization and interoperability (Goldsmith et al. 2010: 261–262)? Standardization and interoperability would not therefore cease at the technical level, but necessarily exhibit highly social and cultural characteristics. Ong's work stands out because she attends to modes of subjectivity like these that advantageously adjust to and, more so, 'mediate between diverse traditions and communities on the global scale' and, for this book's purposes, the vacillations of the supply chain as it travels (Ong 1999: 140–141).

Speaking of entrepreneurs, but with demonstrable pertinence to film workers in the UAE (themselves also perforce highly entrepreneurial), Ong catalogues how, 'They can open doors to new places, translate instructions and values from low- to high-end labor markets, and build the institutional bridges necessary for circulating information, capital, goods, and people' (Ong 2006: 125). Their literal linguistic fluency in global languages coheres with subtler, often draining, eloquence in so-called common grounds, cultural reference points, dominant modes of sociality and attitudes towards work. Addressing the former type of fluency, scholars of international film production routinely underscore the crucial stipulation for either translators or workers with high levels of English (as noted above) in order for the shoot to progress safely and in a prompt, coordinated manner (Szczepanik 2016: 92; Curtin and Sanson 2017: 162–164; Steinhart 2019: 2). To stress, such labour amounts to more than being adequately trained in technical languages. It incorporates a (typically expensive) prerequisite acculturation that must be both multifarious and intercommunicative, serving team members often singularly less cosmopolitan than themselves (as may have been the case with their branch campus professors too). These workers realize that their livelihoods depend on not snarling up the even operation of the supply chain through unfamiliarity, right down to the level of off-duty modes of socialization (where drinking alcohol, say, might enhance camaraderie). They trial all such practices in spaces like branch campuses. Once in the working world, these suitably skilled employees are frequently tasked with feeding back and conveying unfamiliar concepts to local colleagues and vice versa.

Shaima, working on home turf, regales me with snapshots of how, counter to any effortless flow of supply chain cinema production, she has had to stand her ground on and explain herself for maintaining Emirati norms like not shaking hands with the opposite gender and wearing the hijab. I hear of her discomfiture at once being caught by an acquaintance filming (not drinking) in a bar, the late nights out on a shoot that require more justification and defence than they would for her colleagues. She upholds that her values have largely provoked polite and curious questioning from international crew, rather than prejudice, but therein lies the truth about who is asked to expend the most effort to assimilate (themselves and others) into a tightly patrolled sense of diversity.

People like Shaima find ways of navigating difference that are palatable for arriving foreign crews. Shaima identified herself on the *Star Wars* shoot by assuming the label 'the girl with the abaya' (the loose over-garment worn locally) – being the only one and presuming that as a point of interest that overcame other distancing factors like a first name they might find unfamiliar. She took pride in an almost ambassadorial role, answering questions about Islam and the Gulf to co-workers who were generous and well-meaning, yet essentially ignorant of the cultures of where they had been taken for work. Neha Vora and Gayatri Spivak observe such superficiality brimming out of the multicultural syllabus and classroom, finding them resultingly depoliticized, loaded with presumptions of Global Northern superiority and particularly wrongfooted in geographical meeting points like the UAE (Spivak 2012: 77–78). 'The concept of diversity here is very shallow' reflects Pamela of NYUAD; Emilia elaborates the preponderance of one economic class to be the sticking point, associating schooled attitude with moneyed privilege in vicious circle.

The supply chain benefits from these evasions. Despite the high prior costs and considerable effort expended to attain such a multilingual (in many senses) adeptness, national status (flexible non-citizenship, we could call it) utters the final word on a usually lower salary. Translation, patently, does not extend to currency exchange rates. The supply chain extracts coherence, reliability and trustworthiness from its locally based crews, more often leaving their diminished rights unchallenged. This I would highlight as one area where international crews could exert political pressure through solidarity.

In the Gulf context, not just these people's livelihoods, but also their ability to remain within the country (which they largely cannot do without a job or a coveted golden visa), depends upon their successful absorption of these particular behaviours. Their acquiescence, forbearance and education about difference take shape not in a neutral or multivalent fashion, but according to these economic and also social priorities. Muhammad confirms how such attitudes prevail within the hiring practices of media companies: 'When you first get there, someone who is brought in from the UK or Europe or North America is immediately seen as more experienced than you... [as capable of] producing better quality content... even if they are in a lesser position.' Their equivalents in the university system will similarly earn more than their colleagues. Any faculty, though, may be required to teach a syllabus sent over from the Global Northern base campus. This amounts, ultimately, to franchising or, rather, offshoring courses and, in the process, disregarding or undermining local educational cultures and traditions. Speaking with conspicuous pessimism about the rise of transnational private universities, Gari Donn and Yahya Al Manthri bemoan how, 'The exchange of money for curricular products does not also entail an exchange of ideas. There is no long-term scientific collaboration... These institutions and their curricula do not contribute to the internationalisation of higher education... Rather, these institutions are more correctly to be seen as program/degree delivery machines, supported... by the big guns of the G8, the WTO and GATS' (Donn and Al Manthri 2010: 157).

While I side with these two authors, this chapter fundamentally queries claims that branch campuses fail to internationalize higher education. I hope to have demonstrated so far that, in multiple and profound ways, they extend that most global of formations, the supply chain. They do so, as the next section outlines, by accustoming students to creative labour, endowing border-crossing supply chains with a new slew of conveniently precarious workers and, in the process, garnering profits for private enterprise and Emirati sovereign concerns alike.

ARCHITECTURES OF IMPERMANENT EMPLOYABILITY

We've heard it before elsewhere. The Abu Dhabi government means to 'instigate a new paradigm in employment-focused education' (Government of Abu Dhabi 2008: 96). Logically, it intends a workforce from this throng of new universities, particularly urgent for expanding sectors that its own citizens largely eschew because of their long hours and unpredictable salaries.

As ever, the internship emerges as an expeditious means of readying students for this world of work. If not for pipelining them into specific jobs, then at least inserting norms of precarity into their expectations. Alia Yunis and Gaelle Picherit-Duthler describe a not-too-distant past that would seem jaw-dropping in other countries: it used to prove tricky in the UAE, for reasons to do with the taxing conditions and availability of better career options, to recruit student interns, even onto high-profile Hollywood productions (Yunis and Picherit-Duthler 2011: 127). In the intervening years, Zayed University, the American University in Dubai and Wollongong University (as a small sample) have integrated internships into their film and media curricula, often as a compulsory component (Zayed University n.d.; University of Wollongong in Dubai n.d.b).

In tandem with the training it offers in more industry-facing techniques and specialized roles, Abu Dhabi's twofour54 media free zone has been instrumental in arranging internships for academic credit with the companies it houses or temporarily hosts as a condition of the incentives packages it provides (Lodderhose 2010: A12). The emirate's 30 per cent rebate on production spend requires no imperative to hire a proportion of local crew, instead insisting that internships and training be struck as part of the deal (Abu Dhabi Film Commission, n.d.: 4; Abu Dhabi Film Commission 2022). Dubai Media City has instigated internship programmes for UAE students across its companies (Picard and Barkho 2011: 292).

These interns will not be paid, a significant break from established patterns, where no middle-class Emirati (at least) would ever expect to work like this for free. The move represents a distinct infringement of rights through outside influence, one which I emphasize because many studies of the UAE prefer to home in on autocratic rule, rather than the state's provision of sometimes superior social and economic justice. Twofour54's internships, moreover, last a minimum of one month and up to three, with a commitment of no less than forty hours per week. Ruaa, who works in outreach there, rationalizes, 'our job is to convince them that they are the ones who will benefit from the internship, not the company. The company is giving their time, their resources to teach you and you have to appreciate that, you have to pay for that.' Her comment brings to mind Abdullah, the intern from the *Star Wars* making-of, whose placement was facilitated by twofour54, and who marvels to camera, true to this spirit, about his 'once in a lifetime opportunity'.

Like a private higher education, internships that demand this many hours typically rely on considerable family support, as was the case for Shaima, who lived at home with her parents (as most unmarried Emiratis do) while she cut her teeth on *Star Wars*. She told me of another intern who was offered a six-month spot at Pinewood Studios in London through the connections she had made on set. An all-too-rare internship success story for certain, but one that multiplies expenditure while reinforcing a globalized paying-to-work model (for a discussion of the class inequalities bolstered by globe-trotting internship programmes, see Perlin 2011: 187–188).

I cannot conjecture on whether the opportunity financially stretched this woman or her family. As a citizen, her higher education will have been free up to that point, although comparisons to the UK's student and private loan culture may increasingly pertain to those enrolled in the private universities. I need to stress, however, that these institutions are, all the same, built on debt in a decidedly concrete fashion. Many workers arriving into the UAE, particularly within lower-paid sectors like construction, come bonded to a recruitment fee that could run to at least a year's salary (for further factual information, see, for example, Human Rights Watch 2009: 2–4). Until they pay this off, the worker remains at the mercy of their employer, owing labour, often with unanticipated or illicit further deductions for food and lodging. This unequivocally amounts to a form of indenture from which they cannot easily wrestle free and upon which lie the foundations of the 'affordability' of this supply chain infrastructure (Hasha Walia powerfully terms this 'a carceral regime' in Walia 2021: 140).

In Dubai, Knowledge Park, one of the free zones that houses branch campuses, abuts another (Media City), thus animating conveniently proximate alliances between schools and companies. The former educates the future employees of the latter, who also take advantage of the augmenting trend for obliging unpaid intern labour for university course credit (Picard and Barkho 2011: 291 examine these synergies). Both are managed by TECOM, a company dedicated to developing knowledge sector business clusters, itself a subsidiary of the sovereign-owned Dubai Holding. TECOM oversees two university free zones (Knowledge Park and Dubai International Academic City) as well as

Studio City and other creative economy wards. Evidently, the links of the supply chain bonding education and the media economies are not just implicit or loosely aspired, they are already structural, spatial and horizontally administered to invigorate smoother transit between the supply chain's nodes.

The free zones' designed contiguity and its attention to creative sector employability extends beyond how they have been physically located. The free zone model itself matters enormously. In the UAE, it enfolds the film commissions and the production facilities, for example twofour54, as well as other creative and knowledge economy quarters like Dubai Design District and Dubai Internet City. The general image of a free zone persists as a manufacturing quarter allowing for sweatshop-style exploitation. What, then, does it mean to expand this template into knowledge and creative production? At the very least, those studying or working within these related and interrelated architectures habituate to what a free zone actually is: a cordoned space elasticated to certain exceptionalities that accelerate production, historically close to a port (this landmass housed a free port long before it was a nation-state) and, in this respect, carrying the legacy of a border-crossing mercantile crafting of territory. Free zones are also very much characterized by an abdication of governing law and tradition in the name of the needs of specialized manufacturing. Our particular ones block unionization and extend freedom of expression. In providing dispensations unavailable to the country at large, they lubricate the machinery of supply chain cinema, starting at the very point at which someone might decide to enrol in a degree programme.

The free zones profit too from legislatively safeguarding the divisions upon which offshoring flourishes. Real estate, a robust purveyor of income in the UAE, makes money from renting space to campuses, as well as the office and studio accommodation required by freelancers wishing to work within film and its adjacent industries (Chapter 5 further elaborates on this). One such beneficiary is TECOM, which derives returns from rents twice as high as in Dubai city proper (Wilkins 2011: 77). Quite probably, rental revenues transpire to be more reliable for the country than the fruits of creative labour themselves (Ross 2009: 17 argues as much).

Those from whom the free zones garner this income now include the families of workers whose skilled status visas meant they did not have to arrive alone. In previous decades, upon reaching adulthood, any such offspring would have had to travel overseas to continue their studies, look for a sponsor all their own, or move 'back' to their country of citizenship (which may not have been their country of birth). The proliferation of branch campuses now affords these young people the chance to stay on. A smaller number join them as their first expedition to the UAE, eager not only for a globally recognized education, but also the heightened chance of landing a job there afterwards. Student visas for the UAE, I should underscore, are singularly easier to secure for the majority of the world's nationalities than are those for Northern Europe or North America and the tuition fees are more affordable. At branch campuses like that of Middlesex University, a typical three-year degree, say their BA in Film, will cost just over US$45,000 (Middlesex University Dubai 2022). More competitively priced than international fees at their London campus, further savings can be made if a student continues to live, as most expatriates do, in the family home. A home that will almost certainly be rented.

Noting the fundamental impermanence of all these aspects of residence, I circle back to the supply chain's ravenousness for precarity, already hardwired into most people's existence in the UAE. To re-emphasize, migrants make up by far the majority of the population and inter-generationally so. As a consequence, the UAE presents a tenuousness much more pervasive and structurally profound than supply chain cinema (and this book's second and third chapters) find in the UK. While at least some teaching faculty enjoy permanent contracts there, none do in the UAE, a technicality advantageous to their employers, adventurers into their higher educational terra incognita, whose own foreseeable future in the country rests on considerable start-up risks (Becker 2009: 17).

Furthermore, subcontracting, one of the supply chain's favoured modalities, finds its counterpart in how migration is managed. Within the presiding *kafala* system, the governments pass on responsibility for, as well as surveillance of, migrants to an individual Emirati sponsor (a *kafeel*), who earns an income for this service from either a stand-alone freelancer or a company. Suffice to say, and the coming chapter will examine this set-up in more detail, little makes for a lither workforce than does this practice, which is wholeheartedly wed to liberal global capitalism with roots in British colonial administration. The ninth chabter [sic – Arabic has no 'p'] of Deepak Unnikrishnan's novel *Temporary People* conveys some of the scale of this employment instability in the UAE:

> 41,282 BROWN MEN AND WOMEN in their sixties, pravasis [expatriates], every single one of them, will leave the United Arab Emirates in the middle of June. 65 percent of them have lived in the Emirates for over two decades. 18,964 of them will board planes from Abu Dhabi International Airport. All of them were informed of mandatory retirement from their respective companies at the same time. May 13, a Thursday, will be their last working day. Within weeks, they will be expected by the labor ministry to pack up their lives and leave the country for good. (Unnikrishnan 2019: 83)

These perfectly legal large-scale deportations do not just occur at the end of a perceived working life. As Muhammad succinctly puts it, 'You lose your job, you're out in a week, and you may not even have access to your finances.' Ironically, this arrangement reverses a typical impediment to the supply chain's velocity – that humans are largely less mobile than capital – although not at all in favour of the worker, whose assets may be patriated with an effortlessness that they themselves will never experience.

'The notion of insecurity is very present here', Emilia reflects. Muhammad continues, 'I was never there full-time and never invested in it.' Maybe, ultimately, the supply chain wants something of this. How many current creative or education economy migrants, before they arrived, would have stated, as Pamela does, 'I don't see myself living here'? A good amount enjoy their comparatively higher salaries and the other perks they gain, in the moment or as an investment. Many, including academics, have few options regarding where they can move for work. In some ways, the mindset mirrors those that the temporalities of unpaid stints in the film industry set in motion. The employer benefits from the suspension of an intern or migrant in their ambit. The aspirant waits for something better that may never come, allaying their purchase on worker rights in the interim.

All the more reason to strategize, starting first with what happens in the classroom. Neha Vora, Gayatri Spivak and many others argue that, despite its current shortcomings, the multicultural curriculum affords considerable scope to trial new methods of global interaction. For them, we first need to dismantle its suppositions about diversity founded in Global Northern capitalist strongholds and instead conceptualize situationally. Supremely practical with respect to modifying our pedagogy, Gayatri Spivak's essay 'Teaching for the Times' exhorts us to insist on the unevenness of multiculturalism at every point in our syllabi. What is left out of the current images of 'diversity', which populations? When we study international contexts, what might we do to not render them exotic curiosities or something to master for the purposes of domination, for the communication of orders and film commission advertising campaigns? How to lessen rather than perpetuate economic stratification within our walls? Spivak presses each classroom 'to acknowledge our part and hope in capitalism [so] we can bring that hope to a persistent and principled crisis' more specifically, in order to 'distinguish between the varieties of decolonization on the agenda, rather than collapse them as "postcoloniality"' (Spivak 2012: 143 & 152). If supply chains, as well as asserting uniformity for ease of flow and growth, also take strategic advantage of difference – as new markets, as wage differentials – then gestures like Spivak's spur us towards other articulations of difference. Through education, we might refuse (at least at the level of knowledge and outlook) to consolidate current peripheries; we might expose how and why they have been thus relegated. Additionally, as I mentioned in the previous chapter, this remains a distanced dimension of more pressing concerns: interrogating and halting to the best of our abilities unjust (such as unpaid or racialized) labour practices over which we hold a certain jurisdiction.

Tom Looser, in a discussion of the rise in global universities, entreats us to petition for and establish a world citizenry founded less on privileges, mobilities, wealth and expertise than on what we wish our rights to be (Looser 2012: 111). As the policies and profits of a globalized education gallop forwards, I would advocate for a vigorous struggle for workers' rights – including those within universities – so that the concomitant insecurities of liberalism, such as unpredictable income or territorial status, find it hard to recur. The campaigns to expose workplace violations on the construction sites of Abu Dhabi's Saadiyat Island, home to the Louvre as well as NYUAD's campus, effectively mobilize the international purchase of these 'brands', drawing on the cross-sectoral talents of NYU academics, artists, journalists, activists, Human Rights Watch and, most importantly, striking construction workers, to unify along and from outside the supply chain (Human Rights Watch 2015a; Human Rights Watch 2015b; Ross 2015a; NYU Abu Dhabi 2016).

What other rights? I, personally, dream of universal access to higher education, at institutions whose state finances all students, home and international. Like NYUAD as so recently was and almost entirely still is? Confronting aspirations highlights their constitution. For example, where does freedom of expression sit when its victory abets the ascent of the current knowledge and creative economies? What of, let's say, LGBTQIA+ events on campus (NYUAD is a magnet for students who identify in this way) that justifiably feel timid of spreading beyond its boundaries? These examples also highlight sticking points for the 'insourcing' of creative workers and students if we are to go by the fact that I am always asked a question that references criminalized homosexuality when I present this research in the Global North. Do these uneven affordances further flesh out the opportunistic exceptionality of free zoning? Or, more ubiquitously, will the two out gay people I talked to for this chapter ever work on a supply chain action blockbuster starring openly queer performers playing queer characters?

I raise these two questions side-by-side to show up how certain places and people become scapegoats, as the Gulf has with respect to gay rights, for ubiquitous injustices that benefit from being tackled transversally as well as at every site where they erupt. Likewise, the precarity and inequality endemic to the transnational knowledge economies derive from purposefully uneven globalizing initiatives, finding ready counterparts, as I have illustrated, in the UK as well. It therefore does not serve us well to demonize *tout court* singular ports of call when this system's power comes from its omnipresence and dispersal. If we are to struggle against some of the impacts of cinema and education's supply chains, or at least to strive to make them fairer, then these efforts must be multi-sited and between us collectively, as citizens of the world, graduated or otherwise.

5

Production Migrates to the Migrants: Logistics, Service and Precarity in the UAE's Creative Economy Free Zones

I come to *Dune* (Denis Villeneuve, 2021) as a new arrival. I have neither read the books nor even seen David Lynch's 1984 version. I fall for it as a researcher of the Gulf. The eleven days of it shot in Abu Dhabi brought to life a science fictional setting, but the region's aesthetics, never quite outstated, nonetheless vibrate consistently across the movie. Its elegantly sparse sun-shielding architectures, its costumes both exquisite and modest, and its reverence for the desert sublime feel squarely familiar. So too its story-line of monarchy and lacerating resource extraction. The genre which this film observes often means to insinuate the concerns of the present and does so in tension with narrative cinema's conventions of effacing some of its own, its means of production. *Dune* was asking me to pay heed to the territory, the role it plays in fabricating an imaginary space also intended as a warning of the harm we do. Including, for me, through cinema's means of production.

This is what draws me to *Dune*, but what drew *Dune* there? Abu Dhabi Film Commissioner Hans Fraikin, registers the team's interest in 'diverse yet accessible locations' compounded by 'expert local talent, world-class facilities and a supportive environment, all of which Abu Dhabi offers. It really is end-to-end support. Of course, a 30% rebate and year-round sun help too' (Vivarelli 2021a: n.p.). The years of forethought and investment are certainly now paying off. This small country with little appreciable prior industry has transformed itself into a site of partial production for hundreds of films. As with science fiction, what might seem alien or futuristic actually originates in established reality. The hyper-modern cityscapes of Abu Dhabi and, especially, Dubai at one and the same time deliver migrant dreams of advancement, fantastical cinematic mise-en-scene (Dubai plays twenty-second century Yorktown space station in *Star Trek Beyond* (Justin Lin, 2016)) and offshored cinema's resource needs. Although a neophyte to film, the UAE is old friends with the supply chain and now volunteers that expertise to its cinematic output. Film production calls for specialized infrastructure, logistics, service teams and exploitable precarity, all of which have been expertly honed in the UAE, in some cases for centuries.

I begin where many do when the UAE comes to mind: its large-scale real estate and infrastructural developments. Media-specific free zones like Abu Dhabi's twofour54 and Dubai Studio City clamp their outward-facing provisions for offshorers into a host of the country's other amenities. Extensive governmental planning and sovereign ownership patterns horizontally integrate the zones with airlines, freighting and hotels in a fashion that considerably tunes up the machinations of the supply chain. Input from the country's logistics industry (an economic stronghold in which they dominate globally) invigorates this still further. As Chapter 1 revealed, even the army contributes to the complex coordination a big-budget vehicle requires. More regularly so, a compendious and modular team of service workers that excels at everything from construction (building both sets and specialized work environments like studios, as well as other necessary infrastructures, physical and digital), and tourism (proffering a wealth of suitable hotels for accommodating visiting crews). Dedicated film commissions diligently cater to the needs of arriving projects, organizing flight deals and import paperwork, including negotiating how quickly foreign personnel can be granted work permits, hired and released. It often goes unacknowledged the extent to which these factors, essential for the effortless functioning of a film's manufacturing journey, figure in the selection of production sites and, indeed, how skilled work is routinely downgraded under this umbrella to exploit contributors in a variety of ways. This latter issue spotlights particularities of the UAE's labour market that Chapter 4 introduced. Supply chain cinema's lean and just-in-time production preferences capitalize on the country's expendable migrant workforce and differential salary scales. The creative economy free zones have recently pioneered work permits that accommodate freelancers. This move simultaneously accentuates the wage instability that the supply chain appreciates, distances the entrepreneur-creative from the purview of the state and garners dependent rental revenues for the free zones that house them – thus bringing the chapter full circle back to Emirati ventures in real estate.

BUILDING THE CREATIVE ECONOMY: REAL ESTATE AND INFRASTRUCTURE

'A hundred dollars for extras? We pay ten dollars in Morocco.' This is Rami, a prominent producer in the region, mimicking to me a supply chain cinema coordinator sensibility. He continues by explaining why big-budget vehicles come to the UAE all the same:

> They [the UAE] make up for [higher salary costs] in offering services. A lot of the companies here, be it, let's say, Emirates airlines, it's a private company, but, really, it's

government-owned. Jumeirah hotel group is the same story, and, and, and... A lot of the costs for a movie, when it's Americans, is flying here, the crew and the equipment, putting them up in really good hotels. So, you subsidize a lot of that and then, suddenly, you're scraping off quite a bit [of the outlays].

Slickly integrated provision from logistics, services and a range of amenities? The supply chain dreams of this degree of interoperability. In the UAE, it derives from a powerful state with penetrating reach and comprehensive stakes, deft at coordinating its moving parts, aided by the fact that its ruling families own so many of them. Before my subsequent sections burrow deeper into logistics and services, the physical structures that house, support, direct and redirect them require attention.

Chapter 4 characterized a state with a commitment to long-term and large-scale planning. Creative economy policies dictated the building of impressive state-of-the-art facilities for film production, largely from scratch. Dubai Studio City encompasses soundstages of varying scales, water tanks, workshops, offices, warehouses and a commissary. Its supply chain-compliant specifications have allowed it to attract sizeable productions like *Mission: Impossible – Ghost Protocol* (Brad Bird, 2011), *Star Trek Beyond* and *Kung Fu Yoga* (Stanley Tong, 2017). Dubai Studio City's Abu Dhabi counterpart, twofour54, comprises studio space, a backlot and post-production facilities. The emirates' two film commissions dwell in each and both complexes serve as regional bases for media giants like Disney Middle East (in Studio City) and Universal Pictures, Paramount, Lucasfilm, Sony Pictures and Netflix (twofour54). While this chapter, indeed this whole book, does not really tackle production for local markets, it is this, ultimately, that proliferates as the primary output from the media free zones. Most of the people I talked to for this chapter spend the bulk of their time working at this scale. It would be fair to conclude that, over this century, the UAE has ascended to a position where it now dominates Arab media production, from web-based content to glossy advertising to news to reality television to children's animation to *musalsalat* (limited period dramas, typically released an episode per day over the holy month of Ramadan) (Khalil, 2013; Yunis 2020: 163–164). Emirati and other Arabic-language movies emerge from these free zones, so too projects shot in Indian languages like Malayalam and Telugu. All this activity helps spin the UAE's appeal to migrants and its status as a bastion of pride for many in the Arab world: up-to-the-minute and slick, both on-screen and off. The creative economy free zones sprawl over ample tracts of land, spanning millions of square metres, the sizes of villages, yet piled high with multi-storeyed (sometimes skyscraper) office buildings. Ahmad Bin Byat, former Director General of Dubai's three media zones (Internet, Media and Studio

Cities), describes each zone as 'like a tiny little country' (quoted in Sampler and Eigner 2003: 119). He connotes here their magnitude as well as their autonomy (the exceptionality afforded to each).

Financial muscle, autocratic agency, will, investment, expertise and exploitation propel the UAE's leapfrog over other competitors for supply chain trade. The call beyond its borders admits the market for the UAE's own cinematic wares to be unprofitably small and, in fact, this has prompted preferential Emirati investment in big-budget international co-productions like *My Name is Khan* (Karan Johar, 2010) and *The Help* (Tate Taylor, 2011) as well as the joint Emirati–Chinese venture *Home Operation* (Yinxi Song, 2023), which troublingly deploys the real-life bombed-out Syrian ghost town of Hajar al-Aswad as a stand in for war-torn Yemen (Leotta 2015: 30; Hudson 2017: 199–200; Tarnowski 2022). A from-the-ground-up industry with little obligation to home-grown filmmaking proves convenient for supply chain cinema. It can sidestep the conflicting interests or labour histories that plague its undertakings in countries like the UK.

Jamal Al Sharif, Chair of the Dubai Film and TV Commission, rationalizes these prodigious investments and their atypical timelines: 'The whole focus was to build the real estate, build the structure, prepare it as fast as possible because eventually down the road you will have to build the people, build the industry... which is going to drive the real estate' (quoted in Editor in Chief 2016: n.p.). As I hinted in the previous chapter, the governments' stimulus to the creative economy had its eye on rental income too, assured by the country's patterns of ownership. All these complexes are sovereign concerns raised on land that the ruling families by default and law deem themselves to own. An exploited, often-indentured labour force erects these buildings, converting oil capital into diversified income streams (see Hanieh 2011: 110; Buckley and Hanieh 2014: 162–163; Choplin and Vignal 2017: 103–121 for a rigorous understanding of how these real estate markets are globalized and financialized). Dubai Studio City and twofour54 alike fuse into much broader city planning that both incarnates and integrates economic policy, siphoning its proceeds in the same directions. Chapter 4 underlined the consequences of TECOM's joint management of education and media free zones. TECOM, however, is but a subsidiary of Dubai Holding, a government-owned company with a capacious assortment of assets. They include the Jumeirah Group of luxury hotels and resorts, whose A-list-satisfying levels of comfort Rami signals as a draw to supply chain cinema. No small order when a sparsely populated desert is the attached film's shooting location. Thinking beyond short stays, Dubai Holding's sister investment company Dubai World initiated the famous reclaimed land megaprojects, The World and The Palm, while another local (and sovereign-owned) giant, Emaar Properties, claims the Dubai Mall and the Burj Khalifa, the world's tallest building. The latter's Arabian Ranges, an exclusive gated community, replete with a golf course, tellingly neighbours Studio City, intensifying both corporations' convergence on mixed yet intermeshed property portfolios.

Collectively, they shape elaborately detailed environments, for work, leisure and domesticity, resolved to entice international creatives. The media free zones subsume entertainment venues and housing, knitting these activities together and bolstering an interconnected and holistic lifestyle that Chapter 4 relayed as fruitful to creative supply chain productivity. Both internally and in association with each other, free zones choreograph different providers into the offshored cinema economy, whether these be the location services, construction workers for sets and secondary crew members, or the neighbouring educational free zones who supply trainees, interns and, eventually, future freelancers. From the massive water tank to the freelancer's rented office, from the opulent seven-star hotel to the modest family apartment, this real estate orients towards the full range of industry personnel's visa lengths, be that a week or indefinite.

The same adaptive strategy pertains to how the free zones house film-related business, responding dexterously, as Nolwenn Mingant observes, to various scales and temporalities (Mingant 2018: 285). As testament to their adaption to less assuming registers of production, Mushthaque Rahman Kariyaden, director of the Malayalam drama, *Deira Diaries* (2021), confirms, 'We had so much support from the UAE government who went out of their way to make sure everything was in place. It's no wonder that many Indian films are being shot here' (quoted in Tusing 2021: n.p.). During the UAE's sparse weeks of hosting bigger-budget productions, the free zones attune to the supply chain's very raison d'être: stopping off to add on. Locally based personnel help deliver what Ben Goldsmith, Susan Ward and Tom O'Regan label the 'plug in', minor inputs inserted (a film scene here or there), during a much longer journey (Goldsmith et al. 2010: 86). Free zones also regularly market their talent for reducing the costs at planning stages (Scott 2012: 20). Rami notes that, 'Of course, when Americans shoot for three and a half weeks in a country it's a whole production in itself and you're in prep for months.' Landmark blockbusters do not fetch up every day, nor do they linger long (thanks, often, to this sophisticated coordination). Minute for minute, they represent only a meagre proportion of UAE-based content creation, which largely springs from the aforementioned local and multinational media companies regionally headquartered in the free zones. However, just as Tom Cruise atop the Burj Khalifa in *Mission: Impossible – Ghost Protocol* advertises Dubai's glitz to potential tourists who will likely stay somewhere more affordable, the ability of the free zones to cater for blockbusters broadcasts their film-friendliness and stalwart reliability to any media client. The backlots, water tanks and studios also aspire to stretch the duration of a stay that might have intended location shooting only.

At the same time as it effectively channels earnings into state-corporate coffers, the free zone thoroughly harmonizes with the rhythms and flows of transnational capital. Like the universities, the media free zones tailor exceptional legality to suit the purpose of what is produced there. Again, freedom of speech protections unavailable throughout the rest of the country and regularly in contradiction to many of its citizens' belief systems or ways of life. Again, the outlawing of unionization. Again, 100 per cent foreign ownership, this time with minimal set-up paperwork (two to four weeks processing time for any new company), when otherwise non-nationals hold precious few rights and assurances as inhabitants. And, as in the UK, government partiality towards the sector extends a rebate on production spend in Abu Dhabi (30 per cent) (Abu Dhabi Film Commission n.d: 4). Speaking of logistical corridors (and free zones are certainly that), Giorgio Grappi pinpoints how they:

> synchronize the administrative time, procedures, and standards of bordered institutions... Their aim seems to be that of formalizing a third political space between the operations of private capital and political institutions, where these blur in favour of a logistical polity that follows its own temporality, somehow free from the procedures of traditional politics. In this third space, different political systems – whether based on representative politics, state parties, or authoritarian regimes – can meet and share a common ground. (Grappi 2018: 182–184)

Even more so, I would argue, they acrobatically entwine outwardly impossible pairings: freedom and autocracy, mobile and indentured labour. They open gateways and just as surely close them in the name of profit and security. Bindu Menon points out that the free zone expertly draws into tight arrangement the exceptionalism that allows for investment and repatriation of transnational funds, the shunting in and out of capital, as well as honing specialized and multi-layered labour (Menon 2018: n.p.). Ultimately, this architecture connives a particular type of supply chain extractivism that reaches well past its evident spaces of production and into gated communities, labour camps, and, as Chapter 4 evinced, university campuses in order to take advantage of an assiduously diverse workforce (to be examined in more detail presently).

With all this to the fore, I contend that free zone buildings function simultaneously as real estate and as conduits, as infrastructures of passage. In this, they constitute a small wing of something much more sweeping. In 2016, Dubai apportioned a staggering 35 per cent of its budget to infrastructure expansion (from roads and ports to telecommunications). To compare, the USA and Saudi Arabia each spent 3 per cent that year (Unitas Consultancy 2016: 15). To compare again, while India's advanced film industry heartily recommends it to offshorers, it cannot guarantee against power outages as unfailingly as the UAE. In a similar vein, Rami singles out the basic advantage that roads bestow upon competing offshore filming locations, 'The difference between here [the UAE] and Morocco is that here, if you want to shoot in the desert, you drive for forty minutes. In Morocco you've got to fly from Marrakesh to Ouarzazate and then from Ouarzazate drive for I don't know how many hours to get to the really nice desert.' Fuel availability and affordability in the UAE present no hitches to such expeditions, needless to say exemplifying how the post-oil economy is nowhere near post.

Studio City and twofour54, often via their respective film commissions, take advantage of infrastructure and adapt it into human form. They listen to the needs of arriving projects, then reach out their many tentacles. Twofour54 incorporates an on-site travel agent; they are connected to freighting companies, databases of local crews, location managers and scouts, government offices, drivers, hotels. Clients partake of their superlatively fast and secure in-house digital processing, archiving and conveyance of media content. No wonder this expertise in receipt and dispatch, given that the free zones' roots lie in the UAE's ports. The country perseveres with models grown from its enduring position within maritime and colonial-military circuits.

These also stem from the prominence in the UAE of what geographer Thomas J. Sigler labels 'relational cities'. For Sigler, conurbations like Dubai thrive by actively yoking together miscellaneous scales, regions and markets, then amplifying their interaction. The real estate that accommodates different types and durations of media production epitomizes these goals. Sigler's observations about Dubai at large correlate to its nodal point amidst supply chain cinema, 'The Emirate has specialized in connecting nearby regions where free markets have been restricted by social unrest (Iraq), autocratic leadership (Iran, Saudi Arabia), red tape (India), or a combination of all three (former USSR)' (Sigler 2013: 627). The UAE reaps the rewards of its position at a crossroads between continents, a gathering place of skilled film workers from politically unstable countries, a gateway into Gulf markets, all within reach of powerful film production centres like China and India. Relational cities differ from global ones in that they dedicate their energies less to finance and consulting and more to wholesaling, warehousing, logistics, offshore banking, real estate and the institutions of ports, airports and free trade zones (Sigler 2013: 616).

They welcome, too, the 'cluster' model that economists Charlie Karlsson and Robert G. Picard identify as spaces that 'accommodate a large number of planned as well as chance and random encounters with both similar and different producers and customers, i.e. locations that can support the mediation, iteration and heuristic action that is integral to the production of the media industries' (Karlsson and Picard 2011b, 4). With accumulated centuries as a maritime and mercantile axis, the UAE has established trust and track records for such negotiations. Being a new player in filmmaking (as well as higher education), it logically banks on demonstrable capacities to interlink, but more so to broker trade, setting the scene for contracts, within literal architectures of exchange. Shaima, the former *Star Wars* intern featured in the previous chapter, remarks upon twofour54's Creative Lab's primary imperative to 'connect talents' as readily as former NYU president John Sexton gushes about the Abu Dhabi campus's architecture as:

> a genuine *network*, integrated and interlocking – featuring interlocution among its various nodes, and allowing synchronized activity among them with minimal impediments. Faculty, students, and staff at the various sites are available to each other; and they are able to migrate freely among the constituent parts. (Sexton 2010: n.p.)

This real estate, then, discerns itself as much more than a transitory workplace. It endeavours to accrue prodigious income from exploiting the movement, rather than the start-to-finish manufacture of goods. Offshore sites prove themselves all the more inviting if, as relational spaces, they oversee circulation and help chart superior trajectories.

I am struck here by how reminiscent one of the port city's primary architectural forms, the distribution centre, is to the film studio (Dickinson 2020: 267–268). While usually compared to a factory, the studio's windowless functionality suggests this other analogy. In the distribution centre, speed is of the essence, movement complies with modular rather than mass manufacturing needs, must be nimble and trimmed of all waste (Klose 2015: 160–161). Waiting costs money. Dubai Studio City took shape within an historic warehousing district and barely disrupts its visual character. Both building types temporarily house and then dispatch, thanks to the logistical software now solidly bred into their musculature. Studio City boasts integration into fibre-optic networks and satellite services, courtesy of government-owned Samacom, itself both an outcome of the national infrastructural push and now an investor in extra-territorial smart city developments.

LOGISTICAL LABOURS

This is an instance, of many, where built environment, infrastructure and logistics meet. As a reminder from Chapter 1, logistics manages movement, rendering the supply chain's dispersed modes of production feasible. Being a port economy deriving significant proceeds from logistics, the UAE can successfully advertise these capacities to incoming film projects (Dickinson 2016: 140–153). Courtesy of a long history dedicated to aligning flows through its ports, upsurging with oil exportation more recently, the UAE, and Dubai in particular, prides itself on a more advanced logistics economy (along with the world's first 'logistics city' free zone) than any other contemporary site for film offshoring. Ballasted by this top-down reconciliation of transport networks and suppliers (the Emirates airline included), the free zones then fuse these advantages with minimal bureaucracy, openness to foreign capital and the migration system's rigging of labour costs. I start by registering these synchronizations, then progress to how speed and cost reduction impels logistics.

One major theme throughout this book has been that film's dissociable production sequence lends itself to the disaggregation, frequently through offshoring, from which the supply chain profits. Logistics comes good on the necessary relocation of a film's people and objects. More precisely, the UAE specializes in what is variously called re-exporting or trans-shipment, the prompt and reliable onward movement of goods received from elsewhere, splitting, safeguarding, redirecting flows. It sometimes, but not always, enfolds the addition of components (just described as 'plug ins') when labour, transport or fiscal savings surface. This economy where throughput predominates over output duplicates over to the UAE's appeals to supply chain cinema, itself never a unified single-direction journey, but a set of congregations drawn from far and wide.

All filmmaking departments carry tales of the calamitous repercussions of equipment, costumes or props not showing up on time, not clearing customs or arriving damaged. When the cost of big-budget shooting days can run into millions, effective logistics are crucial to making sure everything is where it needs to be. The UAE's global supremacy within air and sea transportation speeds workers, materials and kit across the diffused production line. The country's airline freight divisions carry some of the highest tonne-kilometres in the sector (Emirates sits second only to Federal Express). Sovereign-owned DP World's logistical and port management operations (over eighty terminals across more than forty countries) account for 10 per cent of the planet's container traffic (DP World n.d.). The film commissions roll discounts from these national companies into their incentives packages, booked through free zone travel agencies (Abu Dhabi Film Commission 2018: n.p.). Less overtly, air and seaports assume a role in the variegating of labour and salaries by helping marshal who enters and leaves the country and therefore how the UAE's workforce retains a competitive technical composition (Martin 2012: 368; Dyer-Witheford 2015: 83; Mezzadra and Neilson 2019: 163–164).

In his history of Hollywood's overseas shoots, Daniel Steinhart chronicles a shift from shipping everything required from the US (with incumbent costs, risks and delays) to the rise in the possibility of acquiring resources through local studios and rental houses (Steinhart 2019: 91). Both tendencies rely on logistics. With respect to the latter, Emirati logistics also initiates systems for coordinating multiple state and commercial service sectors, spurring competitive advantage through the sheer reach of what it draws into its ambits. Ruaa from twofour54 stresses what the local team can provide: 'We have post-production facilities, editing and sound recording... We have studios, they can use the studios. We have a travel services team which can provide them with flight tickets, visas and all these logistics. We try to facilitate the thing from A to Z.' Vikram Agrawal, head of content development and production for India's Reliance Entertainment bears this out: 'The kind of facilities that Abu Dhabi gives you to shoot a film are as good as anywhere in the world; it's top notch... you have everything available here, from crew to equipment... the biggest thing is the studio' (quoted in Vivarelli 2021c: 120). Rami has already mentioned the hotels, nodding towards how ownership patterns assure smoother and more expansive interoperability, given that they share their parent company, Dubai Holding, with TECOM. Jebel Ali container port, DP World and multiple real estate interests all reside under the umbrella of Dubai World. Because these are state concerns, they can easily be bundled with tax incentives and tariff reductions. With all this at their fingertips, each emirate's film commission can convincingly describe itself as a 'one-stop shop'.

A short *Variety* article by Nick Vivarelli watches all this come together through the working relationship between the Abu Dhabi Media Zone Authority and big-budget Bollywood production, *Tiger Zinda Hai* (Ali Abbas Zafar, 2017). The emirate's 30 per cent rebate as well as its proximity to India (flights doubtless facilitated by Etihad) attracted the project. Abu Dhabi organized for sets recreating Iraq to be built. As they had for *Star Wars: The Force Awakens*, the army loaned out military equipment, this time vehicles (from a Blackhawk helicopter to Humvees) that would make a splash in an action movie. Vivarelli's inquiries reveal that the team 'got whatever military support it needed because the Media Zone Authority is directly connected with the government' (Vivarelli 2018: 61). Although distinctly less screen-worthy, behind the scenes, these affiliations reduce red tape and keep a look out for how legislation and infrastructural development can support the industry.

More than anything, though, logistics promises pace to market with a competitive product, returns as fast as possible. It aims to dissolve the distinction between production and circulation in capital operations, to eliminate, through a space–time compression, the lag in profit acquisition (for these qualities of logistics, see

Cowen 2014: 11; Budrovich Sáez and Cuevas Valenzuela 2018: 164). 'You can film more in less time in Dubai', affirms the Dubai Film and TV Commission, thanks to 'fast and efficient logistics' (Dubai Film and TV Commission n.d.c: n.p.). Abu Dhabi Film Commissioner Hans Fraikin solidly translates this into industry terms in his portrait of the part they played in *Dune*'s offshoring to the UAE:

> Abu Dhabi Film Commission worked with Denis [Villeneuve, the director] and his team for quite some time to secure the right locations and arrange the logistics, from filming permits to travel and accommodation. This meant that when they arrived they were able to shoot smoothly and seamlessly across 11 days with the support of a number of local businesses and freelancers from twofour54 Abu Dhabi. (Vivarelli 2021a: n.p.)

With an arriving team of around a hundred (all needing to be paid, fed, housed and taken to work), *Dune* reduced its budget considerably through the film commission's efforts. Notably, the CEO of twofour54, Michael Garin, was able to report not a single production day lost to Covid-19, even at the height of the pandemic (Vivarelli 2022: 74). From February 2020 onwards, temperature checks, teams organized into 'bubbles', sterilization and (as soon as available) testing became standard, meaning that shoots like *Mission: Impossible – Dead Reckoning Part One* (Christopher McQuarrie, 2023) could proceed without delay. The Film Commission also pledges to process a rebate application within a fortnight and pay out within 45 days of the final certificate, which ensures exceedingly fast access to capital in the larger scheme of movie budgeting (Abu Dhabi Film Commission 2018). Filming permits can be secured within three days and visas for non-Emirati employees within one.

The logistical state also partners beyond its own agencies, orchestrating the private sector, particularly via its reliance on and provision for outsourcing. The free zones hold databases of suitable local crew and suppliers, poised to contribute in on-demand capacities. Just-in-time manufacturing plays out on several levels here. Local daily rate freelancers retreat off the payroll and out of sight if unneeded. When Shaima interned on *Star Wars: The Force Awakens*, she was packed off to set at extremely short notice. Chapter 4 explicated the touch-and-go nature of whether she would be able to take up this opportunity, her situation exposing how exclusive are the demographic who can simply drop everything when the supply chain calls, and how much workers must surrender if they answer.

Likewise, international personnel can be whisked in quickly. The long reach of UAE logistics draws, at the bat of an eye, the best or cheapest film professionals from around the world. *Star Wars* flew in specialist set builders from Mumbai (Pennington 2015: n.p.). The availability of Emirati airline flights matches the speeds at which work permits can be issued and expired. These junctions within the logistical landscape can dramatically reduce overheads and improve bidding prospects, yet at significant cost to workers. Employees are compelled to keep products perpetually in forward motion, nothing resting in the drive to sublimate resources into capital as swiftly as possible. Logistics means to refigure labour, even broader living conditions, to its whims.

Once more, I find the distribution centre analogy fecund and not just because these spaces notoriously demand harder work at greater pace. They buttress a 'pull economy', sensitively responsive to consumer demand for immediacy, as epitomized by how overlords like Amazon operate through them to distribute physical wares. The streaming wing of this platform, like its counterparts, corresponds its prompt content production as best it can to this priority in its algorithmic processing of viewer data. Both spheres marry the 'pull' objective to a zero-inventory ideal. They keep stock to a minimum so as not to lose money, including on storage itself. 'Storage', when it comes to supply chain cinema, manifests in multiple forms. Chapter 1 gave a glimpse of the supply chain's promises to securely look after intellectual property. As Chapter 2 revealed, film workers more than ever take care of their own kit, saving multinationals significant sums in safeguarding and maintaining it. Storage considerations spread beyond the warehousing of equipment, props or even digital content to engulf how waged workers can be opportunistically codified as 'surplus'. Logistics discharges its international workers just as rapidly as it assembles them, only housing them for as long as absolutely necessary. For local freelancers, far more predictable than their contracts will be the regularity of their rent payments for offices in the zones. They ultimately pay for their own storage in this way.

Just-in-time and zero inventory practices also fulfil supply chain cinema's demands for secrecy. One reason why Shaima was summoned to *Star Wars* at the eleventh hour was because production could not hazard curious crowds flocking to their locations or any resulting compromise to the value of their intellectual property. Better to keep the project covert with workers themselves absorbing the ensuing confusion and last-minute scurrying. Security and trust rise high as quality benchmarks for logistics: reliable handling, the constant traceability of goods and the carefully calculated mitigation of risks (think of the UAE's scrupulous Covid testing and abundance of vaccinations in relation to almost every other shooting location during the pandemic). The supply chain's traditional dependence on the security of trade routes finds cinematic equivalents in the confidence engendered by the UAE as a danger-free place to film desertscapes, a literal port in the Middle East's political storms. Cargo insurance meets its equivalent in the safety measures that rise to extreme conditions. The *Dune* team elected to shoot during the summer because of the particular colour of the sky at that time of year, regardless of the life-threatening temperatures it brings. In a recapitulation of Ben, the British sound mixer's definition of supply chain cinema as the expectation 'that they can throw anything at you', Robbie McAree from Epic Films, the subcontractor providing production services for *Dune* expresses that, 'Logistically it was challenging... Special tents had to be created with air conditioning to keep the heat from affecting the crew and camera equipment' (Sharf 2021: n.p.).

Life or death responsibilities like these group under the 'can do' attitude the UAE wishes to project to international clients. In taking on these challenges, a raft of workers animates Ned Rossiter's claim that 'the logistical city is a city of services' (Rossiter 2012: 25). The classification of service, as a mode of labour, further advantages the supply chain through the division of labour it instantiates.

SERVICING SUPPLY CHAIN CINEMA

Amongst the experienced film personnel with whom I talked in the UAE, there was consensus about being nudged out of a spectrum of expertise. Recalling the mediatory roles delineated in the previous chapter, experienced filmmaker, Muhammad observes how many times he had found himself:

> in that situation where the main producers or the kind of managerial positions had no understanding of the language or the context or whatever, and they would hire people like me to do that work for them, and to kind of be the person who can translate it back to them, be the person who can actually go on the ground and get the work done.

As an accomplished industry professional, he admits that:

> There were certain points when I didn't see why I needed someone else to be supervising this work... when I could just be bypassing them in that sense... you find yourself in weird positions where you feel like you're reporting to someone who's less knowledgeable than you, and the only reason you're here according to them is because of where they're from.

Muhammad's frustrations tally with what anthropologist Kimberly Chong calls 'ontological takeover' (Chong 2018: 62). Her study of Global Northern buyouts of Chinese companies brings to light how incoming firms supplant established procedures with new ones conveniently legible to their interpretations of capitalism.

The ontological takeover actuated in the UAE complies with and perpetuates (largely racialized) hierarchies where incoming projects re-categorize film workers as service personnel. Petr Szczepanik corroborates similar treatment of expert Czech crew hired on home soil by international productions while Ben Goldsmith, Susan Ward and Tom O'Regan stress how 'greenfields' offshore sites like the UAE increase their traffic through adapting deferentially to incoming needs (Szczepanik 2016: 89; Goldsmith et al. 2010: 184). When I ask Rami about his time on offshored projects, he is in no hurry to return to their diminished opportunities for creative contribution:

> When you work on an American film, it's like a job. You get up and go there. Your job's prepared like an extra, literally, that's what they say. Herd the extras out, herd them back in, feed them, change them, send them home, bring them back in the morning.

His musing blurs the line between rallying background performers (a task devolved to the local production services team) and metaphorically becoming one, peripheral to the main action. In Britain, a time-honoured tradition of film craft concedes considerable creative agency to local workers; less such hope in the UAE. Shaima tots up those on *Star Wars* as 'location scouting, the interns, the extras, and that's it'. While these ratios have been rapidly changing since that shoot, for certain many more people will have pitched in (see Vivarelli 2013: 70 for rising statistics in local crew involvement). At a best guess from combing the final credits for likely names, the production also took on: various departments' assistants, government liaison staff, accountants, props and storage support, grips, electricians, set workers (labourers, painters and carpenters), security, transport coordinators and drivers. Shaima's answer reveals how easy it is to imbibe designations of sectoral expertise and overlook those side-lined by such taxonomies.

Even the army, even the government assume production services roles. In the making-of, Mark Somner, the *Star Wars* unit production manager praises the Civil Defence and Ministry of the Interior for facilitating 'the pyrotechnics and the prop weaponry we've brought into the country'. Paul Baker, executive director of twofour54's production services wing, Intaj, overstates, 'We've brought enough C-4 explosive into the UAE to start World War III', underscoring that, to accomplish this, 'you have to have very strong connections and commitment from the government' (quoted in Vivarelli 2015: 109). In what seems almost an allegory of reallocated status, the UAE military loaned *Mission: Impossible – Fallout* (Christopher McQuarrie, 2018) their Boeing C-17 Globemaster III and DHC-6 Twin Otter planes (not easily available at the drop of a hat), skilled pilots, a hanger, decompression chambers, trauma medical teams and security for more than a hundred sky dives over the desert (Ritman 2018: n.p.). Post-production transplanted this footage into the air space above central Paris, consigning the UAE again to stand-in duties, this time leaving no recognizable trace back to source, or to a racialized cadre of labour, save for acknowledgements in the closing credits.

Here they fall into line with other crucial service providers from the hospitality and construction sectors. Hotel accommodation consumes a sizeable portion of a film's location shooting budget. Tellingly, Jamal Al Sharif commences his enumeration of Dubai's contributions to the Bollywood vehicle *Happy New Year* (Farah Khan, 2014) from this angle, 'We customized their hotel requirement, their airline requirement, their logistics in Dubai, the equipment that they wanted, and took care of their visas – we saved them a lot of hassle and cash' (quoted in Vivarelli 2013: 70). Not every supply chain cinema site can promise the high-end lodgings A-list film personalities expect, the full complement of suitable rooms for a large arriving team or such adroitly obeisant staff trained to uphold anticipated standards (for how Eastern Europe used to be considered wanting in these terms, see Goldsmith and O'Regan 2005a: 5–6; Goldsmith et al. 2010: 89). Hosting and, with it, by proxy, facilitation, endure as age-old traditions and points of pride within Arab desert territories. After shooting *Mission: Impossible – Dead Reckoning Part One*, director Christopher McQuarrie was to gush, in advertisement-like alliteration, about Abu Dhabi's 'Grace and graciousness, magic and majesty, hospitality and hope' (quoted in Vivarelli 2021b: n.p.). In return for free rooms at the Atlantis luxury hotel, *Happy New Year* showcased the resort prominently and, in both situations, promotional quid pro quo displaces the effacements described above, mounting to crescendo. Top quality hotels and associated service satisfy film stars whose presence, in reality or diegesis, creates buzz for a place. Screen tourism escalates, be it (location) sightseeing or visits to theme parks like Bollywood Parks or Warner Bros. World Abu Dhabi (largely cartoon-centred, without a wizard in sight). The UAE grows increasingly like a fantasy land to tourists. And the more the film and the tourism sectors harmonize in mutual financial interest, the tighter the connection between their workers' behaviours. Needless to say, the responsibility to care for everyone involved falls chiefly on those employed in tourism, including those who have built its properties to often-lavish standards.

Here we cross into the sector perhaps the most deliberately distanced from the status accrued through creative film labour: construction. In the making-of video, Paul Hayes from the *Star Wars* team acknowledges locally based workers' responsibility for bringing the sets to life. Across the short documentary, most 'above the line' interviewees extol the virtues of a fictional world rendered as 'real' as possible, something that positively struck many fans too. Likewise, in extras found on the

Dune DVD, Denis Villeneuve declares, 'I'm a strong believer that you must build as much as possible because it will influence acting, it will influence the imagination of the actors, it will influence myself as a director.' Both documentaries celebrate the designers, but not the construction teams. While there exists a whole studio tour to exult the skills of named craftspeople in the UK, the labour of builders in the UAE unequivocally classifies as 'unskilled'. In her ethnographic study of equivalent migrant workers in Qatar who, like in the UAE, carry out some of the most challenging and experimental construction in the modern world, Natasha Iskander emphasizes how 'skill functions as a language of political exclusion', as well as an arbiter of hierarchy and wage (Iskander 2021: 10 & 5). 'Unskilled' has excused indenture, a deplorable extreme of supply chain subcontracting where workers' own recruitment debts might negate wages. The cost-cutting their standing provides a film production outstrips that gleaned from the creative sector locals. Neither will add to the hotel bill or request per diem expenses, but construction workers dwell in cramped labour camps, rent and food costs compulsorily deducted. They will be cheaply bussed to and from site together according to just-in-time and hour-intense temporalities. Their treatment has even been named 'containerization' after the shipping units that spearheaded the rise of logistics, so often now repurposed as dormitories for migrants across the world (Hanieh 2016: 48).

In concert with the caterers, drivers, cleaners, freighting company employees and childcare workers, severe consequence colours this filmmaking, hotel and construction staff's superlative service labour. Almost all expatriates' capacities to hold down contracts, continue working and thus stay in the country largely hang on them not angering their bosses or raising complaints. Seldom are conditions so conditional. Muhammad encapsulates, 'Whether I was working in a local company or in the free zone, it always felt like you can't say much because, if you do, then you could get fired, then you lose your visa... then your bank gets notified, your house gets notified, they kind of freeze your accounts.' The UAE's saleable service culture, prised wider now to incorporate creative workers, tempers everyday life and expectation with a justifiable and disciplining anxiety. This country almost never allows its migrants to settle, nor does it offer sanctuary to a humanitarian quota of refugees or asylum seekers, leaving any out-of-favour or even currently contract-less worker entirely prone to deportation.

CALIBRATED PRECARITY, OR 'I JUST WANT TO BE PAID LIKE A WHITE PERSON'

When the Dubai Film and TV Commission's Jamal Al Sharif, once a key player in TECOM's creative free zones, announces, 'Freelancing was part of our strategy', he simultaneously consolidates, broadens and intensifies forms of precarity conducive to supply chain cinema (Picard and Barkho 2011: 299).

Entirely compatible with film's modular production processes, employing freelancers fragments the workforce down into temporary and malleable units. In its UAE configuration, this modality appeases the supply chain's concomitant need for competitive difference by proffering an entirely different scale of impermanence. Migration in the UAE, which accounts for more than eight out of ten workers, is, I have demonstrated, already lean and logistical, already in-step with what employers prize about a casualized sector. Although the UAE may be a newcomer to cinema, it brings considerable experience of managing precarity through migration as a profitable advantage to supply chain operations. Migration law in the UAE summons and blocks a labour force according to its exigencies, matching logistics' frictionless ideals by legally enforcing disposability and flexibility. Consummate service provision and compliant comportment denuded of citizen rights fluidly slipstream into the unique selling points this particular freelancer market tenders.

The same goes for the privilege of relinquishing duties of care. As Chapter 4 laid out, the responsibilities for almost all migrants' welfare, unless they have significantly invested in property or hold a rare golden visa, falls not, in the first instance, to the state but to their *kafeel* (sponsor). It is to them that a temporary worker must appeal for the right to work or to switch jobs and in a system with a woefully small number of regulators (Human Rights Watch 2015a: 6). NYUAD officials, when confronted with proof of how their construction workers had been maltreated, shrugged off culpability by pointing out that this labour had been subcontracted, completed out of view and before they arrived, so was not their dominion (Kaminer and O'Driscoll 2014: A9).

The free zones now expand these tried and tested principles of remaining at arm's length into their new disposition towards self-employment. 'An independent future awaits you... take control of your career!' promises TECOM in its hype for the Dubai Media City free zone (Dubai Media City n.d.a: n.p.). TECOM has spearheaded the relaxation of a migrant's need for an employment contract in order to gain a work permit or trade licence. Instead, the free zones will step up as the sponsor and the worker can be their own boss. Policies like the Abu Dhabi Economic Vision 2030 make it clear that the country aspires towards an even less dependent workforce and the freelancer (as Chapters 1 and 2 contended) will typically suspend benefits, rights and solidarity in the pursuit of entrepreneurial boldness and self-sufficiency (Government of Abu Dhabi 2008: 38–39). The free zones preferentially register your details in their databases, which they furnish to incoming film projects, but, unlike the sponsor of old, they do not promise employment.

Any ensuing precarity remains the worker's own concern, from which the free zone, as will soon emerge, profits. Freelancers in the media free zones include editors, event planners and wardrobe stylists; and in those dedicated to education, autonomously trading advisors, researchers and trainers. The fact that these zones permit workers to conduct business under a 'birth name as opposed to a brand name' speaks to the resulting atomization and casualization (UAE Free Zones n.d.b: n.p.). Tenants band together and split resources on site, from shared secretarial services to equipment rental, but, ultimately, compete with one another for business, cutting the costs for larger enterprises in the process (Picard and Barkho 2011: 297–298). In their study of Dubai Media City, Robert G. Picard and Leon Barkho attribute to this opening up to freelancers a significant structural adjustment towards supple and fluctuating labour markets, both local and global (Picard and Barkho 2011: 297).

Here freelance labour must fall into line with the zones' pre-existing rules, including their prohibitions on organized labour, collective bargaining and striking, aware that contract termination, wage withholding and even imprisonment act as strong deterrents to such behaviour (Human Rights Watch 2012: 4). In these respects, the free zones perpetuate historical reasons for films being shot away from the union protections of Hollywood. Alongside the magnified instability of not being sure when the next contract would appear, Muhammad, once a twofour54 freelancer, catalogues the extra paperwork involved, the constant reporting of hours to the free zone authority, and the implications of job insecurity for his status in the country. The liberties associated with self-employment receded considerably.

When I first began visiting the zones' freelancer webpages, their promotional imagery jarred: eerily similar-looking young, bearded, strawberry blonde hipsters of clearly European descent. How much does this type risk, comparatively, by entering the Emirates' creative economy self-employed? These days, the photos could more realistically deputize for a friend who ended up for a while as a freelancer in twofour54: a Palestinian visual effects artist whom I had met in Damascus and who had since fled his refugee camp home there with only a small bag of possessions. He is just one regional example of many media professionals who have had little choice but to leave countries like Egypt and Syria in the wake of crushed revolutions and the rise of authoritarian power. Solidly middle-class folk, including Chapter 4's Tom, seriously contemplate moves from their economically troubled countries (Lebanon in his case) amidst unstable times. These individuals often bring with them expertise bred of decades of their home countries' investments in cinema and higher education, by the state as well as themselves. The supply chain makes good use of this knowledge, this *skill*.

All the while, the Emirati migration system opens and closes its numerous and regularly replaced valves, setting up a complex tension between various heres and elsewheres. These make the most of heterogenous individual, community and national histories. And they are capricious. As Muhammad, who has Jordanian papers, points out, diplomatic relations can destabilize careers:

> I was to some extent luckier than my Syrian or Iranian friends whose visas really depended on the political situation and Abu Dhabi's relationship with that place... any Syrian friend who was thinking about switching jobs, couldn't because, if they let go of this visa, they were not guaranteed that their new visa would get approved, because now they're a refugee... And so suddenly they just had to leave the country.

Harsha Walia stresses that many such migrants, prompted by displacement crises, have been dispossessed by diminished resources or landlessness that has everything to do with the acquisitive, privatizing and casualizing measures that have already consumed this book (Walia 2021). How cruelly ironic if these workers have been contributing their labour (and their countries' or families' prior outlays) to a film like *Dune*, a critique of colonial extraction.

Extraction persists via the mechanisms of racial capitalism, which, as this chapter has illustrated, demotes people according to skill re-classification, furthering the depression of nation-by-nation variegated salaries. Geographical mobility does not track so tightly to a financial or social mobility. Muhammad bluntly jokes, 'I just want to be paid like a white person', referring as much to either of these tactics for lowering his salary, despite the expensive Anglophone international education that otherwise allows him to be considered 'an equal'. Rami reveals that lots of UAE-based film professionals jump at the chance to work on Hollywood productions for the experience and for the credit, even accepting lower than their usual rate of pay to take up the opportunity. He then lets me know that, 'They don't do that for us, for our movies. Rarely ever for Arab films.'

There are, however, Arab beneficiaries in other sectors. In 2010, when the creative free zones were also coming into being, construction and real estate amounted to 65 per cent of the UAE's economy (Donn and Al Manthri 2010: 39). As Jamal Al Sharif has explicitly outlined, these free zones have been, first and foremost, real estate ventures. The push for infrastructure and the need to diversify away from oil dependency and into the creative and knowledge economy free zones takes advantage not only of labour but also rental income. What happens within generates novel revenue streams at the same time as landlords draw wealth from leasing, in particular as an outcome of the international traffic they attract (Picard and Barkho 2011: 288). Multinationals seeking regional headquarters take up much of the space, though have less to do with feature film production (at least in Dubai, although increasingly so in Abu Dhabi). For the smaller scale company or individual freelancer, costs can prove a challenge. Rents typically come to far more than they would in these migrants' places of origin (even if salaries are pegged thus); the free zone profits considerably from instability elsewhere. My visual effects friend eventually had the option to leave, thankfully so after a jading experience of not feeling that the connections he made justified the high outgoings. The price tag at entry level (granting little more than a permit) sets freelancer applicants back 7,500 dirhams per annum (US$2,042) with a visa and basic business registration fees for the same period costing an additional 8,812 or so dirhams (US$2,400) (twofour54 Abu Dhabi n.d.a). Need it be stressed what a daunting start-up sum this will prove for refugees, like my friend, from Global Southern war zones at the very least?

The restaurants, hotels and other leisure facilities within the free zones, as well as the affiliated domestic housing, make yet more money for these developers with the enlivening creative ambience bestowed by these workers burnishing still further their portfolios. In turn, these types of 'Dubai dream' images attract would-be migrants. Given the obstacles to becoming a property owner and the lack of recourse to state assistance for housing, all such migrants have little choice but to rent. Some of this expenditure will be founded in debt, as was the construction of these sites in the first place. Even departure from the UAE on one's own schedule can prove trying. While lower-paid workers endure the worst versions of this, Muhammad points out that, when he needed to be released early from his sponsorship, he was charged US$1,000, which set him back around a month's wages. All things considered, can we ethically condone the 'savings' that supply chain cinema makes – here and in other countries – in the name of how it delivers our entertainment?

In the UAE, the supply chain gets its way more. Thanks to the country's (and the surrounding world's) particular history within colonization, capitalism and the extreme instabilities they incite, it can protract offshoring into new dimensions here. The remittance it offers, cossetted in narratives of opportunity and plenty, privatizes and absolves other states of their welfare duties. As this book has consistently determined, the supply chain strives tirelessly to dissolve such protections wherever it finds the latitude. It reaches a point in the UAE where it operates beyond the influence of much labour rights activism, criminalizing dissenters, or, more regularly and perfunctorily, simply deporting them within a matter of hours. Here I find it harder to suggest ways around. Despite spending lengthy periods in the country, feeling I have a community there and (for what it's worth) speaking the official language (Arabic) as well as the business one (English), I neither live in the UAE, nor do I work in the film or education industries there; I can only offer glimpses of what could happen from a distance.

We have yet to attain equal pay for equal work, either internally in any country or even more so across the global economy. Such differences, Tsing stresses, motivate the supply chain and induce it most powerfully towards countries like the UAE, which legally protect, rather than suppose to diminish, this injustice. When supply chain cinema routes through the UAE, it exploits disparities for which it would typically have to travel further: a one-stop shop indeed. The film industry holds the power to hire its offshored workers more justly, if it chooses to wield that influence in the name of its current pledges about diversity. More could certainly be done to make audiences aware of film's production conditions, especially when there exist sweatshop-free labels on other commodities and 'no animals were harmed' certifications in movies' end credits. As ever, film education could take on a greater commitment to exposing how, for starters, indentured labour has been conscripted to make blockbusters.

There is much to inspire us in how workers have risen up in the UAE. Interruptions to work schedules hit the fast, frictionless ideal at its core. The frontline struggle against the sharpest edges of offshoring counts stoppages and wild cat strikes with participant numbers in their thousands, including those who build the knowledge and creative economies, the Louvre and NYU Abu Dhabi (Kannan 2014; Hanieh 2015: 226–7; Walia 2021: 154). Natasha Iskander observes that, in Qatar, which arranges its migrant labour force similarly, companies condone short-term, nationality-specific and isolated incidents of this order as a means of 'letting off steam', a paltry concession in the face of unbearable infringements and non-payment of wages. Any more prolonged protest results in summary deportation (Iskander 2021: 157 & 159).

The task then becomes to dismantle this containment. The sheer numbers of migrants holding the UAE together at any given time – whatever their income, paradoxically bonded by insecurity – can also imbue strength here. Gayatri Spivak offers a useful proposition: to think of ethics 'as a problem of relation rather than a problem of knowledge', which I will take here as an invitation towards the prospects for solidarity across the supply chain (Spivak 2012: 104). The supply chain is both a shared experience and a network. It crowds us together as temporary, casualized or service workers in new ways that dissolve certain hierarchies or specialisms of old. It does so for its own ends, yet leaves behind a scaffolding upon which to both collectivize and communicate. How to build alliances across the length of the supply chain with all its designed and promoted differentials that deliberately mitigate against unity in the name of competition?

First it is crucial not to isolate places like the UAE as exceptional; intensifications, perhaps, but more so nodal points in a system (that includes, as Chapters 2 and 3 point out, the UK) to which multitudes contribute. When we understand our place within it – however much we are required to register that as unique (entrepreneurial, self-sufficient or alienated) and competitive – we situate ourselves better for both solidarity and collective action.

How, then, to transfigure these large but varied swathes of exploitation, its contributors in perpetual motion, into a commonality that can serve as a basis for collective struggle? The supply chain's infrastructures build a materiality of interdependence and intermodality that can connect us politically as well, birthing effective strategizing. By thinking and acting transnationally ourselves, we might hope to absorb, for instance, a storied and tested history of non-participation and socialist organizing carried by South Asian migrants from their homelands to the UAE where they temporarily abide in their millions. These tactics temper current campaigns hanging on a distinctly Eurocentric critique of freedom (of expression) infractions by localized authoritarian rulership, itself centrally shaped and propped up by both neo-colonial powers and supply chain capitalism. Extending Aihwa Ong's conceptualization of the graduated citizen, these multilingual migrants bear skills in translation and the transferal of ideas that can also be wielded not as service to the supply chain, but as a means of organizing against it. So, not just: what could a 90 per cent population achieve with so many involved coming in from places with developed vocabularies of workplace activism and organization? But also: what possibilities exist for moving and multiplying struggles across the self-same infrastructures that logistically transport goods and workers?

Conclusion

On the day that I started to write this conclusion, I received one of the semi-regular 'Global Locations' newsletters to which I subscribe from *Variety* (Variety Editors 2022). They aim (often through promotional 'partner content') to equip the reader with fresh information about where to shoot film and television internationally. This issue spotlights Poland, Nigeria, South Africa, Italy, New Zealand, the Cherokee Nation, Spain, Peru, the UK and Saudi Arabia. Some are established offshore destinations (although touting new affordances), some rather surprising new entrants. The familiar inducements repeat: tax credits, skilled and willing workers, specialized facilities and scenic backdrops. A 2020 edition had extolled the virtues of South Korea, France, Jordan, Belgium, Croatia, Uruguay, Norway, the UAE, Australia, the US Virgin Islands and Finland (Variety Editors 2020). Clearly, the jockeying to attract supply chain cinema mounts, each site pledging escalating bountifulness that might undercut the others.

Watching this intensification urges me not to close with a tidy summary of what characterizes the two countries this book has examined, nor to simply reiterate the more alarming and distressing insights gained by analytically installing supply chains centre stage. I would prefer, rather, to spend some time assessing the potential vulnerabilities of a system that, although lissom and inconstant, exerts implacable duress. What margins exist for us as workers, students, film viewers, citizens and non-citizens to access more bearable and humane alternatives to the supply chain's dictates? What can we dismantle or stand up to? How can we communicate, translate, educate and unite along the supply chain? Deploy the commitment and creativity the supply chain extracts from us against the worst of its actions?

Activists pinpoint how defenceless the supply chain leaves itself through its sheer diffusion and loose, last-minute integration. Here lie some prospects for obstructing its passage. In this vein, logistics scholar Charmaine Chua poses the question, 'What would it mean to pay special attention to the *materiality* of capital flows – and to the possibilities that arise from interrupting the massive concentration of commodity capital at sites of its coagulation or through which it flows' (Chua 2014: n.p.)? Because the supply chain's fundamental raison d'être is to moves things, its activities can be halted or detained. In a climate of just-in-time and big-budget shooting days that can cost millions of dollars each, delays wreak substantial havoc (for the vulnerability of the JIT schema, see Bernes 2013 n.p.; Curcio 2014: 376). Logistics researchers typically site the optimum spots for such disruption, which are viscerally titled 'chokepoints', as ports, warehouses or transport interchanges, the switching points of the supply chain (Chua 2014; Boyle 2016: 76; Alimahomed-Wilson and Ness 2018).

Within the portions of cinema's supply chain that this book has scrutinized, the studio and the university similarly protrude as possible chokepoints. Currently, the supply chain must pass through them and, furthermore, they epitomize what political economist Ashok Kumar identifies as 'spatial inflexibility', a limit to the limberness of the supply chain that can bestow opportunity for those abused by it (Kumar 2020: 235). While, for example, the fast fashion supply chain can rapidly replace its small workshops, studios and universities result from expensive and extensive investment of financial and in human capital. These durations clash with the supply chain's dependence on speedy about-turns.

Next question: what is to be done at these chokepoints? Scholars of infrastructure highlight fragilities borne of the supply chain's unmonitorable scale. They celebrate, even advocate for sabotage that, because of this characteristic, becomes difficult to trace back to a perpetrator (Starosielski 2015: 80; Berlant 2016: 394; Calder Williams 2016). However, workers in the film industry and higher education pride themselves in the fruits of their concretely attributable labour, gaining credit and satisfaction from it; few carry the impulse or capacity to trip up or ruin what they do.

Rather, these mainstay junctures amidst cinema's supply chain provide tangible scope for holding firm, for bargaining and making demands. Their highly skilled workers cannot be substituted so easily, although the logistical state confects both law and oversupply to defang them. As the UK–UAE comparison reveals, risks track proportionally to context. Yet tangible examples of consequential protest arise from each: the wildcat construction worker strikes in the UAE and sustained industrial action by UCU (the University and College Union) in Britain specifically militating against casualization and pension cuts (UCU 2022b; UCU 2022c; UCU 2022d).

Attuning to the supply chain's usual leanings reminds us to anticipate offshoring or outsourcing of possibly discrete tasks like grading to zero hours contract workers, local or overseas, who might never even meet the students submitting these assignments. In the moment, when academics launch marking boycotts, they explicitly halt the flow of workers, in the form of qualified graduates, into the supply chain. Intensifying student debt strikes rebuff a financial and disciplinary hold on that future.

Opposition to the supply chain simultaneously persists through contingent and smaller scale gestures. Non-compliance with the insisted norms of entrepreneurial precarity in classrooms and workplaces, drawing on the combined energies of students', teachers' and other employees' insights to impugn this augmenting integration. The university course that does not let up at the moment of fault-finding and critique and commits to discussing rights along with assessing and modelling alternative modes of working. As more autonomous units of counteraction, these certainly play the supply chain's own game of dissociations, concurrently substantiating how revolutions have always truly functioned thus: incremental and ongoing, rather than singular acts of irreversible upheaval.

Slighter operations unshadow the uneven liberties afforded the globalized workforce and the necessity of calibrating resistance accordingly. The supply chain holds many of its subjects in intractable situations while dispatching others against their wishes. Not one film worker traverses the globe as deftly as the heroes who fight the forces of evil in the *Mission: Impossible* or *Fast & Furious* franchises they help make. However, precisely because a production journey cannot cross a border as effortlessly as an on-screen title card signals a new destination, these dispersed workers overlap, converse, compare and learn from each other. Jessica, the British camera trainee who contributed to Chapters 2 and 3, notes that 'change needs to come from inside and outside'. She refers here to absorbed attitudes about never taking time off, something that can modify relationally when film personnel witness different approaches across the chain. She likewise registers how a quick (although 'taboo') conversation with a colleague uncovered their higher pay, allowing her to successfully petition for equal wages.

These communions fall amidst the everyday work of translation that all of this book's chapters have highlighted. Translation need not solely relay orders or instructions all the better for the supply chain to perform. Why stop short at translation's proficiency in rendering legible only what services capitalist exploitation? These workers dexterously transmit and even convert. The supply chain intends to subsume their efforts into the alchemy of transmogrifying, for instance, tuition fees into labour into profit. But they can also be spent on spreading and adapting modes of confronting it (see Mezzadra and Neilson 2013: 273–274).

Supply chain cinema finds itself in a bind here, needing to nourish these skills that could also prove its undoing. For starters, and as witnessed above, this need for expertise can pinion the supply chain to certain concentrations (British crews and facilities, as per Chapters 2 and 3, say). Its volatility then somewhat diminished, it becomes more susceptible to those workers' demands than its overlords would surely wish. Additionally, the way supply chain operations bank on interdependence can surely curb a total ability to divide and conquer (Benvegnù and

Cuppini 2018: 240). The wildfire spread of upstart offshore sites that each *Variety* 'Global Locations' dispatch might list divulges competitive threats to all, but they never stand in isolation. They will be yoked into a sequence motivated by corporate pilfering, but bear the potential for its workers to *relate*, meaning to both impart and connect.

Emphasizing the former, Anna Curcio's militant research within communities of striking logistics workers reveals how participants from the Arab world, fresh from the uprisings in the region, spread tactics from those movements (Curcio 2014: 385). Similarly experienced individuals, from there and beyond, often in uncertain exile, populate the UAE's workforce, including its creative sectors. Their militancy, born of governments' stark preferences for profiting rather than shielding its citizenry from transnational capital, benefits from having been test run. It has faced and overcome impasses that cannot be breached by small-scale defiance and has pushed for regime change. These insurrections materialized as possible pathways around many of the same failings of the state this book has catalogued: income injustice, precarity, prohibitions on collective bargaining, unfair hiring protocols, fiscal incentives for the rich and offshoring's brutal grasp. Rather than sinking lower into insufferable conditions as a means of remaining globally 'competitive', these revolutionaries decided to dismantle the very system imposing them.

Such workers have also modelled means of collectivity. As I have underscored throughout, the supply chain establishes deliberately profitable hierarchies within its cumulative patterning of connection and translation. Consequently, I have dwelt on the latter to lay bare the former and to simultaneously expand the conceptualization of film personnel so it can embrace those in education or construction and thereby accentuate an opportune mutuality. Or, to one extent or another, a shared precarity. What ensues from the segregation of a zero-hours hospitality contract worker from an academic who is hired on identical terms? Or even failing to recognize higher education as a matrix of permanent, offshored and precarious contributors? When weighing up the response of the producer who told her she had to save up for a car in order to accrue deemed-necessary unpaid labour as a runner, Serena reasons, 'Someone who knows the struggle will not say that to you.' Class presumption and aspiration segment labour categorizations, even when, for example, a student might bridge them as an individual worker. University teaching can therefore usefully intervene, not only by engrossing students in how to interrogate these social stratifications, but also by ceasing to perpetuate the suppositions about degrees being the entrepreneurial gateway to upward mobility (as disassembled in Chapter 3). Many educators can input meaningfully into whether or not to shunt students into unpaid labour or to partner with employers who abuse a university association in the name of 'training'. Precarity with a (hollow) promise is still precarity.

Similarly, with the film industry making strides towards inclusivity now, behind the camera as well as in front, we can more easily hold it accountable through its claims of welcoming systemic change. What would it take to extend this groundswell into a shaking up of how the supply chain deliberately exploits globally distributed diversity and to seriously challenge the racialized divisions of labour exposed in Chapters 4 and 5? In more modest on-the-ground terms, might these ventures towards equality offer leverage for transnational crews to insist upon better wages, hours, safety measures or food for the entire team?

Evidently, dispelling these partitions along the supply chain requires conscientious *method*. Fleetingly but recurringly, I have turned to *conricerca* for advice on how to progress here, precisely because its techniques do their utmost to negate such designations, including through how they push back against research paradigms associated with those retaining greater financial and social capital. *Conricerca* also brings us physically into each other's orbits, thriving on what Sandro Mazzadra and Brett Neilson determine as 'the capacity of translation to create the common' (Mezzadra and Neilson 2013: 275). Without foundations in solidarity and mutual- rather than self-reliance, any such liaisons fall prey to dilution into superficial teamwork. The kind the supply chain fashions into interoperability and 'project thinking', or which, like the sharing economy and co-working spaces, poorly compensate for and take advantage of casualization.

A more robust collectivity can reach out to involve consumers too (a category that similarly comprises us all). Activists fighting the abuse of construction workers on Abu Dhabi's Saadiyat Island do so by enmeshing the politics of production and consumption to sully the reputations of the Louvre and NYU, leveraging customers as collateral, but also surely dissuading a few along the way. This particular book did not delve into the complex mechanics of consumer pressure. However, it does acknowledge that, while the supply chain bullies workers, even nation-states, under the threat of recharting its courses away from their livelihoods, it conversely tries its hardest to please the customer. As such, can we mobilize against it to demand a better semblance of, say, international labour standards or tax compliance? All told, I allude here to a diverse and ensconced collectivity. Between us, we possess considerable abilities, uniquely positioned and interrelated, for tackling the supply chain's coercions and deflections.

Of all the diversions and conversions mooted within, the ones most practicable and suited to our context concern creativity and dedication. If the Warner Bros. Studio Tour or both industries' hunger for intellectual property and investment in creative economy precepts are anything to go by, then these qualities carry paramount value. They do to us as well. Despite the hardships film workers endure, not one to whom I talked for this book wished to quit their jobs. Serena reflects, 'However weird and awful it's been, I've not lost my passion for being in this industry... I want this more than anything and there's not a day I wake up and I don't try as hard as I possibly can to make it.' Similarly, Jessica affirms, 'I find the work very fulfilling... it brings me a lot of joy to be good at the job... it's almost like an addiction.' Higher education workers feel the same way, motivated by what process and end result achieves, withstanding levels of exploitation whose structures they squarely comprehend. Such embedded appraisal of the situation suggests latitude to bring about meaningful change. Jessica expresses one of the conundra at stake: 'Every day I think "I don't have a good work–life balance," but I make that sacrifice because I love my work.' The hours she and thousands of others put in, powered by imagination and aptitudes for problem solving and making things flow with greater ease, can simultaneously be apportioned to remedying these situations, to conjuring modes of resistance and alternatives.

Moreover, film sets, like universities, hold true as complex sites where idea generation evolves from exchange and cooperation. In both, we fulsomely appreciate the communal dimension of creativity, even as we watch the supply chain siphoning off its results. The many voices this book comprises testify to that and intend, in small, incremental part and in this spirit of group endeavour, to help orient beyond the obstacles in our path and towards other means and possibilities. These sectors' naturalized sharing of particular predispositions and trainings can be turned to manipulating the openings that appear in some times and places and not in others against the competition they are meant to engender. An embrace of commonality that exceeds intermodality. Together we might conceive of more just ways of being and bring them to life in how we conduct our work. The pleasure these vocations provide lies in just how much they enable the two to merge.

Notes

CHAPTER 2

1   The presence of multinational producers of high-end television in the UK in the early 2020s cannot go unacknowledged. As noted, they contribute more to the British economy than big-budget cinema. Streamer giants such as Amazon and Netflix employ thousands of British crew members across multiple productions, taking advantage of the same tax incentives that will be discussed in this chapter. Given the increasing vertical integration of these corporations (which now make as well as distribute audio-visual content), not to mention the more accurate feedback loops they sustain concerning consumer tastes, I would argue that they are even more supply chain-inclined than big-budget cinema. Ultimately, they bear the capacity to further rationalize the journey to market, exacting ever-new means of just-in-time manufacturing as they do so. These practices are worthy of a comprehensive study in their own right; a digression into this field in the current context could barely do justice to the production techniques at work in contemporary high-end television.

Bibliography

2454abudhabi, 'Exclusive Behind the Abu Dhabi Scenes of Star Wars: The Force Awakens', YouTube 17 December 2015. Available online: https://www.youtube.com/watch?v=LSKrplk0dmQ (accessed 29 December 2022).

Abu Dhabi Film Commission, *Location Guide* (Abu Dhabi: Abu Dhabi Film Commission, n.d.).

Abu Dhabi Film Commission, 'Rebate Guidelines', 2018. Available online: https://www.film.gov.ae/en/wp-content/uploads/sites/2/2020/01/ADFC-Rebate-Guidelines.pdf (accessed 27 December 2022).

Abu Dhabi Film Commission, 'Rebate FAQ's', 2022. Available online: https://www.film.gov.ae/en/30-rebate/rebate-faqs/ (accessed 27 December 2022).

Acland, Charles, 'An Empire of Pixels: Canadian Cultural Enterprise in the Digital Effects Industry', in Gillian Roberts (ed.), *Reading between the Borderlines: Cultural Production and Consumption across the 49th Parallel* (Montreal: McGill-Queen's University Press, 2018), pp. 143–170.

Acland, Charles R., *American Blockbuster: Movies, Technology, and Wonder* (Durham, NC: Duke University Press, 2020).

Alfred, Stephen Richard and John Timothy Lambert Jr, 'Management Factors Influencing Location Selection Decisions of Independent Filmmakers: An Exploratory Case Study', *Systemic Practice and Action Research* vol. 25 no. 4 (2012), pp. 323–354.

Alimahomed-Wilson, Jack and Immanuel Ness (eds), *Choke Points: Logistics Workers Disrupting the Global Supply Chain* (London: Pluto Press, 2018).

Alquati, Romano, 'Co-research and Worker's Inquiry', *The South Atlantic Quarterly* vol. 118 no. 2 (2019), pp. 470–478.

AlShebabi, Omar, 'Rootless Hubs: Migration, Urban Commodification and the "Right to the City" in the GCC', in Abdulhadi Khalaf, Omar AlShebabi and Adam Hanieh (eds), *Transit States: Labour, Migration and Citizenship in the Gulf* (London: Pluto, 2015), pp. 101–131.

Altbach, Philip G., 'Globalisation and the University: Myths and Realities in an Unequal World', *Tertiary Education and Management* vol. 10 no. 1 (2004), pp. 3–25.

Andrijasevic, Rutvica, Julie Yujie Chen, Melissa Gregg and Marc Steinberg, *Media and Management* (Minneapolis: University of Minnesota Press, 2021).

Ashton, Brian, 'Logistics and the Factory without Walls', *Mute* 14 September 2006. Available online: https://www.metamute.org/editorial/articles/logistics-and-factory-without-walls (accessed 27 December 2022).

Ashton, Daniel and Bridget Conor, 'Screenwriting, Higher Education and Digital Ecologies of Expertise', *New Writing* vol.13 no.1 (2016), pp. 98–108.

Ashton, Daniel and Caitriona Noonan (eds), *Cultural Work and Higher Education* (Basingstoke: Palgrave Macmillan, 2013).

Ballon, Hilary, 'Planning from Within: NYU Abu Dhabi', in Harvey Molotch and Davide Ponzini (eds), *The New Arab Urban: Gulf Cities of Wealth, Ambition, and Distress* (New York: New York University Press, 2019), pp. 147–171.

Banks, Mark, *Theorizing Cultural Work: Labour, Continuity and Change in the Cultural and Creative Industries* (London: Routledge, 2013).

Banks, Miranda J. 'Film Schools as Pre-Industry: Fostering Creative Collaboration and Equity in Media Production Programs', *Media Industries* vol. 6 no. 1 (2019), pp. 73–93.

Banks, Miranda, Bridget Conor and Vicki Mayer (eds), *Production Studies, the Sequel!: Cultural Studies of Global Media Industries* (London: Routledge, 2016).

Barkan, Joshua, *Corporate Sovereignty: Law and Government under Capitalism* (Minneapolis: University of Minnesota Press, 2013).

Barraclough, Leo, 'U.K. Shooting Glut Packs Soundstages', *Variety* vol. 326 no. 1, 11 November 2014, p. 148.

Barraclough, Leo, 'Britain is Booming with Film, TV Productions', *Variety* vol. 334 no. 10, 14 December 2016, p. 63.

Barraclough, Leo, 'Europe Takes It Case by Case' in Variety Editors, *Variety's The Big Restart: Our Guide to Global Filming Locations*, 9 September 2020, pp. 62–63. Available online: https://variety.com/2020/film/global/variety-big-restart-global-filming-locations-guide-coronavirus-1234763519/ (accessed 27 December 2022).

Barraclough, Leo, Carole Horst, Jamie Lang and Chris Vourlias, 'Biz on the Rebound: The Entertainment Industry Worked to Put Health and Safety Protocols into Place and the Payoff is a Cautious Return to Work', in Variety Editors, *Variety's The Big Restart: Our Guide to Global Filming Locations*, 9 September 2020, pp. 48–49. Available online: https://variety.com/2020/film/global/variety-big-restart-global-filming-locations-guide-coronavirus-1234763519/ (accessed 27 December 2022).

Becker, Rosa F. J., *International Branch Campuses: Markets and Strategies* (London: The Observatory on Borderless Higher Education, 2009).

BECTU, '#eyeshalfshut', 2017. Available online: https://members.bectu.org.uk›file-grab›bectu-eyeshalfshut-equality-doc.pdf?ref=2635 (accessed 27 December 2022).

BECTU, 'Creative Tool Kit – Work Placements', 2022. Available online: https://www.creativetoolkit.org.uk/your-career/work-placements (accessed 27 December 2022).

Behlil, Melis, *Hollywood is Everywhere: Global Directors in the Blockbuster Era* (Amsterdam: Amsterdam University Press, 2016).

Beller, Jonathan L., 'When "Uberization" Comes to Education', *The Chronicle of Higher Education* 7 October 2016. Available online: http://www.chronicle.com/article/When-Uberization-Comes/238004 (accessed 27 December 2022).

Benvegnù, Carlotta and Niccolò Cuppini, 'Struggles and Grassroots Organizing in an Extended European Choke Point', in Jack Alimahomed-Wilson and Immanuel Ness (eds), *Choke Points: Logistics Workers Disrupting the Global Supply Chain* (London: Pluto Press, 2018), pp. 230–242.

Berardi, Franco 'Bifo', *The Soul at Work: From Alienation to Autonomy* (Los Angeles: Semiotext(e), 2009).

Berger, Richard, Jonathan Wardle and Marketa Zezulkova, 'No Longer Just Making the Tea: Media Work Placements and Work-Based Learning in Higher Education', in Daniel Ashton and Caitriona Noonan (eds), *Cultural Work and Higher Education* (Basingstoke: Palgrave Macmillan, 2013), pp. 87–109.

Berlant, Lauren, *Cruel Optimism* (Durham, NC: Duke University Press, 2011).

Berlant, Lauren, 'The Commons: Infrastructures for Troubling Times', *Environment and Planning D: Society and Space* vol. 34 no. 3 (2016), pp. 393–419.

Bernes, Jasper, 'Logistics, Counterlogistics and the Communist Prospect', *Endnotes* vol. 3 (September 2013). Available online: http://endnotes.org.uk/en/jasper-bernes-logistics-counterlogistics-and-the-communist-prospect (accessed 27 December 2022).

Berti, Lapo (trans. Ettore Lancellotti), *Genealogy of Debt* (Reggio Emilia: Rizosfera, 2019).

BFI, *Future Film Skills: An Action Plan* (London: BFI, 2017).
BFI, 'BFI Stats for 2017 Show New Record for Film Production Spend in the UK', 31 January 2018. Available online: https://www.bfi.org.uk/news-opinion/news-bfi/announcements/bfi-statistics-2017 (accessed 27 December 2022).
BFI, *A Screen New Deal: A Route Map to Sustainable Film Production* (London: BFI: 2020). Available online: https://core-cms.bfi.org.uk/media/2940/download (accessed 27 December 2022).
BFI, 'Screen Culture 2033 – Developing Long-Term Strategies for Education and Skills', 2022. Available online: https://blog.bfi.org.uk/long-read/our-ambitions/developing-long-term-strategies-for-education-and-skills (accessed 27 December 2022).
Bhambra, Gurminder K., Dalia Gebrial and Kerem Nişancıǧlu (eds), *Decolonising the University* (London: Pluto Press, 2018).
Bhayani, Ali, 'The Market Route to Higher Education in the UAE: Its Rationales and Implications', *International Review on Public and Nonprofit Marketing* vol. 11 no. 1 (2014), pp. 75–87.
Bhayani, Ali, 'Building Entrepreneurial Universities in a Specific Culture – Barriers and Opportunities', *International Journal of Nonprofit and Voluntary Sector Marketing* vol. 20 no. 4 (November 2015), pp. 312–330.
Bingen, Steven, *Warner Bros.: Hollywood's Ultimate Backlot* (London: Taylor Trade Publishing, 2014).
Birtchnell, Thomas, Satya Savitzky and John Urry (eds), *Cargomobilities: Moving Materials in a Global Age* (New York and London: Routledge, 2015).
Blair Helen, '"You're Only as Good as Your Last Job": The Labour Process and Labour Market in the British Film Industry', *Work, Employment and Society* vol. 15 no. 1 (2001), pp. 149–169.
Blair, Helen and Al Rainnie, 'Flexible Films?', *Media, Culture & Society* vol. 22 no. 2 (2000), pp. 187–204.
Blair, Helen, Nigel Culkin and Keith Randle, 'From London to Los Angeles: A Comparison of Local Labour Market Processes in the US and UK Film Industries', *International Journal of Human Resource Management* vol. 14 no. 4 (June 2003), pp. 619–633.
Blair, Helen, Susan Grey and Keith Randle, 'Working in Film: Employment in a Project Based Industry', *Personnel Review* vol. 30 no. 2 (2001), pp. 170–185.
Boden, Rebecca and Maria Nedeva, 'Employing Discourse: Universities and Graduate "Employability"', *Journal of Education Policy* vol. 25, no. 1 (2010), pp. 37–54.
Boltanski, Luc and Eve Chiapello (trans. Gregory Elliott), *The New Spirit of Capitalism* (London: Verso, 2005).
Bolton, Paul, *Student Loan Statistics* (London: House of Commons Library, 2022).
Bonacich, Edna and Jake B. Wilson, *Getting the Goods: Ports, Labor, and the Logistics Revolution* (Ithaca: Cornell University Press, 2008).
Boorman, John, Fraser MacDonald and Walter Donohue (eds), *Projections 12: Film-makers on Film Schools* (London: Faber and Faber, 2002).
Bordwell, David, Janet Staiger and Kristin Thompson, *The Classical Hollywood Cinema: Film Style and Mode of Production to 1960* (London: Routledge, 1985).
Borio, Guido, Francesca Pozzi and Gigi Roggero, 'Conricerca as Political Action', in Mark Coté, Richard J. F Day and Greig De Peuter (eds), *Utopian Pedagogy: Radical Experiments against Neoliberal Globalization* (Toronto: University of Toronto Press, 2007), pp. 163–185.
Bousquet, Marc, *How the University Works: Higher Education and the Low Wage Nation* (New York: New York University Press, 2008).

Boyle, Michael Shane, 'Container Aesthetics: The Infrastructural Politics of Shunt's *The Boy Who Climbed Out of His Face*', *Theatre Journal* vol. 68 no. 1 (2016), pp. 57–77.

Brannon Donoghue, Courtney, *Localising Hollywood* (London: BFI, 2017).

Breen, Marcus, 'Offshore Pot o/Gold: The Political Economy of the Australian Film Industry', in Greg Elmer and Mike Gasher (eds), *Contracting Out Hollywood: Runaway Productions and Foreign Location Shooting* (Lanham: Rowman & Littlefield Publishers, 2005), pp. 69–91.

British Film Commission, 'Film Tax Relief', 2022a. Available online: https://britishfilmcommission.org.uk/plan-your-production/tax-reliefs/ (accessed 27 December 2022).

British Film Commission, 'Plan Your Production: Funding', 2022b. Available online: https://britishfilmcommission.org.uk/plan-your-production/funding/ (accessed 27 December 2022).

British Film Commission, 'Why the UK – How We Support You', 2022c. Available online: https://britishfilmcommission.org.uk/why-the-uk/how-we-support-you (accessed 27 December 2022).

British Film Commission, 'Who We Are', 2022d. Available online: https://britishfilmcommission.org.uk/about/who-we-are/ (accessed 27 December 2022).

Brophy, Enda and Sebastián Touza, 'Introduction', in Mark Coté, Richard J. F Day and Greig De Peuter (eds), *Utopian Pedagogy: Radical Experiments against Neoliberal Globalization* (Toronto: University of Toronto Press, 2007), pp. 129–132.

Buckley, Michelle and Adam Hanieh, 'Diversification by Urbanization: Tracing the Property–Finance Nexus in Dubai and the Gulf', *International Journal of Urban and Regional Research* vol. 38 no. 1 (January 2014), pp. 155–175.

Budrovich Sáez, Jorge and Hernán Cuevas Valenzuela, 'Contested Logistics? Neoliberal Modernization and Resistance in the Port City of Valparaíso', in Jack Alimahomed-Wilson and Immanuel Ness (eds), *Choke Points: Logistics Workers Disrupting the Global Supply Chain* (London: Pluto Press, 2018), pp. 162–178.

Burnetts, Charles, '"New Weapons" for the Precariat in Film and Media Studies', *Cinema Journal Teaching Dossier* vol. 4 no. 2 (2016). Available online: http://www.teachingmedia.org/new-weapons-precariat-film-media-studies (accessed 27 December 2022).

Calder Williams, Evan, 'Manual Override', *The New Inquiry Magazine* vol. 50 (21 March 2016). Available online: https://thenewinquiry.com/manual-override (accessed 27 December 2022).

Caldwell, John Thornton, *Production Culture: Industrial Reflexivity and Critical Practice in Film and Television* (Durham, NC: Duke University Press, 2008).

Cant, Callum, Sai Englert, Lydia Hughes, Wendy Liu, Achille Marotta, Seth Wheeler and Jamie Woodcock, '*Notes from Below*: A Brief Survey of Class Composition in the UK', in Robert Ovetz (ed.), *Workers' Inquiry and Global Class Struggle* (London: Pluto Press, 2021), pp. 174–193.

Chakravartty, Paula and Denise Ferreira da Silva, 'Accumulation, Dispossession, and Debt: The Racial Logic of Global Capitalism – An Introduction', *American Quarterly* vol. 64 no. 3 (2012), pp. 361–385.

Champion, Katherine M., 'A Risky Business? The Role of Incentives and Runaway Production in Securing a Screen Industries Production Base in Scotland', *M/C Journal* vol. 19 no. 3 (2016). Available online: https://journal.media-culture.org.au/index.php/mcjournal/article/view/1101 (accessed 27 December 2022).

Champion, Katherine M. and Lisa Kelly, '"I'm Just the Lucky One I Guess": Accounts of Scottish Screen Industries Workers from *Outlander*'s Trainee Placement Scheme', Mediating Culture Work, University of Leicester, September 2017 (unpublished).

Chan, Jenny, Ngai Pun and Mark Selden, 'The Politics of Global Production: Apple, Foxconn and China's New Working Class', *New Technology, Work and Employment* vol. 28 no. 2 (2013), pp. 100–115.

Chiba, Yushi, 'Location, Regulation, and Media Production in the Arab World: A Case Study of Media Cities', in Nele Lenze, Charlotte Schriwer and Zubaidah Abdul Jalil (eds), *Media in the Middle East: Activism, Politics, and Culture* (New York: Palgrave Macmillan, 2017), pp. 71–88.

Chong, Kimberly, *Best Practice: Management Consulting and the Ethics of Financialization in China* (Durham, NC: Duke University Press, 2018).

Choplin, Armelle and Leïla Vignal, 'Gulf Investments in the Middle East: Linking Places, Shaping a Region', in Leïla Vignal (ed.), *The Transnational Middle East: People, Places, Borders* (Abingdon, Oxon: Routledge, 2017), pp. 103–121.

Choudry, Aziz and Mondli Hlatshwayo (eds), *Just Work? Migrant Workers' Struggles Today* (London: Pluto Press, 2016).

Christopherson, Susan, 'Divide and Conquer: Regional Competition in a Concentrated Media Industry', in Greg Elmer and Mike Gasher (eds), *Contracting Out Hollywood: Runaway Productions and Foreign Location Shooting* (Lanham: Rowman & Littlefield Publishers, 2005), pp. 21–40.

Christopherson, Susan, 'Labor: The Effects of Media Concentration on the Film and Television Workforce', in Paul McDonald and Janet Wasko (eds), *The Contemporary Hollywood Film Industry* (Oxford: Blackwell Publishing, 2008), pp. 155–166.

Christopherson, Susan, 'Connecting the Dots: Structure, Strategy, and Subjectivity in Entertainment Media', in Mark Deuze (ed.), *Managing Media Work* (London: Sage, 2011), pp. 179–190.

Chua, Charmaine, 'Logistics, Capitalist Circulation, Chokepoints', *The Disorder of Things* (9 September, 2014). Available online: https://thedisorderofthings.com/2014/09/09/logistics-capitalist-circulation-chokepoints. (accessed 27 December 2022).

Chua, Charmaine, Martin Danyluk, Deborah Cowen and Laleh Khalili, 'Introduction: Turbulent Circulation: Building a Critical Engagement with Logistics', *Environment and Planning D: Society and Space* vol. 36, no. 4 (2018), pp. 617–629.

Chung, Hye Jean, *Media Heterotopias: Digital Effects and Material Labor in Global Film Production* (Durham, NC: Duke University Press, 2021).

Clarke, Stewart, 'Brexit Concerns Abound', *Variety* vol. 339 no. 16, 2 May 2018, pp. 68–69.

Clarke, Stewart, 'Netflix Stretches U.K. Production Limits', *Variety* vol. 334 no. 17, 18 July 2019, pp. 17–18.

Cohen, Joseph N., *Investing in Movies: Strategies for Investors and Producers* (New York: Routledge, 2017).

Cohen, Nicole S. and Greig de Peuter, 'Interns Talk Back', *The Political Economy of Communication* vol. 6 no.2 (2018), pp. 3–24.

Colectivo Situaciones, 'On the Researcher-Militant', in Mark Coté, Richard J. F Day and Greig De Peuter (eds), *Utopian Pedagogy: Radical Experiments against Neoliberal Globalization* (Toronto: University of Toronto Press, 2007), pp. 186–200.

Collini, Stefan, *Speaking of Universities* (London and New York: Verso, 2017).

Conor, Bridget, *Screenwriting: Creative Labor and Professional Practice* (London and New York: Routledge, 2014).

Coté, Mark, Richard J. F Day and Greig De Peuter, *Utopian Pedagogy: Radical Experiments against Neoliberal Globalization* (Toronto: University of Toronto Press, 2007).

Cowan, T.L. and Jasmine Rault, 'The Labour of Being Studied in a Free Love Economy: The Politics of Workers' Inquiry', *Ephemera* vol. 13 no. 3 (2014), pp. 471–488.

Cowen, Deborah, *The Deadly Life of Logistics: Mapping Violence in Global Trade* (Minneapolis: University of Minnesota Press, 2014).

Cox, George, *Cox Review of Creativity in Business: Building on the UK's Strengths* (Norwich: HMSO/HM Treasury, 2005).

Crary, Jonathan, *24/7: Late Capitalism and the Ends of Sleep* (London: Verso, 2013).

Creative England, 'Filming in England', 2022. Available online: https://www.filmingin-england.co.uk (accessed 27 December 2022).

Creative UK, 'Statistics', 2021. Available online: https://www.wearecreative.uk/champion/statistics (accessed 27 December 2022).

Cucco, Marco, 'Blockbuster Outsourcing: Is There Really No Place Like Home?' *Film Studies* vol. 13 (Autumn 2015), pp. 73–93.

Curcio, Anna, 'Practicing Militant Inquiry: Composition, Strike and Betting in the Logistics Workers Struggles in Italy', *ephemera: theory and politics in organization* vol. 14, no. 3 (2014), pp. 375–390.

Curtin, Michael, 'Media Capital: Towards the Study of Spatial Flows', *International Journal of Cultural Studies* vol. 6 no. 2 (2003), pp. 202–228.

Curtin, Michael, 'Regulating the Global Infrastructure of Film Labor Exploitation', *International Journal of Cultural Policy* vol. 22 no.5 (2016), pp. 673–685.

Curtin, Michael, 'Post Americana: Twenty-First Century Media Globalization', *Media Industries* vol. 7 no. 1 (2020), pp. 89–109.

Curtin, Michael and Kevin Sanson, 'Precarious Creativity: Global Media, Local Labor', in Michael Curtin and Kevin Sanson (eds), *Precarious Creativity: Global Media, Local Labor* (Oakland CA: California University Press, 2016a), pp. 1–18.

Curtin, Michael and Kevin Sanson (eds), *Precarious Creativity: Global Media, Local Labor* (Oakland CA: California University Press, 2016b).

Curtin, Michael and Kevin Sanson (eds), *Voices of Labor: Creativity, Craft, and Conflict in Global Hollywood* (Oakland CA: California University Press, 2017).

Daley, Suzanne, 'N.Y.U. in the U.A.E.', *New York Times* 17 April 2011: pp. A24–A26.

Dams, Tim, 'UK Film and TV Production Total Production Spend Hits Record High in 2021, With Indie Film Up 39%', *Screen Daily*, 4 February 2022. Available online: https://www.screendaily.com/news/uk-film-and-tv-production-total-spend-hits-record-high-in-2021-with-indie-film-up-39/5167251.article (accessed 27 December 2022).

Danyluk, Martin, 'Capital's Logistical Fix: Accumulation, Globalization, and the Survival of Capitalism', *Environment and Planning D: Society and Space* vol. 36 no.4 (2018), pp. 630–647.

Davenport, John, 'UK Film Companies: Project-Based Organizations Lacking Entrepreneurship and Innovativeness?' *Creativity and Innovation Management* vol. 15 no. 3 (2006), pp. 250–257.

Dawtrey, Adam, 'Here to Help: Several Agencies Provide Financial or Location Services for Films Shooting in the U.K.', *Variety* vol. 412 no. 10, 20–26 October 2008, p. 10.

Dawtrey, Adam, 'Snaring the Big H'Wood Pictures', *Variety* vol. 421 no. 3, 29 November–5 December 2010a, pp. A13–A14. [sic]

Dawtrey, Adam, 'Transfer of Power: Pending Demise of the U.K. Film Council Will Change the Landscape', *Variety* vol. 421 no. 3, 29 November–5 December 2010b, p. A13.

Dawtrey, Adam, 'Studio Schools Visitors on "Potter"', *Variety* vol. 426 no. 8, 2–8 April 2012, p. 11.

Dawtrey, Adam and Dave McNary, 'House that Harry Built', *Variety* vol. 426 no. 8, 2–8 April 2012, pp. 1 & 11.

Deuze, Mark (ed.), *Managing Media Work* (London: Sage, 2011).
deWaard, Andrew, 'Financialized Hollywood: Institutional Investment, Venture Capital, and Private Equity in the Film and Television Industry', *JCMS: Journal of Cinema and Media Studies* vol. 59 no. 4 (2020), pp. 54–84.
Dickinson, Kay, *Arab Cinema Travels: Syria, Palestine, Dubai and Beyond* (London: BFI Publishing, 2016).
Dickinson, Kay, '"Make It What You Want It to Be": Logistics, Labor and Land Financialization Via the Globalized Free Zone Studio', in Brian R. Jacobson (ed.), *In the Studio: Visual Creation and Its Material Environments* (Berkeley: University of California Press, 2020), pp. 261–280.
Dickinson, Margaret and Sylvia Harvey, 'Film Policy in the United Kingdom: New Labour at the Movies', *Political Quarterly* vol. 76 no. 3 (2005), pp. 240–249.
Donn, Gari and Yahya Al Manthri, *Globalisation and Higher Education in the Arab Gulf States* (Didcot, UK: Symposium Books, 2010).
Doyle, Gillian, Philip Schlesinger, Raymond Boyle and Lisa Kelly, *The Rise and Fall of the UK Film Council* (Edinburgh: Edinburgh University Press, 2015).
DP World, 'Our Global Reach', n.d. Available online: https://www.dpworld.com/about-us/our-locations (accessed 27 December 2022).
Dubai Film and TV Commission, *Limitless Possibilities* (Dubai: Government of Dubai, n.d.a).
Dubai Film and TV Commission, 'Services', n.d.b. Available online: http://www.dubaifilmcommission.ae/why-dubai/services (accessed 27 December 2022).
Dubai Film and TV Commission, 'Why Dubai', n.d.c. Available online: https://www.filmdubai.gov.ae/s/site/filming-in-dubai (accessed 27 December 2022).
Dubai Media City, 'Join Our Freelance Community', n.d.a. Available online: https://dmc.ae/offerings/gofreelance (accessed 27 December 2022).
Dubai Media City, 'Freelance Activities', n.d.b. Available online: https://dmc.ae/offerings/gofreelance (accessed 27 December 2022).
Dyer-Witheford, Nick, *Cyber-Proletariat: Global Labour in the Digital Vortex* (London: Pluto Press, 2015).
Dyer-Witheford, Nick and Greig de Peuter, *Games of Empire: Global Capitalism and Video Games* (Minneapolis: University of Minnesota Press, 2009).
Easterling, Keller, *Extrastatecraft: The Power of Infrastructure Space* (New York: Verso, 2016).
Editor in Chief, 'Dubai's Prime for Film Production', *Leaders Middle East*, 11 February 2016. Available online: http://www.leadersme.com/dubais-prime-for-film-production (accessed 17 July 2017).
Edu-Factory Collective, 'The Double Crisis: Living on the Borders', *EduFactory Webjournal* Issue Zero (2010), pp. 4–9, https://transversal.at/media/attachments/edufactory-journal-0_D4OhC4O.pdf.
Einstein, Mara, 'Nothing for Money and Your Work for Free: Internships and the Marketing of Higher Education', *tripleC: Communication, Capitalism & Critique* vol. 13 no. 2 (2015), pp. 471–485.
El Khachab, Chihab, *Making Film in Egypt: How Labor, Technology, and Mediation Shape the Industry* (Cairo: American University in Cairo Press, 2021).
Elmer, Greg and Mike Gasher (eds), *Contracting Out Hollywood: Runaway Productions and Foreign Location Shooting* (Lanham: Rowman & Littlefield Publishers, 2005).
Evans, Paul and Jonathan Green, *Eyes Half Shut: A Report on Long Hours and Productivity in the UK Film and TV Industry* (London: BECTU, 2017).
Ewers, Michael C. and Edward J. Malecki, 'Leapfrogging into the Knowledge Economy: Assessing the Economic Development Strategies of the Arab Gulf States', *Tijdschrift voor Economische en Sociale Geografie* vol. 101 no. 5 (2010), pp. 494–508.

Fazackerley, Anna, 'Why are Many Academics on Short Term Contracts for Years?', *The Guardian*, 4 February 2013. Available online: https://www.theguardian.com/education/2013/feb/04/academic-casual-contracts-higher-education (accessed 27 December 2022).

Ferrer-Roca, Natàlia, 'The Political Economy of The Hobbit Labour Dispute: Global Hollywood, National Interests and Film Policy', *The Political Economy of Communication* vol. 8 no. 1 (2020), pp. 18–33.

Film Policy Review Group, *A Bigger Picture: The Report of the Film Policy Review Group* (London: Department for Culture, Media and Sport, 1998).

Fishman, Charles, *The Wal-Mart Effect: How an Out-of-Town Superstore Became a Superpower* (London: Penguin Books, 2007).

Foderaro, Lisa W., 'Talented Students are Sought Worldwide for N.Y.U.'s Mideast Campus', *New York Times*, 21 June 2010, p. A24.

Foucault, Michel, (trans. David Macey) (ed. Mauro Bertani and Allesandro Fontana), *Society Must Be Defended: Lectures at the Collège de France, 1975–76* (New York: Picador, 2003).

Foucault, Michel, (trans. Graham Burchell) (ed. Michel Senellart), *The Birth of Biopolitics: Lectures at the Collège de France, 1978–79* (Basingstoke, UK: Palgrave Macmillan, 2008).

Freeman, Matthew, 'Transmedia Attractions: The Case of *Warner Bros. Studio Tour—The Making of Harry Potter*', in Matthew Freeman and Renira Rampazzo Gambarato (eds), *The Routledge Companion to Transmedia Studies* (New York: Routledge, 2019), pp. 124–140.

Freire, Paulo (trans. Myra Bergman Ramos), *Pedagogy of the Oppressed* (London: Continuum, 2005).

Friedman, Yael and Steve Whitford, 'On the Edge of Practice: Reflections on Filmmaking Pedagogy in the Age of the Creative Industries', *Cinema Journal Teaching Dossier* vol. 5 no. 1 (2018). Available online: https://teachingmedia.org/on-the-edge-practice-reflections-on-filmmaking-pedagogy-in-the-age-of-the-creative-industries/ (accessed 27 December 2022).

Fumagalli, Andrea and Sandro Mezzadra (eds) (trans. Jason Francis Mc Gimsey), *Crisis in the Global Economy: Financial Markets, Social Struggles, and New Political Scenarios* (Los Angeles: Semiotext(e), 2009).

Furgang, Adam, *Internship & Volunteer Opportunities for TV and Movie Buffs* (New York: Rosen Publishing Group, 2013).

Gago, Verónica (trans. Liz Mason-Deese), *Neoliberalism from Below: Popular Pragmatics and Baroque Economies* (Durham, NC: Duke University Press, 2017).

Ganti, Tejaswini, *Producing Bollywood: Inside the Contemporary Film Industry* (Durham, NC: Duke University Press, 2012).

Ganti, Tejaswini, '"No One Thinks in Hindi Here": Language Hierarchies in Bollywood', in Michael Curtin and Kevin Sanson (eds), *Precarious Creativity: Global Media, Local Labor* (Oakland CA: California University Press, 2016), pp. 118–131.

Gardner, Andrew M., 'Engulfed: Indian Guest Workers, Bahraini Citizens, and the Structural Violence of the Kafala System', in Nicholas De Genova and Nathalie Peutz (eds), *The Deportation Regime: Sovereignty, Space and the Freedom of Movement* (Durham, NC: Duke University Press, 2010), pp. 196–223.

Gasher, Mike, *Hollywood North: The Feature Film Industry in British Columbia* (Vancouver: UBC Press, 2002).

Gill, Rosalind, 'Breaking the Silence: The Hidden Injuries of the Neoliberal University', in Róisín Ryan-Flood and Rosalind Gill (eds), *Secrecy and Silence in the Research Process: Feminist Reflections* (London: Routledge, 2009) pp. 228–244.

Gill, Rosalind, 'Academics, Cultural Workers and Critical Labour Studies', *Journal of Cultural Economy* vol. 7 no. 1 (2014), pp. 12–30.
Gill, Rosalind, 'Beyond Individualism: The Psychosocial Life of the Neoliberal University', in James McNinch and Marc Spooner (eds), *Dissident Knowledge in Higher Education* (Saskatchewan: University of Regina Press, 2017), pp. 193–216.
Gill, Rosalind and Ngaire Donaghue, 'Resilience, Apps and Reluctant Individualism: Technologies of Self in the Neoliberal Academy', *Women's Studies International Forum* vol. 54 (2016), pp. 91–99.
Giroux, Henry A., *Neoliberalism's War on Higher Education* (Chicago: Haymarket Books, 2014).
Gleich, Joshua and Lawrence Webb (eds), *Hollywood on Location: An Industry History* (New Brunswick, NJ: Rutgers University Press, 2019).
Goby, Valerie Priscilla, 'Financialization and Outsourcing in a Different Guise: The Ethical Chaos of Workforce Localization in the United Arab Emirates', *Journal of Business Ethics* vol. 131 no, 2 (2015), pp. 415–421.
Goldsmith, Ben and Tom O'Regan, *Cinema Cities, Media Cities: The Contemporary International Studio Complex* (Woolloomooloo NSW: Australian Film Commission, 2003).
Goldsmith, Ben and Tom O'Regan, 'Locomotives and Stargates: Inner-city Studio Complexes in Sydney, Melbourne and Toronto', *International Journal of Cultural Policy* vol. 10 no.1 (2004), pp. 29–45.
Goldsmith, Ben and Tom O'Regan, *The Film Studio: Film Production in the Global Economy* (Oxford: Rowman & Littlefield Publishers, 2005a).
Goldsmith, Ben and Tom O'Regan "The Policy Environment of the Contemporary Film Studio in Greg Elmer and Mike Gasher (eds), *Contracting Out Hollywood: Runaway Productions and Foreign Location Shooting* (Lanham: Rowman & Littlefield Publishers, 2005b), pp. 41–66.
Goldsmith, Ben, Susan Ward and Tom O'Regan, *Local Hollywood: Global Film Production and the Gold Coast* (St Lucia, Queensland: University of Queensland Press, 2010).
Goodley, Simon, Luke Harding, Rowena Mason and Harry Davies, 'Revealed: How Tory Co-Chair's Offshore Film Company Indirectly Benefited from £121K Tax Credits', *The Guardian* 5 October 2021. Available online: https://www.theguardian.com/news/2021/oct/05/revealed-how-tory-co-chairs-offshore-film-company-indirectly-benefited-from-121k-tax-credits (accessed 27 December 2022).
Gornostaeva, Galina, 'The Film and Television Industry in London's Suburbs: Lifestyle of the Rich or Losers' Retreat?', *Creative Industries Journal* vol. 1 no. 1 (2008), pp. 47–71.
Gornostaeva, Galina and Johanne Brunet, 'Internationalization of the Production Process in the US Film Industry: The Case of the United Kingdom', *International Journal of Arts Management* vol. 12, no. 1 (2009), pp. 21–30.
Government of Abu Dhabi, *The Abu Dhabi Economic Vision 2030*. (Abu Dhabi: General Secretariat of the Executive Council/Department of Planning & Economy/Abu Dhabi Council for Economic Development, 2008).
Graeber, David, *Debt: The First 5,000 Years* (New York: Melville House Publishing, 2011).
Grappi, Giorgio, 'Asia's Era of Infrastructure and the Politics of Corridors: Decoding the Language of Logistical Governance' in Brett Neilson, Ned Rossiter and Ranabir Samaddar (eds), *Logistical Asia: The Labour of Making a World Region* (Singapore: Palgrave Macmillan, 2018), pp. 175–194.
Grater, Tom, 'Creative Skillset Rebrands as ScreenSkills, Urges Increased Training to Support Production Boom', *Screen Daily*, 4 October 2018. Available online: https://www.screendaily.com/news/creative-skillset-rebrands-as-screenskills-urges-

increased-training-to-support-production-boom/5133241.article. (accessed 27 December 2022).
Guidali, Fabio, 'Intellectuals at the Factory Gates: Early Italian *Operaismo* from Raniero Panzieri to Mario Tronti', *Labor History* vol. 62, no. 4 (2021), pp. 454–469.
Haider, Asad and Salar Mohandesi, 'Workers' Inquiry: A Genealogy', *Notes from Below* Vol. 1 (2018). Available online: https://notesfrombelow.org/article/workers-inquiry (accessed 27 December 2022).
Hall, Gary, *The Uberfication of the University* (Minneapolis: University of Minnesota Press, 2016).
Halpern, Orit, Robert Mitchell and Bernard Geoghegan, 'The Smartness Mandate: Notes toward a Critique', *Grey Room* vol. 68 (Summer 2017), pp. 106–129.
Hanieh, Adam, *Capitalism and Class in the Gulf Arab States* (New York: Palgrave Macmillan, 2011).
Hanieh, Adam, 'Migrant Rights in the Gulf: Charting the Way Forward', in Abdulhadi Khalaf, Omar AlShebabi and Adam Hanieh (eds), *Transit States: Labour, Migration and Citizenship in the Gulf* (London: Pluto, 2015), pp. 223–232.
Hanieh, Adam, 'States of Exclusion: Migrant Work in the Gulf Arab States', in Aziz Choudry and Mondli Hlatshwayo (eds), *Just Work? Migrant Workers' Struggles Today* (London: Pluto Press, 2016), pp. 41–60.
Hanieh, Adam, *Money, Markets, and Monarchies: The Gulf Cooperation Council and the Political Economy of the Middle East* (Cambridge: Cambridge University Press, 2018).
Harabi, Najib, 'Knowledge Intensive Industries: Four Case Studies of Creative Industries in Arab Countries (World Bank Project)', Paper presented at Learning Event on Developing Knowledge Economy Strategies to Improve Competitiveness in the MENA Region conference on 17–21 May 2009, Alexandria, Egypt. Available online: https://1library.net/document/q0n4gely-knowledge-intensive-industries-case-studies-creative-industries-countries.html (accessed 29 December 2022).
Harney, Stefano and Fred Moten, *The Undercommons: Fugitive Planning and Black Study* (Wivenhoe: Minor Compositions, 2013).
Harvey, David, *The Condition of Postmodernity: An Enquiry into the Origins of Cultural Change* (Oxford: Blackwell Publishers, 1990).
Heery, Edmund, Hazel Conley, Rick Delbridge and Paul Stewart, 'Beyond the Enterprise: Trade Union Representation of Freelances in the UK', *Human Resource Management Journal* vol. 14 no. 2 pp. 20–35.
Herb, Michael, *The Wages of Oil: Parliaments and Economic Development in Kuwait and the UAE* (Ithaca: Cornell University Press, 2014).
Hesmondhalgh, David, 'Exploitation and Media Labor', in Richard Maxwell (ed.), *The Routledge Companion to Labor and Media* (New York and London: Routledge, 2016), pp. 30–39.
Hesmondhalgh, David and Sarah Baker, *Creative Labour: Media Work in Three Cultural Industries* (London: Routledge, 2011).
Hjort, Mette (ed.), *The Education of the Filmmaker in Africa, the Middle East, and the Americas* (New York: Palgrave Macmillan, 2013a).
Hjort, Mette (ed.), *The Education of the Filmmaker in Europe, Australia, and Asia* (New York: Palgrave Macmillan, 2013b).
HM Revenue & Customs, 'Use the Enterprise Investment Scheme (EIS) to Raise Money for Your Company', 2016. Available online: https://www.gov.uk/guidance/venture-capital-schemes-apply-for-the-enterprise-investment-scheme (accessed 27 December 2022).
Ho, Karen, *Liquidated: An Ethnography of Wall Street* (Durham, NC: Duke University Press, 2009).

Hockenberry, Matthew, Nicole Starosielski and Susan Zieger (eds), *Assembly Codes: The Logistics of Media* (Durham, NC: Duke University Press, 2021).

Hofmann, Katja and Melanie Goodfellow, 'U.K. Gov't Taxes Film Industry's Patience', *Variety* vol. 400 no. 6, 26 September–2 October 2005, pp. 2-A1 & A4.

Holmes, Brian, 'The Flexible Personality: For a New Cultural Critique', 2011. Available online: http://www.tacticalmediafiles.net/articles/3438/The-Flexible-Personality_-For-a-New-Cultural-Critique (accessed 27 December 2022).

Holt, Jennifer and Alisa Perren (eds), *Media Industries: History, Theory, and Method* (Chichester UK: Wiley-Blackwell, 2009).

Hope, Sophie and Joanna Figiel, 'Interning and Investing: Rethinking Unpaid Work, Social Capital, and the "Human Capital Regime"', *tripleC: Communication, Capitalism & Critique* vol. 13 no. 2 (2015), pp. 361–374.

House of Lords Select Committee on Communications, *The British Film and Television Industries – Decline or Opportunity? Volume I: Report* (London: Authority of the House of Lords, 2010).

Hudson, Dale, 'Locating Emirati Filmmaking within Globalizing Media Ecologies', in Nele Lenze, Charlotte Schriwer and Zubaidah Abdul Jalil (eds), *Media in the Middle East: Activism, Politics, and Culture* (New York: Palgrave Macmillan, 2017), pp. 165–202.

Human Rights Watch, *'The Island of Happiness': Exploitation of Migrant Workers on Saadiyat Island, Abu Dhabi* (New York: Human Rights Watch, 2009).

Human Rights Watch, *The Island of Happiness Revisited: A Progress Report on Institutional Commitments to Address Abuses of Migrant Workers on Abu Dhabi's Saadiyat Island* (New York: Human Rights Watch, 2012).

Human Rights Watch, *Migrant Workers' Rights on Saadiyat Island in the United Arab Emirates: 2015 Progress Report* (New York: Human Rights Watch, 2015a).

Human Rights Watch, 'UAE: NYU to Compensate Migrant Workers', 21 April 2015b. Available online: https://www.hrw.org/news/2015/04/21/uae-nyu-compensate-migrant-workers-0 (accessed 27 December 2022).

Iskander, Natasha, *Does Skill Make Us Human? Migrant Workers in 21st-Century Qatar and Beyond* (Princeton: Princeton University Press, 2021).

Jaafar, Ali, 'Brits Wolf Down Films', *Variety* vol. 412 no. 10, 20–26 October 2008, pp. 3-A1, A15 & A20.

Jaikumar, Priya, *Where History Resides: India as Filmed Space* (Durham, NC: Duke University Press, 2019).

Johnson, Chris, 'HMRC Criticised Over Film Industry Tax Avoidance Probes', *BBC News*, 27 February 2017. Available online: https://www.bbc.co.uk/news/business-39080743 (accessed 27 December 2022).

Kamenetz, Anya, 'Take This Internship and Shove It', *The New York Times*, 30 May 2006, p. A19.

Kaminer, Ariel and Sean O'Driscoll, 'Workers at N.Y.U.'s Abu Dhabi Site Faced Harsh Conditions', *New York Times*, 19 May 2014, pp. A1 & 8–9.

Kamrava, Mehran (ed.), *Gateways to the World: Port Cities in the Persian Gulf* (New York: Oxford University Press, 2016).

Kanna, Ahmed, 'Flexible Citizenship in Dubai: Neoliberal Subjectivity in the Emerging "City-Corporation"', *Cultural Anthropology* vol. 25 no. 1 (2010), pp. 100–129.

Kanna, Ahmed, *Dubai, the City as Corporation* (Minneapolis: University of Minnesota Press, 2011).

Kannan, Preeti, 'Number of Labour Strikes in Dubai Falls Almost 25%', *The National*, 16 April 2014. Available online: https://www.thenationalnews.com/uae/government/number-of-labouikes-in-dubai-falls-almost-25-1.251813 (accessed 27 December 2022).

Karlsson, Charlie and Robert G. Picard (eds), *Media Clusters: Spatial Agglomeration and Content Capabilities* (Northampton, MA: Edward Elgar Publishing, 2011a).
Karlsson, Charlie and Robert G. Picard, 'Media Clusters: What Makes Them Unique?', in Karlsson and Picard, Charlie Karlsson and Robert G. Picard (eds), *Media Clusters: Spatial Agglomeration and Content Capabilities* (Northampton, MA: Edward Elgar Publishing, 2011b) pp. 3–29.
Kerr, Aphra, 'Placing International Media Production', *Media Industries Journal* vol. 1 no. 1 (2014), pp. 27–32.
Kezar, Adrianna, Tom DePaola and Daniel T. Scott, *The Gig Academy: Mapping Labor in the Neoliberal University* (Baltimore: Johns Hopkins University Press, 2019).
Khalaf, Abdulhadi, Omar AlShebabi and Adam Hanieh (eds), *Transit States: Labour, Migration and Citizenship in the Gulf* (London: Pluto, 2015).
Khalil, Joe F., 'Towards a Supranational Analysis of Arab Media: The Role of Cities', in Tourya Guaaybess (ed.), *National Broadcasting and State Policy in Arab Countries* (London: Palgrave Macmillan, 2013), pp. 188–208.
Khalili, Laleh, *Sinews of War and Trade: Shipping and Capitalism in the Arabian Peninsula* (London and New York: Verso, 2020).
Klose, Alexander (trans. Charles Marcrum II), *The Container Principle: How a Box Changes the Way We Think* (Cambridge, MA: MIT Press, 2015).
Knight, Jane, 'Education Hubs: A Fad, a Brand, an Innovation?' *Journal of Studies in International Education* vol. 15 no.3 (2011), pp. 221–240.
Koch, Natalie, 'We Entrepreneurial Academics: Governing Globalized Higher Education in "Illiberal" States', *Territory, Politics, Governance* vol. 4 no. 4 (2016), pp. 438–452.
Kokas, Aynne, *Hollywood Made in China* (Berkeley: University of California Press, 2017).
Krieger, Zvika, 'Desert Bloom', *The Chronicle of Higher Education* vol. 54 no. 29, 28 March 2008, n.p.
Kumar, Ashok, *Monopsony Capitalism: Power and Production in the Twilight of the Sweatshop Age* (Cambridge: Cambridge University Press, 2020).
Lawton, Kayte and Dom Potter (for Public Policy Research and Internocracy), 'Why Interns Need a Fair Wage', 2010. Available online: https://www.ippr.org/publications/why-interns-need-a-fair-wage (accessed 27 December 2022).
Lazzarato, Maurizio (trans. and ed. Couze Venn), 'Neoliberalism, the Financial Crisis, and the End of the Liberal State', *Theory, Culture & Society* vol. 32 no. 7–8 (2015), pp. 67–83.
Lazzarato, Maurizio (trans. Joshua David Jordan), *The Making of the Indebted Man: An Essay on the Neoliberal Condition* (Los Angeles: Semiotext(e), 2012).
LeCavalier, Jesse, *The Rule of Logistics: Walmart and the Architecture of Fulfillment* (Minneapolis: University of Minnesota Press, 2016).
Lee, David, 'Creative Networks and Social Capital', in Daniel Ashton and Caitriona Noonan (eds), *Cultural Work and Higher Education* (Basingstoke: Palgrave Macmillan, 2013), pp. 195–213.
Lenin, Vladimir (trans. Tim Delaney), *What is to be Done?* (Marxist Internet Archive, 1902). Available online: https://www.marxists.org/archive/lenin/works/download/what-itd.pdf (accessed 27 December 2022).
Leotta, Alfio, 'Small Nations and the Global Dispersal of Film Production: A Comparative Analysis of the Film Industries in New Zealand and the United Arab Emirates', *The Political Economy of Communication* vol. 2 no.2 (2015), pp. 20–35.
Leslie, Stuart W., *The Cold War and American Science: The Military-Industrial-Academic Complex at MIT and Stanford* (New York: Columbia University Press, 1993).

Levinson, Marc, *The Box: How the Shipping Container Made the World Smaller and the World Economy Bigger* (Princeton: Princeton University Press, 2006).
Lewin, Tamar, 'Universities Rush to Set Up Outposts Abroad', *New York Times*, 10 February, 2008, pp. N1 & N14.
Lightfoot, Michael, 'Promoting the Knowledge Economy in the Arab World', *SAGE Open* vol.1 no.2 (2011), pp. 1–8.
Lim, Eng-Ben, 'Performing the Global University', *Social Text* vol. 27 no. 4 (Winter 2009), pp. 25–44.
Littler, Jo, *Against Meritocracy: Culture, Power and Myths of Mobility* (London: Routledge, 2018).
Lodderhose, Diana, 'Below the Line Focus Builds on Tech Skills', *Variety* vol. 420 no. 4, 6 September 2010, p. A12.
Lodderhose, Diana, '"Star Wars" Deal Marks Latest Coup for the U.K.', *Variety* vol. 321 no. 7, 26 August 2013, p. 57.
Lodderhose, Diana, 'Mighty Blighty', *Variety* vol. 325 no. 1, 12 August 2014, pp. 128–129.
Looser, Tom, 'The Global University, Area Studies, and the World Citizen: Neoliberal Geography's Redistribution of the "World"', *Cultural Anthropology* vol. 27 no.1 (2012), pp. 97–117.
Lorey, Isabell, 'Becoming Common: Precarization as Political Constituting', *E-flux* 17 (June 2010). Available online: https://www.e-flux.com/journal/17/67385/becoming-common-precarization-as-political-constituting/ (accessed 27 December 2022).
Lorey, Isabell, *State of Insecurity: Government of Insecurity* (London: Verso, 2015).
Lovink, Geert and Ned Rossiter (eds), *MyCreativity Reader: A Critique of Creative Industries* (Amsterdam: Institute of Network Cultures, 2007).
Low, Linda, *Abu Dhabi's Vision 2030: An Ongoing Journey of Economic Development* (Singapore: World Scientific Publishing, 2012).
Lowe, Lisa, *The Intimacies of Four Continents* (Durham, NC: Duke University Press, 2015).
Macdonald, Ian W., 'Mindset and Skillset; the Persistence of Division in Media Education', *Journal of Media Practice* vol. 7 no. 2 (2006), pp. 135–142.
Magor, Maggie and Philip Schlesinger, "For this Relief Much Thanks': Taxation, Film Policy and the UK Government', *Screen* vol. 50 no.3 (2009), pp. 299–317.
Mandler, Peter, *The Crisis of the Meritocracy: Britain's Transition to Mass Education Since the Second World War* (Oxford: Oxford University Press, 2020).
Marciniak, Katarzyna and Bruce Bennett (eds), *Teaching Transnational Cinema: Politics and Pedagogy* (New York and London: Routledge, 2016).
Martin, Craig, 'Desperate Mobilities: Logistics, Security and the Extra-Logistical Knowledge of "Appropriation"', *Geopolitics* vol. 17 no. 2 (2012), pp. 355–376.
Martin, Stewart, 'Pedagogy of Human Capital', *Mute* (21 February 2008). Available online: http://www.metamute.org/editorial/articles/pedagogy-human-capital (accessed 31 December 2022).
Marx, Karl (trans. Ben Fowkes), *Capital Volume 1* (London: Penguin Classics/New Left Review, 1990).
Marx, Karl, *Wage Labour and Capital* (originally published as a pamphlet in 1891). Available online: https://www.marxists.org/archive/marx/works/download/pdf/wage-labour-capital.pdf (accessed 27 December 2022).
Mathew, Johan, *Margins of the Market: Trafficking and Capitalism Across the Arabian Sea* (Oakland, CA: University of California Press, 2016).
Mathew, Johan, 'Sindbad's Ocean: Reframing the Market in the Middle East', *International Journal of Middle East Studies* vol. 48 (2016), pp. 754–757.

Maxwell, Richard (ed.), *The Routledge Companion to Labor and Media* (New York and London: Routledge, 2016).

Mayer, Vicki, 'Bringing the Social Back In: Studies of Production Cultures and Social Theory', in Vicki Mayer, Miranda J. Banks and John Caldwell (eds), *Production Studies: Cultural Studies of Media Industries* (New York: Routledge, 2009), pp. 15–24.

Mayer, Vicki, *Almost Hollywood, Nearly New Orleans: The Lure of the Local Film Economy* (Oakland, CA: University of California Press, 2017).

Mayer, Vicki, 'Pedagogies of Paradox in Media Studies and Media Labour', *Synoptique* vol. 8 no.2 (2019), pp. 8–10.

Mayer, Vicki, Miranda J. Banks and John Caldwell (eds), *Production Studies: Cultural Studies of Media Industries* (New York: Routledge, 2009).

Mayer, Vicki and Jocelyn Horner, 'Student Media Labor in the Digital Age: MediaNOLA in the Classroom and the University', in Richard Maxwell (ed.), *The Routledge Companion to Labor and Media* (New York and London: Routledge, 2016), pp. 242–251.

McCarthy, Cameron, 'Afterword: The Unmaking of Education in the Age of Globalization, Neoliberalism and Information', in Michael A. Peters and Ergin Bulut (eds), *Cognitive Capitalism, Education and Digital Labor* (New York: Peter Lang, 2011), pp. 301–321.

McClanahan, Annie, 'The Living Indebted" Student Militancy and the Financialization of Debt', *Qui Parle: Critical Humanities and Social Sciences* vol. 20 no. 1 (2011), pp. 57–77.

McDonald, Paul, 'Britain: Hollywood UK', in Paul McDonald and Janet Wasko (eds), *The Contemporary Hollywood Film Industry* (Oxford: Blackwell Publishing, 2008), pp. 220–231.

McNary, Adam, 'House That Harry Built', *Variety* vol. 426 no. 8, 2–8 April 2012, pp. 1 & 11.

McNutt, Myles, 'Mobile Production: Spatialized Labor, Location Professionals, and the Expanding Geography of Television Production', *Media Industries* vol. 2 no. 1 (2015), n.p.

McRobbie, Angela, *Be Creative: Making a Living in the New Culture Industries* (Cambridge: Polity Press, 2016).

Menon, Bindu, 'Media Free Zones: Precarious Labour and Migrant Vernacular of Emirati Cities', *IIAS Newsletter* vol. 79 (2018). Available online: https://www.iias.asia/the-newsletter/article/media-free-zones-precarious-labour-migrant-vernaculars-emirati-cities (accessed 27 December 2022).

Menon, Bindu, 'Migrant Images: Lateral Agency and Affective Citizenship in Dubai', *Middle East Journal of Culture and Communication* vol. 14 (2021), pp. 225–249.

Mezzandra, Sandro in interview with Garelli, Glenda and Martina Tazzioli, 'Double Opening, Split Temporality, and New Spatialities: An Interview with Sandro Mezzadra on "Militant Research"', *Postcolonial Studies* vol. 16 no. 3 (2013), pp. 309–319.

Mezzadra, Sandro and Brett Neilson, *Border as Method, or, the Multiplication of Labor* (Durham and London: Duke University Press, 2013a).

Mezzadra, Sandro and Brett Neilson, 'Extraction, Logistics, Finance: Global Crisis and the Politics of Operations', *Radical Philosophy* vol. 178 (March/April 2013b), pp. 8–18.

Mezzadra, Sandro and Brett Neilson, *The Politics of Operations: Excavating Contemporary Capitalism* (Durham, NC: Duke University Press, 2019).

Middlesex University Dubai, 'Fees & Finance: Tuition Fee Charges', 2022. Available online: https://www.mdx.ac.ae/studentfinance/tuition-fees (accessed 27 December 2022).

Miège, Bernard, *The Capitalization of Cultural Production* (Bagnolet, France: International General, 1989).
Mignolo, Walter D., 'Enacting the Archives, Decentring the Muses: The Museum of Islamic Art in Doha and the Asian Civilizations Museum in Singapore', *Ibraaz*, 6 November 2013. Available online: https://www.ibraaz.org/essays/77 (accessed 27 December 2022).
Milburn, Alan and Cabinet Office, *Fair Access to Professional Careers: A Progress Report by the Independent Reviewer on Social Mobility and Child Poverty* (London: Information Policy Team/Crown Copyright, 2012).
Miller, Toby, Nitin Govil, John McMurria, Richard Maxwell and Ting Wang, *Global Hollywood 2* (London: BFI Publishing, 2005).
Mingant, Nolwenn, 'Films *Ex-Nihilo*: Abu Dhabi's Greenfields Film and Media Policy Model', in Nolwenn Mingant and Cecilia Tirtaine (eds), *Reconceptualising Film Policies* (New York: Routledge, 2018), pp. 282–295.
Mongin, Olivier, 'Mega-ports: On the New Geography of Containerization', *Eurozine*, 27 July 2012, https://www.eurozine.com/mega-ports.
Moore, Phoebe V., *The Quantified Self in Precarity: Work, Technology and What Counts* (London and New York: Routledge, 2018).
Moore, Schuyler M., *Taxation of the Entertainment Industry, 2016 Edition* (Chicago: Wolters Kluwer, 2016).
Morawetz, Norbert, Jane Hardy, Colin Haslam and Keith Randle, 'Finance, Policy and Industrial Dynamics – The Rise of Co-Productions in the Film Industry', *Industry and Innovation* vol. 14 no. 4 (2007), pp. 421–443.
Moreton, Simon, 'Contributing to the Creative Economy Imaginary: Universities and the Creative Sector', *Cultural Trends* vol. 27 no. 5 (2018), pp. 327–338.
Morgan, George and Pariece Nelligan, *The Creativity Hoax: Precarious Work in the Gig Economy* (London: Anthem Press, 2018).
Mould, Oli, 'Mediating the City: The Role of Planned Media Cities in the Geographies of Creative Industry Activity', in Sven Conventz, Ben Derudder, Alain Thierstein, Frank Witlox, Prof Dr Markus Hesse and Professor Richard Knowles (eds), *Hub Cities in the Knowledge Economy: Seaports, Airports, Brainports* (New York: Routledge, 2016), pp. 163–180.
Mould, Oli, *Against Creativity* (London: Verso, 2018).
Mukherjee, Arpita, Parthapratim Pal, Saubhik Deb, Subhobrota Ray and Tanu M Goyal, *Special Economic Zones in India: Status, Issues and Potential* (New Delhi: Springer India, 2016).
Nachum, Lilach and David Keeble, 'MNE Linkages and Localised Clusters: Foreign and Indigenous Firms in the Media Cluster of Central London', *Journal of International Management* vol. 9 no. 2 (2003a), pp. 171–192.
Nachum, Lilach and David Keeble, 'Neo-Marshallian Clusters and Global Networks: The Linkages of Media Firms in Central London', *Long Range Planning* vol. 36 no. 5 (2003b), pp. 459–480.
Naficy, Hamid, 'Branch-Campus Initiatives to Train Media-Maters and Journalists: Northwestern University's Branch Campus in Doha, Qatar', in Mette Hjort (ed.), *The Education of the Filmmaker in Africa, the Middle East, and the Americas* (New York: Palgrave, 2013), pp. 81–98.
Neilson, Brett, 'Five Theses on Understanding Logistics as Power', *Distinktion: Scandinavian Journal of Social Theory* vol.13 no.3 (2012), pp. 322–339.
Neilson, Brett, Ned Rossiter and Ranabir Samaddar (eds), *Logistical Asia: The Labour of Making a World Region* (Singapore: Palgrave Macmillan, 2018).

Neilson, Brett, Ned Rossiter and Soenke Zehle, 'From Flows of Culture to the Circuits of Logistics: Borders, Regions, Labour in Transit', *Transit Labor* 2 (2010), pp. 1–4.

Newsinger, Jack 'British Film Policy in an Age of Austerity', *Journal of British Film and Television* vol. 9 no. 1 (2012), pp. 133–144.

Noonan, Caitriona, 'Smashing Childlike Wonder? The Early Journey into Higher Education', in Daniel Ashton and Caitriona Noonan (eds), *Cultural Work and Higher Education* (Basingstoke: Palgrave Macmillan, 2013), pp. 133–153.

Noonan, Caitriona, 'Constructing Creativities: Higher Education and the Cultural Industries Workforce', in Kate Oakley and Justin O'Connor (eds), *The Routledge Companion to the Cultural Industries* (London: Routledge, 2015), pp. 442–451.

NYU Abu Dhabi, 'Film and New Media Major', n.d. Available online: https://nyuad.nyu.edu/en/academics/undergraduate/majors-and-minors/film-and-new-media-major.html (accessed 27 December 2022).

NYU Abu Dhabi, 'Supplier Code of Conduct', 2016. Available online: https://nyuad.nyu.edu/content/dam/nyuad/about/social-responsibility/nyuad-project-supplier-code-of-conduct.pdf (accessed 27 December 2022).

NYU Abu Dhabi, 'Community Life', 2021a. Available online: https://nyuad.nyu.edu/en/news/latest-news/community-life/2021/november/530-students-from-over-85-countries-join-nyuad-as-the-class-of-2025.html (accessed 27 December 2022).

NYU Abu Dhabi, 'Graduate Outcomes', 2021b. Available online: https://nyuad.nyu.edu/en/academics/undergraduate/career-development/graduate-outcomes.html (accessed 27 December 2022).

Oakley, Kate, 'Making Workers: Higher Education and the Cultural Industries Workplace', in Daniel Ashton and Caitriona Noonan (eds), *Cultural Work and Higher Education* (Basingstoke: Palgrave Macmillan, 2013), pp. 25–44.

Ohanian, Tom, 'Moving Media through the Digital Media Supply Chain', *Guide2iptv* (September 2007), pp. 14–15.

Olds, Kris, 'Global Assemblage: Singapore, Foreign Universities, and the Construction of a "Global Education Hub"', *World Development* vol. 35, no. 6 (2007), pp. 959–975.

Olds, Kris and Nigel Thrift, 'Cultures on the Brink: Reengineering the Soul of Capitalism – on a Global Scale', in Aihwa Ong and Stephen J. Collier (eds), *Global Assemblages: Technology, Politics, and Ethics as Anthropological Problems* (Malden, MA: Blackwell, 2005), pp. 270–290.

Ong, Aihwa, *Flexible Citizenship: The Cultural Logics of Transnationality* (Durham, NC: Duke University Press, 1999).

Ong, Aihwa, *Neoliberalism as Exception: Mutations in Citizenship and Sovereignty* (Durham and London: Duke University Press, 2006).

Ooyala, *Why Media Logistics Matters: Accelerating your Content from Concept to Cash* (White Paper, 2016). Available online: http://go.ooyala.com/wf-whitepaper-why-media-logistics-matters (accessed 27 December 2022).

Orenstein, Dara, 'Foreign-Trade Zones and the Cultural Logic of Frictionless – Production', *Radical History Review* vol. 109 (Winter 2011), pp. 36–61.

Ovetz, Robert, 'Introduction', in Robert Ovetz (ed.), *Workers' Inquiry and Global Class Struggle* (London: Pluto Press, 2021a), pp. 1–42.

Ovetz, Robert, 'Making Threats: Credible Strike Threats in the US, 2012–2016', in Robert Ovetz (ed.), *Workers' Inquiry and Global Class Struggle* (London: Pluto Press, 2021b), pp. 105–147.

Ovetz, Robert (ed.), *Workers' Inquiry and Global Class Struggle* (London: Pluto Press, 2021c).

PACT/BECTU, *PACT/BECTU Agreement – Terms Applicable to Major Motion Pictures* (2021).

Parker, Alan, *Building a Sustainable UK Film Industry: A Presentation to the UK Film Industry* (London: UKFC, 2002).
Parks, Lisa, '"Stuff You Can Kick": Toward a Theory of Media Infrastructures', in Patrik Svensson and David Theo Goldberg (eds), *Between Humanities and the Digital* (Cambridge, MA: MIT Press, 2015), pp. 355–373.
Partridge, Damani James, 'Activist Capitalism and Supply-Chain Citizenship: Producing Ethical Regimes and Ready-to-Wear Clothes', *Current Anthropology* vol. 52 no. S3 (April 2011), pp. S97–S111.
Paterson, Richard, 'Partnerships with a Purpose: Creating Cultural and Commercial Value in the UK Film Sector' in David Greenaway and Chris D. Rudd (eds), *Business Growth Benefits of Higher Education* (London: Palgrave Macmillan, 2014), pp. 136–148.
Pennington, Adrian, 'International Studios: A World of Opportunity', *Broadcast*, 1 October 2015. Available online: https://www-proquest-com.ezproxy.lib.gla.ac.uk/docview/1919405369?accountid=14540. (accessed 27 December 2022).
Percival, Neil and David Hesmondhalgh, 'Should You Work for Free in TV?', *Broadcast*, 18 October 2012. Available online: www.proquest.com/trade-journals/should-you-work-free-tv/docview/1112926841/se-2 (accessed 27 December 2022).
Percival, Neil and David Hesmondhalgh, 'Unpaid Work in the UK Television and Film Industries: Resistance and Changing Attitudes', *European Journal of Communication* vol. 29 no. 2 (2014), pp. 188–203.
Perlin, Ross, *Intern Nation: How to Earn Nothing and Learn Little in the Brave New Economy* (London and New York: Verso, 2011).
Peters, Michael A. and Ergin Bulut (eds), *Cognitive Capitalism, Education and Digital Labor* (New York: Peter Lang, 2011).
Petrie, Duncan, 'Creative Industries and Skills: Film Education and Training in the Era of New Labour', *Journal of British Cinema and Television* vol. 9 no.3 (2012), pp. 357–376.
Petrie, Duncan and Rod Stoneman, *Educating Film-makers: Past, Present and Future* (Bristol: Intellect Books, 2014).
Picard, Robert G. and Leon Barkho, 'Dubai Media City: Creating Benefits from Foreign Media Developments', in Charlie Karlsson and Robert G. Picard (eds), *Media Clusters: Spatial Agglomeration and Content Capabilities* (Northampton, MA: Edward Elgar Publishing, 2011) pp. 281–305.
Pitts, Frederick H., 'Follow the Money? Value Theory and Social Inquiry', *Ephemera* vol. 13 no. 3 (2014), pp. 335–356.
Posner, Miriam, 'Breakpoints and Black Boxes: Information in Global Supply Chains', *Postmodern Culture* vol. 31, no. 3 (2021).
Powdermaker, Hortense, *Hollywood, the Dream Factory: An Anthropologist Looks at the Movie Makers* (London: Secker and Warburg, 1951).
Precarious Workers Brigade, *Training for Exploitation? Politicising Employability and Reclaiming Education* (London: Journal of Aesthetics & Protest Press, 2017). Available online: https://joaap.org/press/trainingforexploitation.htm (accessed 31 December 2022).
Punathambekar, Aswin, *From Bombay to Bollywood: The Making of a Global Media Industry* (New York: New York University Press, 2013).
Qiu, Jack Linchuan, *Goodbye iSlave: A Manifesto for Digital Abolition* (Urbana, IL: University of Illinois Press, 2016).
Ramsey, Phil, Stephen Baker and Robert Porter, 'Screen Production on the "Biggest Set in the World": Northern Ireland Screen and the Case of *Game of Thrones*', *Media, Culture & Society* vol. 41 no. 6 (2019), pp. 845–862.

Ramsey, Phil and Andrew White, 'Art for Art's Sake? A Critique of the Instrumentalist Turn in the Teaching of Media and Communications in UK Universities', *International Journal of Cultural Policy* vol. 21 no. 1 (2015), pp. 78–96.

Randle, Keith, 'The Organization of Film and Television Production', in Mark Deuze (ed.), *Managing Media Work* (London: Sage, 2011), pp. 145–153.

Randle, Keith, 'Class and Exclusion at Work: The Case of UK Film and Television', in Kate Oakley and Justin O'Connor (eds), *The Routledge Companion to the Cultural Industries* (London: Routledge, 2015), pp. 330–343.

Redfern, Nick, Connecting the Regional and the Global in the UK Film Industry', *Transnational Cinemas* vol. 1 no. 2 (2010), pp. 145–160.

Ritman, Alex, 'Why the Biggest Stunt in "Mission: Impossible – Fallout" Saw Abu Dhabi Stand in for Paris', *The Hollywood Reporter*, 27 July 2018. Available online: https://www.hollywoodreporter.com/movies/movie-news/mission-impossible-fallout-why-biggest-stunt-saw-abu-dhabi-stand-paris-1130267 (accessed 27 December 2022).

Rodino-Colocino, Michelle and Stephanie N. Beberick, '"You Kind of Have to Bite the Bullet and Do Bitch Work": How Internships Teach Students to Unthink Exploitation in Public Relations', *tripleC: Communication, Capitalism & Critique* vol. 13 no. 2 (2015), pp. 486–500.

Roggero, Gigi (trans. Enda Brophy), *The Production of Living Knowledge: The Crisis of the University and the Transformation of Labor in Europe and North America* (Philadelphia: Temple University Press, 2011).

Ross, Andrew, *Fast Boat to China: High-Tech Outsourcing and the Consequence of Free Trade Lessons from Shanghai* (New York: Vintage Books, 2006).

Ross Andrew, 'The New Geography of Work: Power to the Precarious?', *Theory, Culture and Society* vol. 25, no. 7–8 (2008), pp. 31–49.

Ross, Andrew, *Nice Work If You Can Get It: Life and Labor in Precarious Times* (New York: New York University Press, 2009).

Ross, Andrew, 'Leveraging the Brand: A History of Gulf Labor' in Andrew Ross (for Gulf Labor) (ed.), *The Gulf: High Culture/Hard Labor* (New York and London: OR Books, 2015a), pp. 11–35.

Ross, Andrew (for Gulf Labor) (ed.), *The Gulf: High Culture/Hard Labor* (New York and London: OR Books, 2015b).

Rossiter, Ned, 'The Logistical City: Software, Infrastructure, Labour', *Transit Labour* 4 (2012), pp. 25–27.

Rossiter, Ned, *Software, Infrastructure, Labor: A Media Theory of Logistical Nightmares* (New York and London: Routledge, 2016).

Rossoukh, Ramyar D. and Steven C. Caton (eds), *Anthropology, Film Industries, Modularity* (Durham, NC: Duke University Press, 2021).

Rushton, Katherine, 'Warner Bros Contributes £1bn a Year to UK Economy', *The Telegraph*, 25 April 2013. Available online: http://www.telegraph.co.uk/finance/newsbysector/mediatechnologyandtelecoms/10019472/Warner-Bros-contributes-1bn-a-year-to-UK-economy.html (accessed 27 December 2022).

Ryan-Flood, Róisín and Rosalind Gill (eds), *Secrecy and Silence in the Research Process: Feminist Reflections* (London: Routledge, 2009).

Sabbagh, Dan and Mark Sweney, 'Warner Bros Buys Harry Potter Studios in £100m Boost for UK films', *The Guardian*, 9 November 2010. Available online: http://www.guardian.co.uk/media/2010/nov/09/warner-bros-leavesden-studios (accessed 27 December 2022).

Saha, Anamik, *Race and the Cultural Industries* (Cambridge: Polity Press, 2018).

Samaddar, Ranabir, 'Zones and Corridors', *Transit Labour*, 15 October 2012. Available online: https://transitlabour.asia/blogs/zones_corridors (accessed 27 December 2022).

Sampler, Jeffrey and Saeb Eigner, *Sand to Silicon: Achieving Rapid Growth Lessons from Dubai* (London: Profile Books, 2003).

Sanson, Kevin, 'Stitching it All Together: Service Producers and the Spatial Dynamics of Screen Media Labor', *International Journal of Cultural Studies* vol. 21 no. 4 (2018), pp. 359–374.

Sassen, Saskia, *Expulsions: Brutality and Complexity in the Global Economy* (Cambridge, MA: Harvard University Press, 2014).

Saundry, Richard, Valerie Antcliff and Mark Stuart, '"It's More Than Who You Know" – Networks and Trade Unions in the Audio-Visual Industries', *Human Resources Management Journal* vol. 16 no. 4 (2006), pp. 376–392.

Sayfo, Omar, 'Set for Success: Hollywood Runaway Productions in Socialist and Post-socialist Hungary', *Media Industries* vol. 7 no. 1 (2020), pp. 43–63.

Schlesinger, Philip, 'Creativity: From Discourse to Doctrine?', *Screen* vol. 48, no. 3 (Autumn 2007), pp. 377–387.

Schroeder, Christopher M., *Startup Rising: The Entrepreneurial Revolution Remaking the Middle East* (London: Palgrave Macmillan, 2013).

Scott, Allen J., *The Cultural Economy of Cities: Essays on the Geography of Image-Producing Industries* (London: Sage Publications, 2000).

Scott, Allen J., *On Hollywood: The Place, the Industry* (Princeton, NJ: Princeton University Press, 2005).

Scott, Allen J., 'A World in Emergence: Notes Toward a Resynthesis of Urban-Economic Geography for the 21st Century', *Urban Geography* vol. 32 no. 6 (2011), pp. 845–870.

Scott, Allen J., *A World in Emergence: Cities and Regions in the 21st Century* (Cheltenham UK: Edward Elgar Publishing, 2012).

Scott, Allen J. and Naomi E. Pope, 'Hollywood, Vancouver, and the World: Employment Relocation and the Emergence of Satellite Production Centers in the Motion-Picture Industry', *Environment and Planning A* vol. 39 (2007), pp. 1364–1381.

Screen Scotland, 'Filming in Scotland', 2021a. Available online: https://www.screen.scot/film-in-scotland (accessed 27 December 2022).

Screen Scotland, '*Outlander* Training Programme', 2021b. Available online: https://www.screen.scot/skills-and-talent/skills-development/outlander-training-programme (accessed 27 December 2022).

ScreenSkills, 'Apprenticeships', 2022a. Available online: https://www.screenskills.com/training/apprenticeships (accessed 27 December 2022).

ScreenSkills, 'Become a Trainee Finder Trainee', 2022b. Available online: https://www.screenskills.com/training/trainee-finder/become-a-trainee-finder-trainee (accessed 27 December 2022).

ScreenSkills, 'How to Apply for ScreenSkills Select Endorsement, 2022c. Available online: https://www.screenskills.com/training/screenskills-select/how-to-apply-for-screenskills-select-endorsement/ (accessed 27 December 2022).

ScreenSkills, 'ScreenSkills Select Application Guidelines', 2022d. Available online: https://www.screenskills.com/training/screenskills-select/screenskills-select-application-guidelines (accessed 27 December 2022).

ScreenSkills, 'Skills Forecasting Service', 2022e. Available online: https://www.screenskills.com/industry/screenskills-research/skills-forecasting-service (accessed 27 December 2022).

ScreenSkills, 'Why Be Endorsed by ScreenSkills Select?', 2022f. Available online: https://www.screenskills.com/online-learning/series/work-well-series (accessed 27 December 2022).

ScreenSkills, 'Work Well Series', 2022g. Available online: https://www.screenskills.com/online-learning/series/work-well-series (accessed 27 December 2022).

ScreenSkills, 'ScreenSkills Select: Application Guidelines and Endorsement Criteria – Guidelines for Undergraduate, Postgraduate and Vocational Courses', n.d.a. Available online: https://www.screenskills.com/media/5231/screenskills-select-application-guidelines.pdf (accessed 27 December 2022).

ScreenSkills, 'ScreenSkills Select: Leaflet for Course Leaders', n.d.b. https://www.screenskills.com/media/5339/screenskills-select-leaflet-for-course-leaders.pdf (accessed 27 December 2022).

ScreenSkills, Nordicity and Saffery Champness, *Forecast of Labour Market Shortages and Training Investment Needs in Film and High-End TV Production* (London: ScreenSkills, 2022).

Sen, Samita, 'Engaging with the Idea of "Transit Labour"', *Transit Labour* 4 (2012), pp. 15–18.

Sennett, Richard, *The Corrosion of Character: The Personal Consequences of Work in the New Capitalism* (New York: W. W. Norton & Company, 1998).

Sennett, Richard, *The Culture of the New Capitalism* (New Haven and London: Yale University Press, 2006).

Sexton, John, 'Global Network University Reflection', *NYU* 21 December 2010. Available online: https://www.nyu.edu/about/leadership-university-administration/office-of-the-president-emeritus/communications/global-network-university-reflection.html (accessed 27 December 2022).

Shaginian, Diana, 'Unpaid Internships in the Entertainment Industry: The Need for a Clear and Practical Intern Standard after the *Black Swan* Lawsuit', *Southwestern Journal of International Law* vol. 21 no. 2 (2015), pp. 509–533.

Sharf, Jack, 'Why Denis Villeneuve Shot "Dune" During Abu Dhabi's Hottest Months: "Strange Haze in the Air"', *IndieWire* 27 September 2021. Available online: https://www.indiewire.com/2021/09/denis-villeneuve-shot-dune-hottest-months-abu-dhabi-1234667710 (accessed 27 December 2022).

Shaxson, Nicolas, *Treasure Islands: Uncovering the Damage of Offshore Banking and Tax Havens* (London: Vintage, 2012).

Shukla, Ajay, 'The UAE – A Higher Education Hub for International Students and Foreign University Branch Campuses', *GN Focus* 3 August 2021. Available online: https://gulfnews.com/uae/education/the-uae---a-higher-education-hub-for-international-students-and-foreign-university-branch-campuses-1.1627982146370 (accessed 27 December 2022).

Sigler, Thomas J., 'Relational Cities: Doha, Panama City, and Dubai as 21st Century Entrepôts', *Urban Geography* vol. 35 no. 5 (2013), pp. 612–633.

Sorkin, Andrew Ross, 'N.Y.U. Crisis in Abu Dhabi Stretches to Wall Street', *New York Times*, 27 May 2014, pp. 1 & 5.

Spivak, Gayatri Chakravorty, *An Aesthetic Education in the Era of Globalization* (Cambridge, MA: Harvard University Press: 2012).

Srnicek, Nick, *Platform Capitalism* (Cambridge: Polity Press, 2017).

Srnicek, Nick and Alex Williams, *Inventing the Future: Postcapitalism and a World Without Work* (London and New York: Verso, 2016).

Standing, Guy, *The Precariat: The New Dangerous Class* (New York: Bloomsbury Academic, 2011).

Starosielski, Nicole, *The Undersea Network* (Durham, NC: Duke University Press, 2015).

Steinhart, Daniel, *Runaway Hollywood: Internationalizing Postwar Production and Location Shooting* (Berkeley: University of California Press, 2019).

Steyerl, Hito, *The Wretched of the Screen* (Berlin: Sternberg Press, 2012).

Strauss-Kahn, Vanessa and Xavier Vives, 'Why and Where Do Headquarters Move?' Working Paper. IESE Business School – University of Navarra, 17 July 2006. Available online: http://www.iese.edu/research/pdfs/DI-0650-E.pdf. (accessed 27 December 2022).

The Student Handjob: So Radical It's Fucking Bodacious (Pamphlet, 29 September 2011). Available online: https://studenthandjob.wordpress.com (accessed 29 December 2022).

Szalai, Georg, 'London Tax Tribunal to Evaluate U.K. Film Investment Vehicles', *Hollywood Reporter*, 11 March 2014. Available online: https://www.hollywoodreporter.com/news/general-news/london-tax-tribunal-evaluate-uk-745757/#!. (accessed 27 December 2022).

Szczepanik, Petr, 'Globalization through the Eyes of Runners: Student Interns as Ethnographers on Runaway Productions in Prague', *Media Industries* vol. 1 no. 1 (2014), pp. 56–61.

Szczepanik, Petr, 'Transnational Crews and Postsocialist Precarity: Globalizing Screen Media Labor in Prague', in Michael Curtin and Kevin Sanson (eds), *Precarious Creativity: Global Media, Local Labor* (Oakland, CA: California University Press, 2016), pp. 88–103.

Tarnowski, Stefan, 'Cinematic Looting', *LRB*, 8 September 2022. Available online: https://www.lrb.co.uk/blog/2022/september/cinematic-looting (accessed 27 December 2022).

Terranova, Tiziana, 'Free Labor: Producing Culture for the Digital Economy', *Social Text* 63, vol. 18, no. 2 (2000), pp. 33–58.

Thornham, Sue and Tim O'Sullivan, 'Chasing the Real: "Employability" and the Media Studies Curriculum', *Media, Culture & Society* vol. 26, no. 5 (2004), pp. 717–735.

Tinic, Serra, *On Location: Canada's Television Industry in a Global Market* (Toronto: University of Toronto Press, 2005).

Tokumitsu, Miya, 'In the Name of Love', *Jacobin* 12 January 2014. Available online: https://jacobin.com/2014/01/in-the-name-of-love/ (accessed 27 December 2022).

Toscano, Alberto and Jeff Kinkle, *Cartographies of the Absolute* (Winchester: Zero Books, 2015).

Tsing, Anna, 'Supply Chains and the Human Condition', *Rethinking Marxism* vol. 21 no. 2 (2009), pp. 148–176.

Tsing, Anna, 'On Nonscalability: The Living World Is Not Amenable to Precision-Nested Scales', *Common Knowledge* vol. 18 no. 3 (2012), pp. 505–524.

Tsing, Anna, *The Mushroom at the End of the World: On the Possibility of Life in Capitalist Ruins* (Princeton, NJ and Oxford: Princeton University Press, 2015).

Tusing, David, '"Deira Diaries": Dubai-Shot Malayalam Film Showcases Different Side of Life in the Gulf', *The National* 21 March 2021. Available online: https://www.thenationalnews.com/arts-culture/film/deira-diaries-dubai-shot-malayalam-film-showcases-different-side-of-life-in-the-gulf-1.1188221 (accessed 27 December 2022).

twofour54 Abu Dhabi, 'Frequently Asked Questions', n.d.a. Available online: https://www.twofour54.com/en/who-we-are/frequently-asked-questions/ (accessed 27 December 2022).

twofour54 Abu Dhabi, 'Make It a Passion, Make it a Career', n.d.b. Available online: https://internships.twofour54.com/ (accessed 27 December 2022).

twofour54 Abu Dhabi, 'Production Services', n.d.c. Available online: https://www.twofour54.com/en/production-services/our-talent/ (accessed 27 December 2022).

UAE Free Zones, 'Dubai International Academic City', n.d.a. Available online: https://www.uaefreezones.com/dubai_international_academic_city_free_zone.html (accessed 27 December 2022).
UAE Free Zones, 'Dubai Studio City', n.d.b. Available online: https://www.uaefreezones.com/dubai_studio_city_free_zone.html (accessed 27 December 2022).
UAE Free Zones, 'twofour54 Abu Dhabi', n.d.c. Available online: https://www.uaefreezones.com/twofour54_free_zone.html (accessed 27 December 2022).
UCU, *Precarious Work in Higher Education (November 2016 Update)* (London: UCU, 2016).
UCU, *Counting the Costs of Casualisation in Higher Education* (London: UCU, 2019).
UCU, *Precarious Work in Higher Education: Insecure Contracts and How They Have Changed Over Time (October 2021 Update)* (London: UCU, 2021).
UCU, 'Precarious Contracts in HE: Institution Snapshot', 2020. Available online: https://www.ucu.org.uk/article/8154/Precarious-contracts-in-HE---institution-snapshot (accessed 27 December 2022).
UCU, *Workload Survey 2021: Data Report* (London: UCU, 2022a).
UCU, 'Action for USS', 2022b. Available online: https://www.ucu.org.uk/strikeforuss (accessed 27 December 2022).
UCU, 'Four Fights 2: Casualisation', 2022c. Available online: https://www.ucu.org.uk/media/11908/Four-fights-casualisation/pdf/Casualisation_1200_x_675_px.pdf (accessed 27 December 2022).
UCU, 'UCU Rising', 2022d. Available online: https://www.ucu.org.uk/rising (accessed 27 December 2022).
UNESCO, *Cultural and Creative Industries in the Face of Covid-19: An Economic Impact Outlook* (Paris: UNESCO, 2021).
Unitas Consultancy, *Dubai: Financialization and its Discontents* (Dubai: GCP and Reidin Real Estate Information, 2016).
United Nations, *Creative Economy Report 2008* (Geneva: United Nations, 2008).
University of Wollongong in Dubai, 'Master of Media and Communication', n.d.a. Available online: https://uowdubai.ac.ae/degrees/masters/media/master-media-and-communication (accessed 27 December 2022).
University of Wollongong in Dubai, 'Media and Design', n.d.b. Available online: https://uowdubai.ac.ae/degrees/bachelors/media (accessed 27 December 2022).
Unnikrishnan, Deepak, *Temporary People* (Crawley, Western Australia: UWA Publishing, 2019).
Urry, John, *Offshoring* (Cambridge: Polity Press, 2014).
Variety Editors, *Variety's The Big Restart: Our Guide to Global Filming Locations*, 9 September 2020. Available online: https://variety.com/2020/film/global/variety-big-restart-global-filming-locations-guide-coronavirus-1234763519/ (accessed 27 December 2022).
Variety Editors, *Variety Global Locations*, 2022. Available online: https://edition.pagesuite.com/html5/reader/production/default.aspx?pubname=&edid=198e152f-b9a0-4c8b-bc52-43460d13042b (accessed 27 December 2022).
Vercellone, Carlo, 'From Formal Subsumption to General Intellect: Elements for a Marxist Reading of the Thesis of Cognitive Capitalism', *Historical Materialism* vol. 15 no. 1 (2007), pp. 13–36.
Vignal, Leïla (ed.), *The Transnational Middle East: People, Places, Borders* (Abingdon, Oxon: Routledge, 2017).
Vivarelli, Nick, 'Dubai Tailors its Perks to Foreign Projects', *Variety* vol. 322 no. 6, 3 December 2013, pp. 70–71.
Vivarelli, Nick, 'Twofour54 Thrives as Region's Content Capital', *Variety* vol. 325 no. 10, 14 October 2014, p. 80.

Vivarelli, Nick, 'Sheikhdoms Spawn "Star Wars"', *Variety* vol. 330 no. 5, 1 December 2015, p. 109.
Vivarelli, Nick, 'Dubai Studio City Chief Jamal Al-Sharif Talks New Strategy to Stimulate Local Production', *Variety* 9 December 2016. Available online: https://variety.com/2016/film/news/dubai-studio-city-chief-jamal-al-sharif-on-new-strategy-to-stimulate-local-content-industry-1201938058 (accessed 27 December 2022).
Vivarelli, Nick, 'Bollywood Hears Call of Abu Dhabi', *Variety* vol. 340 no. 2, 15 May 2018, p. 61.
Vivarelli, Nick, '*Dune*: Watch Denis Villeneuve Reveal Why He Chose Abu Dhabi's Liwa Desert as a Double for Arrakis (EXCLUSIVE)', *Variety* 22 September 2021a. Available online: https://variety.com/2021/film/news/dune-arrakis-abu-dhabi-liwa-desert-denis-villeneuve-1235070287/ (accessed 27 December 2022).
Vivarelli, Nick, 'How the Middle East Has Enticed Hollywood with Stunning Locales and Generous Incentives', *Variety* 29 November 2021b. Available online: https://variety.com/2021/film/filming-locations/middle-east-production-hollywood-dune-mission-impossible-1235117536/#recipient_hashed=65b5b113c612faf39022e10eca d6c97e7b6e7ee8afc98716b9cc9185aa68a507&utm_medium=email&utm_source=exacttarget&utm_campaign=eshowdaily_cairo&utm_content=316488&utm_term=1705044 (accessed 27 December 2022).
Vivarelli, Nick, 'United Arab Emirates Leads the Way in Luring Foreign Shoots', *Variety* vol. 354, no. 7, 15 December 2021c, p. 120.
Vivarelli, Nick, 'Middle East Gears Up', in Variety Editors, *Variety Global Locations*, 2022. Available online: https://edition.pagesuite.com/html5/reader/production/default.aspx?pubname=&edid=198e152f-b9a0-4c8b-bc52-43460d13042b, pp. 74–75 (accessed 27 December 2022).
Vora, Neha, *Impossible Citizens: Dubai's Indian Diaspora* (Durham, NC: Duke University Press, 2013).
Vora, Neha, 'Expat/Expert Camps: Redefining "Labour" Within Gulf Migration', in Abdulhadi Khalaf, Omar AlShebabi and Adam Hanieh (eds), *Transit States: Labour, Migration and Citizenship in the Gulf* (London: Pluto, 2015a), pp. 170–197.
Vora, Neha, 'Is the University Universal? Mobile (Re)Constitutions of American Academia in the Gulf States', *Anthropology & Education Quarterly* vol. 46 no.1 (2015b), pp. 19–36.
Vora, Neha, *Teach for Arabia: American Universities, Liberalism, and Transnational Qatar* (Stanford: Stanford University Press, 2019).
Wacquant, Loïc, *Punishing the Poor: The Neoliberal Government of Social Insecurity* (Durham, NC: Duke University Press, 2009).
Wages for Students Students [sic], *Wages for Students* (Pamphlet, 1975). Available online: https://libcom.org/article/wages-students (accessed 29 December 2022).
Walia, Harsha, *Border and Rule: Global Migration, Capitalism and the Rise of Racist Nationalism* (Chicago: Haymarket Books, 2021).
Wang, Jackie, *Carceral Capitalism* (South Pasadena, CA.: Semiotext(e), 2018).
Wang, Sin-Yi, Ying-Ting Chuang and Bertrand M. T. Lin, 'Minimizing Talent Cost and Operating Cost in Film Production', *Journal of Industrial and Production Engineering* vol. 33 no. 1 (2016), pp. 17–31.
Ward, Steven C., *Neoliberalism and the Global Restructuring of Knowledge and Education* (London: Routledge, 2012).
Warner Bros. Studios Leavesden, 'Apprenticeships', 2022. Available online: https://www.wbsl.com/studios/careers/reach (accessed 27 December 2022).

Watt, Andrew, 'The Impact of Private Equity on European Companies and Workers: Key Issues and a Review of the Evidence', *Industrial Relations Journal* vol. 39 no. 6 (2008), pp. 548–568.

Wilkins, Stephen, 'Who Benefits from Foreign Universities in the Arab Gulf States?', *The Australian Universities' Review* vol. 53 no. 1 (2011), pp. 73–83.

Williams, Raymond, *The Long Revolution* (London: Chatto & Windus, 1961).

Wilson, Tim, *A Review of Business-University Collaboration: The Wilson Review* (London: Department for Business, Innovation and Skills, 2012).

Woodcock, Jamie, Brendan Donegan and Sølvi Goard, 'A Workers' Inquiry Among Academics: Hourly-Paid Teaching Staff at Goldsmiths College, London', *Notes from Below*, 29 January 2018. Available online: https://notesfrombelow.org/article/workers-inquiry-among-academics (accessed 27 December 2022).

World Economic Forum, *Global Gender Gap Report 2022: Insight Report July 2022* (Geneva: World Economic Forum, 2022).

Xiang Biao, *Global 'Body Shopping': An Indian Labor System in the Information Technology Industry* (Princeton, NJ: Princeton University Press, 2007).

Yossman, K. J., 'A United Kingdom', *Variety* vol. 354 no. 4, 24 November 2021, pp. 60–65.

Yunis, Alia, 'Coming Soon: Encounters on the Road to Heritage and Film in the UAE' (PhD diss., University of Amsterdam, 2020).

Yunis, Alia and Gaelle Picherit-Duthler, 'Lights, Camera, Education: An Overview of the Future of Film Education in the United Arab Emirates', *Journal of Middle East Media* vol. 7 (2011), pp. 119–140.

Zaslove, Jerry, 'Exiled Pedagogy: From the "Guerrilla" Classroom to the University of Excess', in Mark Coté, Richard J. F. Day and Greig De Peuter (eds), *Utopian Pedagogy: Radical Experiments against Neoliberal Globalization* (Toronto: University of Toronto Press, 2007), pp. 93–107.

Zayed University, 'BS in Communication & Media Sciences (Concentration in Media Production and Storytelling)', n.d. Available online: https://www.zu.ac.ae/main/en/colleges/colleges/__college_of_comm_media_sciences/undergraduate-programs/bs-film-and-video-communications-mps.aspx (accessed 27 December 2022).

Index

20th Century Fox 39
6 Underground 89

Abu Dhabi 1, 6, 10, 13, 17, 87–88, 89, 90, 91, 92, 94, 96, 97, 98, 99, 100, 102, 105, 108, 110, 113, 114, 115, 118, 120, 122, 123, 127, 129, 131, 132, 133, 139
Abu Dhabi Economic Vision 2030 88, 91, 98, 129
Abu Dhabi Film Commission 6, 17, 105, 113, 118, 121, 123
academic freedom, *see* freedom
academic labour, *see* labour
academics 30, 31, 32, 33, 67, 68, 69, 71, 73, 77, 81, 83, 84, 85–86, 94, 99, 103, 109, 110, 136
accommodation, temporary (for cast and crew) 13, 17, 48, 50, 123
  see also hotels
accountability 14, 21, 139
  see also care
Acland, Charles 5, 7, 9, 11, 14
activism 31, 33, 59, 78, 85, 90, 110, 132, 134, 135, 139
  see also resistance to supply chains
Afghanistan 89
Airlift 87
airlines 2, 114, 121, 124, 127
  see also transportation and travel arrangements
airports 92, 108, 119
Al Manthri, Yahya 94, 104, 131
Al Sharif, Jamal 116, 127, 128, 131
Al-Azhar University 94, 95
Amazon 3, 17, 61, 65, 124
American University in Beirut 96
Andrijasevic, Rutvica 15
Apple 16

apprenticeships 25, 63, 65
  see also trainees
Aquaman and the Lost Kingdom 39
architecture 12, 30, 40, 47, 79, 107, 113, 118, 120
army, *see* military
artificial intelligence 18
artisanship 55
  see also craft
Arts Council England 66
assembly line production, 4, 7, 33
  see also Fordism
Australia 10, 46, 93, 94, 135
autonomy 16, 25, 27, 28
  see also freedom

Baker, Paul 126
Baker, Sarah 25
Baker, Stephen 13
Barrandov Studios 8
Batman, The 37, 39
Batman Begins 44
BBC 37
Beberick, Stephanie N. 75
BECTU, *see* Broadcasting, Entertainment, Communications and Theatre Union
Belgium 135
'below-the-line' workers 6
  see also film crews
Berardi, Franco 'Bifo' 22–23, 24, 70
Berlant, Lauren 72, 136
BFC, *see* British Film Commission
BFI, *see* British Film Institute
Bharat 87
big-budget films and filmmaking 1, 3, 5, 6, 8, 10, 14, 13, 16, 17, 18, 21, 27, 33, 43, 47, 60, 61, 114, 116, 117, 121, 122, 136
  see also blockbusters
Bin Byat, Ahmad 115–116

biopolitics 81, 83, 85, 102
biopower 24
Black Swan 76
Blair, Tony 40
blockbusters 1, 2, 5, 22, 37, 46, 110, 117, 133
  see also big-budget films and filmmaking
Boden, Rebecca 68
Bollywood 27, 87, 122, 127
Bollywood Parks (theme park) 127
borders 6–7, 12, 23, 44, 48, 50, 89, 90, 95, 96, 102, 105, 107, 116, 118, 137
Bourne Legacy, The 87, 89
Bousquet, Marc 30
boycotts 136
  see also strikes
branch campuses 3, 30, 88, 92–95, 96, 97, 98, 99, 100, 102, 103, 104, 106, 107–108
  see also universities
Brannon Donoghue, Courtney 27, 40, 44
Brexit 36
British cinema 37–38, 43, 53, 54, 60
British Columbia 50
British Film Commission 42, 44, 47, 64
British Film Institute 53
Broadcasting, Entertainment, Communications and Theatre Union 48–49, 54, 55, 56, 57, 60, 65, 73, 74, 77, 83
Budrovich Sáez, Jorge 5, 123
building, *see* construction and the construction sector
Bunty Aur Babli 2 87
Burj Khalifa 116, 117
Burnetts, Charles 72
Button, Roy 35, 36, 44

Caldwell, John 15
California 6, 13, 38, 46, 89
Canada 6, 10, 14, 50
Cardington Studios 42
care 53, 57, 58, 77
  childcare 39, 53, 57, 58, 61, 129
  duties of (renounced) 7, 8, 21, 22, 26, 41, 46, 51, 53, 56, 57, 64, 70, 95, 108, 129, 132; *see also* accountability

casualization 7, 25, 33, 36, 41, 46, 59, 63, 65, 68, 70, 71, 72, 76, 77, 83, 84, 85, 95, 129, 130, 131, 133, 136, 139
catering 1, 17, 60, 128
Caton, Steven C. 5
Chalamet, Timothée 91
Champion, Katherine M. 76
Chen, Julie Yujie 15
Cherokee Nation 135
childcare, *see* care
China 8, 47–48, 87, 116, 119, 125
chokepoints 32, 136
Chong, Kimberly 8, 20, 125
Christopherson, Susan 10, 44
Chua, Charmaine 135
Chung, Hye Jean 23, 50
citizenship (and lack thereof) 6, 28, 89, 90, 102, 104, 106, 107, 110, 111, 129, 135
  see also graduated citizenship
Civil Defence of the United Arab Emirates 1, 17, 126
class systems and classism 6, 9, 13, 26, 33, 34, 53, 60, 70, 73, 78, 90, 91, 95, 104, 105, 106, 130, 138
Cohen, Joseph N. 11
Colectivo Situaciones 33–34
collective bargaining 8, 10, 52, 130, 136, 138
  see also unions and unionization
collectivity and collective struggle 8, 23, 29, 32, 34, 70, 71, 82–83, 85, 110, 111, 133, 134, 138, 139
  see also resistance to the supply chain; solidarity
Collini, Stefan 79
Columbus, Chris 43, 78
Commune, La 85
competition, competitiveness and competitive advantage 2, 5, 7, 8, 10, 17, 21, 26, 28, 29, 34, 37, 38, 42, 43, 45, 47, 48, 50, 52, 59, 64, 73, 78, 79, 83, 88, 92, 93, 96, 98, 119, 121, 122, 129, 130, 133, 134, 138, 140
conricerca 32–33, 85, 139
construction and the construction sector 1, 6, 7, 13, 40, 90–91, 92, 106, 110, 114, 115, 116, 117, 124, 127–128, 129, 131, 132, 133, 136, 138, 139
containerization 4, 38, 128

continuous working 59
contracts and contracting (short-term and temporary) 6, 7, 12, 13, 14, 15, 27, 29, 40, 41, 46, 51, 54, 57, 58, 68, 71, 75, 77, 81, 83, 84, 89, 95, 96, 108, 120, 124, 128, 129, 130, 136, 140
   see also labour (temporary); subcontracting
coordination 2, 7, 13, 14, 17, 18–19, 27, 50, 54, 55, 64, 66, 87, 100, 103, 114, 115, 117, 122, 126
   see also interoperability
cosmopolitanism 28, 52, 102, 103
Covid-19 56, 59, 87, 123, 124
craft 24, 43, 48, 55, 126, 128
Crary, Jonathan 56, 57
creative economy 3, 25, 36, 42, 44, 71, 78, 88, 89, 93, 97, 100, 101, 107, 109, 110, 114, 115, 116, 130, 131, 133, 139
creative class 34, 91
creative industries and the creative sector 24, 28, 33, 39, 40, 41, 42, 52, 60, 67, 70, 88, 91, 138
Creative Lab, Abu Dhabi 100, 120
creative labour, *see* labour
Creative UK 41
Creative Skillset, *see* ScreenSkills
critical thinking 97–98
Croatia 135
Cruise, Tom 91, 117
Cuarón, Alfonso 37
Cucco, Marco, 13
Cuevas Valenzuela, Hernán 5
cultural industries 7
cultural quarters 91
Curcio, Anna 138
Curtin, Michael 10, 12, 13, 14, 16, 17, 20, 21, 27, 57
Czech Republic 8–9, 50, 74, 101, 126

Dabangg 87
Darkest Hour, The 39
Dawtrey, Adam 43
debt 11, 19, 22, 25, 26, 28, 29, 76, 78, 80, 81–82, 106, 128, 132
   student debt, 21, 23, 26, 28 , 64, 80, 81, 136; *see also* student loans
Deira Diaries 117

DePaola, Tom 30
Department for Digital, Culture, Media & Sport, UK 64
deportation 108–109, 128, 132, 133
deregulation 10, 36
deserts 1, 2, 4, 10, 13, 89, 113, 116, 119, 124, 127
deWaard, Andrew 19
difference and differences 5, 14, 21, 27, 33, 34, 43, 48, 52, 88, 95, 101, 103, 104, 109, 129, 133
digital effects 23, 50, 55
discipline (modes of social disciplining) 26, 63, 70, 81, 82, 98, 128
Disney 37, 115
distribution 3, 4, 16, 18
   film distribution 4, 5, 18, 38, 39, 124
distribution centres 120, 124
diversity 4, 5, 14, 59, 87, 88, 89, 93, 97, 100–101, 102, 103, 104, 109, 118, 133, 139
divisions of labour, *see* labour
do what you love (DWYL) 71
Donaghue, Ngaire 72
Donn, Gari 94, 104
DP World 121, 122
Dubai Design District 107
Dubai Film and TV Commission 87, 116, 123, 128
Dubai Holding 106, 116, 122
Dubai International Academic City 94, 106
Dubai Internet City 107, 115
Dubai Knowledge Park 106
Dubai Media City 105, 106, 115, 129, 130
Dubai Studio City 107, 114, 115, 116, 117, 119, 120
Dune 87, 113, 123, 125, 128, 131
Dyer-Witheford, Nick 18, 21, 24, 81

Ealing Studios 77
education
   critical and radical 28, 31, 32–34, 68, 82–86, 109–111, 133, 135, 137, 138
   liberal arts 88, 96–100, 102
   privatized 26, 27, 28, 63, 66, 78–79, 82–83, 90, 92, 93, 94, 96, 98, 101, 106, 108

public 21, 75, 78, 90, 96, 99, 100, 101, 106
  see also branch campuses; English (English-medium education); supply chain education; universities
Egypt 16, 94, 130
Einstein, Mara 74
El Khachab, Chihab 16
emotional labour, see labour
employability 28, 33, 64, 68, 69, 70, 71, 72, 74, 79, 80, 81, 82, 83, 84, 98, 105
English
  necessity for fluency in 27, 48, 96, 101, 103, 125
  English-medium education 3, 88, 96, 101, 102, 131
enterprise 12, 26–27, 36, 64, 68, 69, 98
  see also entrepreneurs and entrepreneurship
Enterprise Investment Scheme 44, 45
entrepreneurs and entrepreneurship 14, 21, 24, 26–27, 28, 29, 41, 51, 64, 68–70, 71, 72, 75, 79, 88, 97, 98, 103, 114, 129, 134, 137, 138
  see also enterprise
equal opportunities 51
Europe and Europeans 5, 39, 54, 89–90, 92, 96, 104, 108, 127, 130
exchange rates 9, 21, 36, 104
Exclusive Behind the Abu Dhabi Scenes of Star Wars: The Force Awakens (making-of video) 1, 2, 6, 13, 17, 24, 27, 55, 96, 106, 126, 127
exhaustion 29, 35, 57–58
  see also long hours; sleep, rest and breaks
expatriates 89, 93, 101, 108, 128
  see also migrants

fair trade 23
family connections, see nepotism
Fantastic Beasts series 39
Fast & Furious 9 39, 50
Fast & Furious franchise 137
Figiel, Joanna 70, 79
file transfer systems 18
film commissions 6, 10, 12–13, 17, 27, 36, 42, 47, 48, 50, 87, 88–89, 107, 109, 114, 115, 116, 119, 121, 122, 123

film crews 1, 7, 10, 12, 14, 15, 17, 18, 24, 33, 35, 36, 37, 38, 41, 42, 43, 44, 45, 47, 48, 49, 50, 51, 52, 54, 55, 56, 57, 58, 59, 60, 61, 63, 64, 72, 77, 80, 83, 89–90, 96, 100, 101, 103, 104, 105, 114, 115, 117, 119, 122, 123, 125, 126, 137, 139
film friendliness 10, 12, 14, 43, 47, 117
Film London 64
film schools 64–66, 68, 76
film studios, see studio facilities; Hollywood studios
financialization and the financial sector 5, 9, 11, 19–22, 26, 36, 45, 55, 58, 78, 79–82, 87, 116, 119
Finland 135
flexible citizenship 102, 104, 111, 134
flexibility 12, 14, 17, 25, 30, 41, 49, 53, 69, 90, 96, 97, 102, 104, 129, 136
fluency (technical and linguistic) 2, 27, 48–49, 51, 67, 85, 88, 103, 125
  see also English
Fordism 4, 64
  see also assembly line production
Foucault, Michel 24, 26, 50, 98
Fraikin, Hans 113, 123
France 54, 93, 135
franchise universities, see branch campuses
free zones 1, 12, 14, 30, 88, 91, 94, 98, 100, 102, 105, 106–107, 110, 114, 115–119, 121, 123, 128, 129–130, 131–132
freedom 24, 25, 26, 27, 41, 81, 94, 97, 101, 107, 110, 118, 134
  academic 97
  of speech and expression 94, 97, 107, 110, 118, 134
  see also autonomy
freelancers and freelancing 36, 40, 41, 42, 60, 63, 65, 75, 89, 98, 107, 108, 114, 117, 123, 124, 128–130, 132
Freeman, Matthew 40
freighting 38, 114, 119, 121, 128
  see also shipping; transportation and travel arrangements
Freire, Paulo 80
frictionlessness 5, 17, 23, 31, 49, 129, 133
Friedman, Yael 67

INDEX

Furgang, Adam 74
Furious 7 87

Gago, Verónica 98
Game of Thrones 13
Gasher, Mike 50
gated communities 91, 117, 118
gender inequality and discrimination 26, 52, 55, 56, 57, 70, 76, 77, 94, 101
Gill, Rosalind 29, 72
Global North 7, 38, 101, 104, 109, 110, 125
Global South and Global Majority 6, 92, 132
golden visa, *see* visas
Goldeneye 38
Goldsmith, Ben 9, 10, 12, 13, 14, 46–47, 102, 117, 126
graduated citizenship, *see* flexible citizenship
Grappi, Giorgio 118
Gravity 37
Gregg, Melissa 15
Guardians of the Galaxy 37
Gulf (Arabian/Persian) 93, 94, 103, 104, 110, 113, 119

Happy New Year 87, 127
Harney, Stefano 49, 82
Harry Potter franchise 37, 39, 40, 41, 43, 44, 46, 53, 55, 63, 72, 79
Harry Potter and the Chamber of Secrets 78
Harry Potter and the Goblet of Fire 63
Harry Potter and the Order of the Phoenix 56
Harry Potter Studio Tour, *see* Warner Bros. Studio Tour – the Making of Harry Potter
health insurance 36, 46
healthcare services 21, 36, 46, 57, 90
hedge funds 11, 19, 20
HEFCE, *see* Higher Education Funding Council for England
Help, The 116
HESA, *see* Higher Education Statistics Agency
Hesmondhalgh, David 25, 73, 74
high-end television 36, 61, 64
Higher Education Funding Council for England 65

Higher Education Statistics Agency 71
hiring practices 1, 7, 8, 10, 12, 13, 14, 16, 17, 28, 33, 36, 38, 40, 44, 51–53, 54, 58, 63, 65, 71, 74–75, 77, 85, 104, 105, 114, 125–126, 133, 138
Ho, Karen 22
Hollywood 3, 4, 5–6, 8–9, 10–11, 13, 14, 36–37, 38, 42, 43, 45, 46, 47, 48, 50, 57, 60, 64, 96, 102, 105, 122, 130, 131
Hollywood studios 11, 15, 16, 19, 20, 43, 45, 48
  see also studio facilities
Home Operation 116
Hong Kong 89
Hope, Sophie 70, 79
hope labour, *see* labour
hospitality and hosting 13, 49, 71, 91, 94, 117, 127, 138
hotels 37, 91, 114, 115, 116, 117, 119, 122, 127, 128, 132
  see also accommodation
Housefull 3 87
housing 81, 90, 92, 117, 132
human capital 14, 26, 27, 28, 30, 31, 41, 64, 69, 74, 75, 79, 85, 91, 98, 136
Human Rights Watch 106, 110
Hungary 10, 50, 61

incentives
  fiscal 5, 138
  for film- or education-based investment 5, 10, 11, 20, 38, 46, 94, 105, 113, 115, 118, 121
  tax (credits, breaks, relief, exemptions) 9, 10, 11, 30, 35, 36, 38, 43, 44, 45, 46, 47, 51, 61, 94, 105, 113, 118, 122, 123, 135
IMF, *see* International Monetary Fund
indenture 81, 106, 116, 118, 128, 133
Independence Day: Resurgence 87
India and Indians 89, 90, 93, 96, 101, 115, 117, 119, 122
individualism 26, 28, 31, 52, 69, 72, 74, 82, 83, 84, 98, 99
industrial action, *see* strikes
infrastructure 2, 5, 10, 12, 14, 21, 32, 36, 37, 38, 42, 45, 47, 48, 49, 87, 92, 106,

113–114, 118–119, 120, 122, 131, 134, 136
insourcing 89, 110
intellectual property 9, 18, 30, 31, 43, 59, 69, 83, 100, 124, 139
intermodality 17, 38, 134, 140
see also interoperability
International Monetary Fund 80
interns, internships and work placements 1, 24, 25–26, 27, 30, 31, 53, 63, 72–75, 76, 79, 80, 84–85, 99–100, 105–106, 109, 117, 120, 126
see also runners; trainees
interoperability, integration and interdependence 2, 4–5, 17, 18, 37, 47, 52, 97, 102, 115, 120, 122, 134, 135, 137, 139
see also coordination; standardization
Ireland 13
Islam 97, 103
Italy 32, 54, 135

Jaikumar, Priya 13
James Bond 38
Japan 15, 51
Jason Bourne 39
Hunt, Jeremy 38
JIT, *see* just-in-time
Jordan, 2, 131, 135
Jurassic World: Fallen Kingdom 37
Justice League 39
just-in-time 2, 14–15, 18, 22, 24, 25, 30, 36, 41, 49, 51, 52, 53, 59, 61, 64, 71, 83, 88, 90, 94, 114, 123–124, 128, 136
see also speed

Kabul 89
kafala, *see* sponsors and sponsorship
kafeel, *see* sponsors and sponsorship
Kamenetz, Anya 76
Karachi 89
Kariyaden, Mushthaque Rahman 117
Karlsson, Charlie 100, 119
Kelly, Lisa 76
Kezar, Adrianna 30
Ki & Ka 87
Kid Who Would Be King, The 39

Kingdom, The 37, 87, 89
Klose, Alexander 4, 10
knowledge economy 24, 31, 67, 78, 88, 89, 93, 97, 100, 101, 106, 107, 110, 131, 133
Kokas, Aynne 47–48
Kumar, Ashok 136
Kung Fu Yoga 87, 115

labour
   academic 25, 29
   creative 6, 9, 8, 22, 24, 29, 34, 44, 50, 71, 77, 79, 85, 88, 91, 98, 100, 105, 107, 110, 117, 127, 128
   divisions of 6, 13, 23, 44, 102, 125, 139; *see also* racialized divisions of labour
   emotional 29, 52, 101
   hope 72
   low wage 6, 9, 10, 18, 21, 30, 47, 53, 55, 58, 64, 71, 72, 78, 90, 91, 97, 104, 106, 132
   migrant 3, 90, 95, 121, 128, 129, 133; *see also* migrants and migration
   permanent 30, 51, 69, 90, 93
   precarious 5, 51; *see also* precarity
   racialized (divisions of) 6–7, 13, 53, 89–91, 101–103, 104, 110, 114, 121, 125–127, 128, 131, 132, 139
   service 13, 14, 17, 27–28, 27–28, 36, 44, 45, 47–48, 50, 55, 64, 67, 91, 96, 100, 114, 125–128, 129; *see also* services
   skilled 5, 8, 24, 26, 27, 36, 39, 43, 52, 63, 64, 67, 75, 76, 88, 89, 93, 94, 98, 103, 107, 114, 119; *see also* skill and de-skilling
   student and study 28, 33, 75–76, 81
   temporary, impermanent and insecure 6, 7, 11, 13, 14, 15, 16, 21, 27, 29, 40, 46, 50, 51, 52, 71, 78, 83, 90, 96, 109, 129, 133
   unpaid 1, 18, 25–26, 28, 31, 53, 64, 72–77, 78, 80, 83, 84, 85, 91, 105, 106, 109, 110, 138; *see also* indenture
Labour Party 38, 40, 42
labour camps 91, 118, 128
labour power 26, 58, 75
Las Vegas 89
Lawton, Kayte 72
Lazzarato, Maurizio 81–82
leadership qualities 98–99

Leavesden Studios 37–42, 43–44, 47, 50, 53, 54, 61, 63, 65, 72
  see also Warner Bros. Studio Tour – the Making of Harry Potter
Lebanon 90, 93, 130
Lee, David 74
liberal arts, *see* education (liberal arts)
liberalism 100, 110
Lightfoot, Michael 97
living knowledge 31, 34
living labour 31
loans, *see* debt; student loans
logistical city 12, 125
logistical state 18, 42, 45, 87, 94, 123, 136
logistics 1, 2, 5, 7, 12, 16–19, 20, 21, 23, 30, 35, 36, 38, 42, 45, 47, 49–50, 54, 55, 57, 59, 87, 94, 113, 114, 115, 118, 119, 120–125, 127, 128, 129, 134, 135, 136, 138
London 35, 37, 73, 98, 106, 108
London Film School 65
long hours 15, 24, 35, 36, 52, 54–60, 61, 64, 71, 72, 73, 76–77, 85, 90, 105
  see also exhaustion; overtime; sleep, rest and breaks
Longcross Studios 42
Looser, Tom 95, 110
Lorey, Isabell 23, 24, 41
Los Angeles 15, 35, 42
Louvre (Abu Dhabi) 91, 110, 133, 139
Low, Linda 90
low wages, *see* labour (low wage); pay scales
Lucasfilm 115
Lynch, David 113

McLanahan, Annie 81, 82
McRobbie, Angela 24–25, 52, 64, 70
Martin, Stewart 28
Marx, Karl 26, 31, 32, 57–59, 75
Mayer, Vicki 10, 11, 20, 85
measures 46–48, 51, 63, 88
Men in Black: International 39
meritocracy 53, 73
Mezzadra, Sandro 6, 21, 90, 139
Middlesex University 94, 98, 108
migrants and migration 3, 6, 10, 22, 53, 81, 88–91, 92, 95, 98, 100–101, 108–109, 113, 114, 115, 121, 128, 129, 130, 131, 132, 133, 134
  see also expatriates; labour (migrant)
Milburn Report 73
militant research 32, 85, 138
military 1, 2, 17, 87, 114, 119, 122, 126
Mingant, Nolwenn 117
minimum wage 26, 74
Ministry of the Interior (UAE) 1, 17, 126
Mission: Impossible franchise 87, 137
Mission: Impossible – Dead Reckoning Part One 87, 123, 127
Mission: Impossible – Fallout 39, 50, 126
Mission: Impossible – Ghost Protocol 115, 117
mobilization, *see* resistance to the supply chain
Moore, Schuyler M. 11
Morgan, George 28, 40, 69
Morocco 2, 114, 119
Morris, William 55
Morrissey, Gerry 54
Moten, Fred 49, 82
Motion Picture Patents Company 46
multiculturalism 88, 94–95, 100–101, 102, 104, 109
musalsalat 115
My Name is Khan 116

National Film and Television School 65, 68
Nedeva, Maria 68
Neilson, Brett 6, 21, 90, 139
Nelligan, Pariece 28, 40, 69
neoliberalism 28, 30, 41, 89
nepotism 52–53, 65, 73, 74, 82
Netflix 3, 15, 17, 37, 61, 65, 115
networking 51, 64, 69, 82, 99
New York University 68, 95, 99, 110, 120, 139
New York University Abu Dhabi 90, 92, 93, 94–95, 96, 97–98, 99, 100, 101–102, 104, 110, 120, 129, 133
New Zealand 94, 135
Newsinger, Jack 40, 45
NFTS, *see* National Film and Television School
NHS 46
Nigeria 135
non-disclosure agreements 18, 32, 33, 100
Noonan, Caitriona 69

Norway 135
Notes from Below 33
NYU, *see* New York University
NYUAD, *see* New York University Abu Dhabi

Oakley, Kate 68
OECD, *see* Organisation for Economic Co-operation and Development
offshoring 2, 5, 8–9, 11, 12, 17, 20, 21, 27, 29, 30, 34, 36, 37, 38, 41, 42, 45–46, 50, 60, 67, 86, 87, 88, 93, 94, 95, 96, 98, 102, 104, 107, 113, 114, 117, 119, 120, 121, 123, 126, 132, 133, 135, 136, 138
Ong, Aihwa 102–103, 134
ontological takeover 125–126
Open University 30
operaismo 32, 33
O'Regan, Tom 9, 10, 12, 13, 14, 38, 46–47, 102, 117, 126, 127
Organisation for Economic Co-operation and Development 78
organized labour, *see* unions and unionization
Out on the Street 85
Outlander 65, 76–77
outsourcing 2, 7–8, 14, 18–19, 21, 59, 95, 123, 136
overtime 15–16, 54, 56, 58, 60
Ovetz, Robert 32

PACT, *see* Producers Alliance for Cinema and Television
Paddington 35, 39
Paddington 2 35
Palestine 89, 90, 93, 130
Panama Papers 46
Paramount 39, 115
Paris 127
Parker, Alan 43–44
passion 24, 30, 41, 55, 71–72, 77, 82, 139
Pathaan 87
pay scales, salaries and wages 6, 7, 8, 10, 19, 25, 26, 28, 29, 42, 46, 47, 49, 50, 51, 52, 53, 55, 56–57, 58, 59, 60, 61, 69, 71–72, 75, 76, 77, 81, 83, 89–90, 97, 104, 105, 109, 114, 121, 123, 128, 130, 131, 132, 133, 137, 139

pensions 9, 83, 136
Percival, Neil 73, 74
Perlin, Ross 25, 26, 28–29, 76, 106
Peru 135
Petrie, Duncan 65, 67
PhDs, 29, 30, 71, 81, 91
    see also qualifications; university degrees
Picard, Robert G. 100, 119, 130
Picherit-Duthler, Gaelle 92, 97, 105
Pinewood Studios 37, 106
Pirates of the Caribbean: On Stranger Tides 37
Poland 135
policy 2, 10, 11, 12, 13, 17, 19, 32, 35, 42, 44, 47, 51, 70, 88, 116, 129
    creative economy 3, 36, 39, 44, 47, 88, 115
    education 26, 27, 28, 67, 68, 69, 73, 78, 79, 87–88, 93, 98, 100
    fiscal 42, 44, 80
    migrant labour 22, 90, 91, 129
political organizing, *see* resistance to the supply chain
Porter, Robert 13
ports 92, 107, 111, 118, 119, 120, 121, 122, 124, 136
Posner, Miriam 3, 6, 18, 50
Potter, Dom 72
Prague 5
Precarious Workers Brigade 83–85
precarity 2, 3, 7, 14, 19, 22–23, 24, 25, 29, 30, 33, 34, 45, 70–71, 73, 75, 77, 78, 79, 83, 87, 90, 91, 92–93, 102, 105, 108, 110, 113, 129, 130, 137, 138
    see also labour (precarious)
principal photography 2, 17, 51, 59
private equity 11, 19, 20, 45
private sector, 12, 13, 57, 87, 89, 98, 105, 114, 118, 122, 123
    see also education (privatized)
privatization 24, 26, 28, 30, 34, 51, 72, 77, 80–81, 82, 106, 131, 132
privilege 7, 23, 29, 70, 72, 84, 99, 104, 129
Producers Alliance for Cinema and Television 48–49, 60
production line 3, 40, 121
production services 13–14, 15, 19, 27, 50, 64, 100, 113, 114, 117, 125, 126, 127, 133
    see also labour (service); services

professors, *see* academics
project thinking 14, 27, 52, 139
public funds and resources 2, 5, 10–14, 17, 18, 19, 21, 28, 30, 41, 43, 44, 45, 46, 59, 65, 66, 69, 70, 71, 75, 80–81, 90, 93, 94, 96, 97, 98, 102, 105, 110, 115, 118, 132
public sector 6, 12, 13, 42, 46, 70, 87, 88, 90, 115, 116, 120, 122
  see also education (public)
Puzzlewood 48

Qatar 99, 128, 133
qualifications 23, 29, 66, 71
  see also university degrees

Race 3 87
race to the bottom 9
racial inequality and prejudice 52, 53, 70, 71, 76, 95, 101, 131
racialized divisions of labour, *see* labour (racialized divisions of)
Ramsey, Phil 13, 42, 68
ranking systems for universities 28, 69, 78, 79
real estate 89, 107, 114, 116–117, 118, 119–120, 122, 129, 131
  see also rental economy
refugees 128, 130, 131, 132
  see also migrants and migration
relational cities 119–120
rental economy 39, 41, 75, 94, 107, 108, 114, 116, 117, 124, 128, 130, 131–132
  see also real estate
residence permits and residence restrictions 88, 92, 93, 108–109
  see also visas
resistance to the supply chain 23, 29, 31–34, 59–61, 68, 76, 77, 82–86, 109–111, 132–134, 135–140
  see also activism; solidarity
responsibility, *see* care (duties of)
rest, *see* sleep, rest and breaks
Ridley, Daisy 91
rights 75, 76, 84–85, 104, 110, 118, 129, 137
  to education 94, 110
  gay 110
  political 90, 95

worker 6, 8, 9, 10, 20, 25, 36, 42, 50, 52, 71, 73, 74, 76, 85, 95, 105, 109, 110, 132, 139
Rodino-Colocino, Michelle 75
Roggero, Gigi 31, 69, 81
Rolls-Royce 38
Ross, Andrew 7, 8, 94–95
Ross, Dick 68
Rossiter, Ned 12, 18, 30, 42, 125
Rossoukh, Ramyar D. 5
runaway productions 8–9, 95
runners, 73, 138
  see also interns; trainees
Ruskin, John 55

Saadiyat Island 110, 139
salaries, *see* pay scales, salaries and wages
Sanson, Kevin 10, 13, 16, 17, 27, 57
Saudi Arabia 89, 118–119, 135
Sayfo, Omar 50
Scott, Allen J. 49
Scott, Daniel T. 30
Scotland 47, 78
Screen Scotland 65
ScreenSkills 65, 66–69, 70, 72, 74, 79, 81, 97, 98
Second World War 5, 8, 38, 96
self-employment 26, 40, 64, 68, 70, 129, 130
self-reliance and self-sufficiency 2, 24, 28, 41, 42, 57, 69–70, 71, 97, 98, 129, 134, 139
Sennett, Richard 25, 55
services 1, 10, 12, 15, 30, 36, 43, 44, 67, 93, 94, 114–115, 122, 125–127, 128, 129, 134
  see also labour (service); production services
Shaxson, Nicolas 45–46
Shepperton Studios 37
shipping 2, 122, 128
  see also freighting
Sigler, Thomas, J. 119
skill and de-skilling 26, 27, 50, 55, 67, 75, 80, 99, 114, 119, 125–126, 128, 130, 131, 135, 137
  see also labour (skilled)
Skillset, *see* ScreenSkills
sleep, rest and breaks 15, 16, 24, 29, 36, 46, 50, 51, 54, 56–60, 76, 118
  see also exhaustion; long hours

Sleepy Hollow 39
social capital 69, 75, 101, 139
social class, *see* class systems and classism
solidarity 52, 82, 104, 129, 133–134, 139
    see also collectivity and collective struggle
Sonic the Hedgehog 87
Sony 39, 115
South Africa 10, 135
South Korea 135
Spain 135
speed 3, 11, 15–22, 49–50, 59, 109 119, 120, 122, 123
    see also just-in-time
Spiderman: Far From Home 39
Spivak, Gayatri 100, 104, 109, 133
sponsors and sponsorship 89, 92, 95, 107, 108, 129, 132
standardization 4, 5, 11–12, 14, 37, 38, 43, 47, 48, 60, 66, 67, 69, 70, 96, 98, 102
    see also interoperability
Standing, Guy 78
Star Trek Beyond 87, 113, 115
Star Wars franchise 1, 2, 13, 90
Star Wars: Episode I – The Phantom Menace 39
Star Wars: The Force Awakens 1, 3, 4, 6, 7, 10, 17, 24, 26, 48, 87, 90, 96, 99, 103, 106, 120, 122, 123–124, 126, 127
Steinberg, Marc 15
Steinhart, Daniel 122
streaming services 3, 15, 16, 17, 50, 61, 124
strikes, 83, 110, 130, 133, 136, 138
    see also unions and unionization
struggle, *see* resistance to the supply chain
student debt, *see* debt
student loans 22, 80–81
    see also debt
students 25, 26, 28–29, 31, 32, 33, 34, 63, 64, 66, 68, 69, 70, 71, 73, 74–83, 84–85, 88, 92, 93, 94, 95, 96, 97, 98, 99, 101–102, 105, 108, 110, 120, 135, 136, 137, 138
    see also labour (student and study)
studio facilities 4, 5, 8, 12, 35, 37–39, 43, 47, 49, 50, 53, 54, 55, 61, 65, 107, 114, 115, 117, 120, 122, 136
studio system 4, 59
subcontracting 2, 7, 34, 108, 125, 128, 129

subsidies, *see* public funds and resources; incentives
supply chain (definition and characteristics) 1–34
supply chain cinema 1–9, 10, 13, 15, 16, 17, 18, 19, 20, 21, 23, 24, 25, 27, 28, 31, 33, 35, 36, 37, 38, 45, 46, 50, 51, 53, 54, 55, 56, 57, 60, 63, 64, 70, 72, 76, 78, 80, 83, 85, 89, 90, 96, 99, 102, 103, 107, 108, 111, 114, 116, 119, 121, 124, 125, 127, 129, 132, 133, 135, 137–138
supply chain capitalism 4, 12, 134
supply chain education 2–3, 4, 12, 21, 24, 28–31, 63–69, 77, 78, 87, 88, 93–96, 106–107, 111, 117, 135, 136
Syria 116, 130, 131
Szczepanik, Petr 50, 74, 101, 126

tax and taxpayers 8, 11, 14, 21, 45–6, 80, 94, 139
    see also incentives (tax)
tax evasion and havens 2, 11, 45–46
    see also incentives (tax)
teamwork 1, 14, 52, 55, 57, 58, 70, 97, 99, 101, 139
TECOM 106–107, 116, 122, 128, 129
Tiger Zinda Hai 122
Tinic, Serra 6, 10
Toronto 89
tourism 11, 13, 39, 44, 50, 97, 114, 117, 127
trades unions, *see* unions and unionization
trainees 51, 59, 65, 72, 73, 76–77, 85, 117, 137
    see also interns; apprenticeships
translation 24, 27, 34, 47–48, 49, 50, 86, 88, 96, 97, 100, 103, 104, 125, 134, 135, 137, 138, 139
    see also English
transportation and travel arrangements 1, 5, 12, 13, 17, 18, 37, 38, 48, 119, 121–122, 123, 126, 134, 136
    see also airlines; freighting; shipping
Tsing, Anna 4, 5, 14, 27, 43, 47, 48, 59–60, 81, 133
tuition fees 26, 28, 66, 74, 75, 78, 81, 83, 92, 108, 137
twofour54 1, 6, 17, 100, 105–106, 107, 114, 115, 116, 119, 120, 122, 123, 126, 130

Uber 19, 30, 71
UCU, *see* University and College Union
UK Film Council 42, 43
unions and unionization 9, 14, 30, 41, 42, 46, 48–49, 50, 52, 60, 65, 68, 77, 83, 107, 118, 130, 136
  see also collective bargaining; strikes
United World Colleges 96
Universal Pictures/Studios 39, 115
universities 2, 3, 12, 26, 28, 30, 31, 32, 33, 63, 65–69, 70–71, 73–74, 76, 78–79, 80, 81, 82–85, 88, 90, 92, 93–96, 97, 99, 100, 101, 102, 104, 105, 106, 110, 118, 136, 137, 138, 140
  see also branch campuses
University and College Union 77, 83, 136
university degrees 64, 65–66, 69–70, 71, 74, 78, 79, 80, 91, 94, 95, 96, 97, 104, 107, 108, 138
  see also PhDs
University of Wollongong 92, 94
  in Dubai 91, 94, 105
Unnikrishnan, Deepak 108
unpaid labour, *see* labour
Urry, John 9
Uruguay 135
UWC, *see* United World Colleges
Uzbekistan 89

Vancouver 6
Vanguard 87
Variety 43, 122, 135, 138
Villeneuve, Denis 123, 128
Virgin Islands 135
visas 17, 47, 89, 90, 92, 107, 108, 177, 122, 123, 127, 128, 131, 132
  golden (UAE) 89, 90, 92, 104, 129
  see also work permits
Vivarelli, Nick 122
volunteering 52, 74
  see also interns and internships
Vora, Neha 94, 99, 102, 104, 109

wages, *see* pay scales, salaries and wages
Wages for Students 75, 83

Walia, Harsha 89, 90, 106, 131
Wall Street, Money Never Sleeps 87
War Machine 89
Ward, Susan 9, 10, 12, 14, 78, 102, 117, 126
warehouses and warehousing 115, 119, 120, 124, 136
Warner Bros. 35, 37, 38, 39, 43, 44, 46, 127
Warner Bros. Studio Tour – the Making of Harry Potter 39–40, 41, 43–44, 48, 52, 55, 56, 63, 139
Warner Bros. World Abu Dhabi 127
Welcome Back 87
welfare benefits 2, 9, 25, 57, 70, 71, 80, 83, 90, 129
  see also pensions
Wexler, Haskell 56
White, Andrew 42, 68
Whitford, Steve 67
Who Needs Sleep? 56, 57, 58, 60
Wilson Review 67–69, 73
Witches, The 39
Wonder Woman 35
Wonder Woman 1984 39
Wootton, Adrian 64
work permits 12, 17, 80, 90, 114, 124, 129, 132
  see also visas
work-based learning 28, 29
worker inquiry 33
Working Class Goes to Heaven, The 85
working hours, *see* long hours
World Bank 28, 78, 80
World Trade Organization 94

Xiang Biao 90

Yates, David 39, 56
Yemen 116
YouTube 1, 13
Yunis, Alia 92, 97, 105

Zaslove, Jerry 95
Zayed University 99, 105

www.ingramcontent.com/pod-product-compliance
Lightning Source LLC
Chambersburg PA
CBHW052047300426
44117CB00012B/2006